To my family, Mom & Dad, Chet, Chase, and Christine, for showing that passion, potential, and possibilities are connected by always working toward being a better student, athlete, and person, and believing that success in life is found in the journey.

Linda

To the three men in my life who are the epitome of true student-athletes: my husband, David, and my two sons, Jimmy and Matt. For my parents who encouraged me and taught me that if you work hard in life, you WILL be successful.

Suzanne

Acknowledgments

We want to give a special thanks to the student-athletes who were willing to share their personal academic and athletic stories. Some of these stories are included in this book while many of the stories may not be cited here but they gave us an understanding and broader perspective of how high school and college athletics work. We would like to thank all student-athletes, coaches, administrators, admissions' personnel, compliance officers, parents of recruited athletes, and guest speakers in the sports culture class who shared their insights and experiences over the years.

Thank you, student-athletes, for sharing your academic and athletic stories.

Ryan Adkins, Shannon Adkins, Erik Akre, Condrew Allen, Alyssa Anderson, Gavin Andrews, Elena Banister, Tim Bardet, Jamie Bardwil, Betsy Barr, Emmy Barr, Katie Bauer, Mikey Beck, Brian Benson, Jordan Blake, Eric Blank, Geoff Blumenfeld, Jimmy Bosco, Farrah Bradford, Preston Bramow, Joe Burke, Aaron Burney, Miles Burris, Jordan Caines, Chris Campbell, Hunter Carnival, Megan Cobbin, Christy Cooper, Keslie Cooper, Grant Currey, Pat Devenny, Chase Dickson, Christine Dickson, Alexandra Diemer, Austin Diemer, Riley Drongesen, Allyse Duffin, Brent Edwards, Scotty Enos, Megan Erkel, Nate Esposito, Ryan Fehr, Tyler Fitzgerald, Jillian Garton, Peter Gibbs, Chad Gielow, Jay Gill, Nolan de Graaff, Natalie Gulbis, Alison Guzenski, Andy Guzenski, Alison Hamby, Jessica Hamby, Spencer Hamby, Robert Haney, Thomas Haney, Liz Harkin, Brian Harrison, AJ Herlitz, Jodie Higgins, Cliff Hinkle, Brooke Holt, Holden Huff, Avery Hutchinson, Travis Israel, Adam Jennings, Dorien Johnk, Kayla Karlsson, Matt Kasner, Brendan Keeney, Jake Keester, Jacob Keys, James Kinloch, Andrew Knapp, Alexis Knudtson, Kristin Kurpershoek, Jimmy Laughrea, Matt Laughrea, Paige Lee, Caresse Little, Nick Little, Ryan Loder, Kyle Loria, Garrett Marion, Joe McIntosh, Brandon Michalkiewicz, Ryan Miller, Nico Molino, Lydell Moseby, Jacob Moss, Ryan Motsenbocker, Andrew Murch, Caitlyn Murphy, Gregory Neale, Bobby Neary, Katie Oddo, Mark Palmer, Eric Parker, Hilary Perry-Smith, Suzy Peterson, Jessie Pleis, Kendra Postell, Morgan Ragan, Andrew Reego, Ian Rhodes, Jeff Ringholm, Dereck Roth, Kendall Roth, Scott Roth, Kurt Russell, Rocky Russo, Gina Saldana, Dallas Sartz, Kyle Saukko, Kyle Schlehofer, Scott Shaull, Michelle Slagle, Bryce Smith, Matt Smock, Annelise Spargo, Brian Sprinkle, Max Stassi, Kaellie Stone, Sammy Stroughter, Rachael Gross Thomas, Ronnie Thomas, Peyton Thompson, Amanda Threde, Katryna Ton, Derek Tough, Jeff Tyrell, Corey Vanderbeek, Jared Vanderbeek, James Vigeant, Max Vigeant, Max Vogt, Adam Wagner, Scotty Walker, Madison Wallace, Kristi Whalen Horwitz, Mitchell White, Scotty Williams, Andrew Wilson, Jill Wirt, Noah Wright, Devon Wylie, Ryan Xepoleas, Braden Young, Nick Young, Jameel Ziadeh, Katie Zingheim, and all our students in Sports Culture.

The *Academic* ATHLETE

A Step-by-Step Guide for Success in the Classroom, Recruiting, and College Admissions

Linda Luther Dickson & Suzanne Packard Laughrea

This book is a concise yet comprehensive guide and planner for any high school student-athlete in today's competitive world of high school sports and college admission. Its purpose is to give you the knowledge, insights, and guidance so you can go through high school successfully and give you the best opportunity to play high school and college sports. Hopefully, it will inspire you to find your strengths. This guide will help you prepare athletically and academically. We've seen the NCAA advertisements reminding us there are 400,000+ college student-athletes who are going pro in something other than their sport. **Your education is most important; academics are first and athletics are second. Have a plan and do it.**

DCI
press

Design · Collaborate · Innovate

The authors and publisher have made every effort to ensure that the information in this book was accurate as of its publication although it may have subsequently become outdated by new regulations, laws, or other circumstances. This publication contains the authors' insights and advice on the college prep process from a coach/teacher/administrator/parent perspective. This publication is sold with the understanding that the authors are not engaged in rendering professional services. If legal, accounting, medical, psychological, academic counseling, or any other expert assistance is required, the services of a competent professional should be sought.

All brand names and product names used in this book are trademarks, registered trademarks, or trade names of their respective holders. The authors and publisher are not associated with any product or vendor in this book.

Copyright 2013 Linda Dickson and Suzanne Laughrea
Cover, internal design, and illustrations by Alison Sale
Supplemental design by Chris Dickson
Cover Photo by Julia Williams, Letterman Jacket provided by NorCal Jackets, Orangevale, CA
Editing by Alison Sale, Laura Preston, and Shannon Wagner

First Edition

Library of Congress Control Number: 2012944714

ISBN: 978-0-9858619-0-2

Published by DCI Press
www.dcipress.com

Printed by Delta Web Printing, W. Sacramento, California

We would also like to thank many coaches, athletic directors, trainers, doctors, teachers, admissions personnel, and parents for sharing their insights.

Skip Albano, Brian Alvarez, Rob Awalt, Jim Barr, Terry Battenberg, Bill Baxter, Ryan Beidler, Al Biancani, Whitney Bibbins, Fred Biletnikoff, Guin Boggs, Ruthie Bolton, Kim Boone, Bill Bowman, Phil Boyte, Stu Brokowsky, Dave Brown, Kim Brown, Danny Bunz, Keith Burcham, Rob Burger, Doug Casebier, Rachael Conway, Robert Cooley, Ernie Cooper, Brandon Coupe, Roger Crawford, Paul Diemer, Tim Dixon, Gary Donnell, Linda Drever, Kristie Dunham, Pat Esposito, Lee Evans, Lance Fischer, Steve Fischer, Brian Flajole, Mel Fontes, Sterling Forbes, Patrick Gallagher, Leslie Gallimore, Craig Garabedian, Bryan Geist, Scottie Geist, Tiffany Gieck, Rick Gielow, Tamara Givens, Pablo Gonzalez, Phil Grams, Kyle Grossert, Scott Hall, Bob Haney, Larry Harmon, Tim Healy, Lain Hensley, Brian Hewitt, John Howarth, Jim Jack, Bobby Jackson, Lars Jensen, Kurt Johnson, Kevin Kelly, Roosevelt Kent, Richie Kim, Julie Knapp, Duki Kuresa, Scott Laverty, Leon Lee, Josh Levin, Tom Lininger, Ron Loder, Brittany Luther, David Luther, Mark Luther, Mike Lynch, John MacLeane, Jenny Mann, Greg Marjama, Johnny McDowell, Tim McFerran, Cassie McMillen, Mike Meggers, Ed Michalkiewicz, Cary Moore, Dale Mortensen, Lloyd Moseby, Tom Murphy, Bill Neal, Les Nederveld, Joe Oddo, Mikela Olsen, Jim Phillips, Scott Pink, Gary Powers, Cathy Raycraft, Kathy Ritter-Anderson, Mike Rodriguez, Rick Rodriquez, Mirna Romero, Andi Rothman, John Roza, Lucy Sakagishi-Judd, Jeannie Sampson, Steve Sax, John Segale, Ron Severson, John Sherman, Jeff Shuman, Ron Silvia, George Sirovy, Jason Sitterud, Marty Slimak, Terry Smith, Mark Speckman, Jamie Sprague, Terry Stafford, Aaron Swick, Mike Takayama, Jennifer Thomas, Jeff Threde, Chase Tidwell, Randy Town, Steve Treadway, Nathan Trosky, Mack Tucker, Cindi Underwood, Mike Valentine, Bob Valletta, Tony Vargas, Mike Verbitski, Danielle Viglione, David Vujovich, Dede Walker, Jerry Weinberg, Dale White, Walt Wild, Steve Williams, Barbara Wilson, Billy Wiskel, Anthony Wong, Jason Zemanovic, and Charlie Zink.
And a special thank you to Coach Rick Sundberg for believing in Chase.

In addition, a number of college students worked diligently on this book, enabling us to finally get it published. Alison Sale designed the cover, layout for the book, as well as all of the creative illustrations. She also brought her expert editing and writing skills to our team. Laura Preston and Shannon Wagner spent hours editing multiple drafts, providing brevity and clarity where we really needed it. Jim Barr, Walt Wild, Barbara Wilson, Lauren Neal, Jessica Reese, and the Sale Family made wonderful edits. Brooke Bohan and Katie Gezi typed drafts, and Adam Tilford saved us by designing math problems with answer keys. Chris Dickson assisted whereever needed. Guin Boggs encouraged and inspired us to believe in the value of our book.

Our families have allowed us to work together for five years on this book, often asking us, "When are you going to finish that book?" We would like to thank our children, Chase, Chris, Jimmy and Matt, for years of enjoyment watching them excel in school and in sports. Some of our fondest memories are of sitting in the stands watching them compete. Our husbands have been unbelievably patient with us as we wrote and rewrote this book. Chet Dickson provided excellent insights and wisdom on many stages of the book, and was always available for help when we got stuck. Thanks to Linda's parents, Bill and Linda, who supported this project from its inception.

CONTENTS

PRE-GAME: PURPOSE & DESIGN

Playbook Purpose:
To guide high
school student-
athletes and their
parents through
high school and
into college

The Academic Athlete is not just a book, but it is a resource in the form of a playbook for students, athletes, parents, coaches, counselors, and anyone else assisting student-athletes in understanding college athletic opportunities. The purpose of this playbook is to serve as a resource and give you the information needed to understand the high school system, as well as the college recruiting and application process. The most successful athletes and business executives agree that desire and hard work—over talent—are the keys to success. Student-athletes need a plan, and more importantly, they need to execute the plan! Executing the plan means building a strong student-athlete profile, which will be the sum of your experiences and relationships established throughout your high school years.

As authors of this book, we bring our personal and professional experiences as parents, teachers, and coaches. Between the two of us, we have had three sons and a daughter play high school sports and work hard to succeed in the classroom. They earned good grades in school which gave them the opportunity to attend schools where they could get a good education and play college sports. Our husbands are also high school teachers and coaches, and the four of us have worked with student-athletes over the past 30 years. As a result, we understand the high school system, have experienced successful teacher-parent-coach communication, and have learned how parents can help their teens through high school.

Over the years, we have watched our children and other teens play numerous sports. We often found ourselves chatting with parents about how to prepare our kids for college, and how to start navigating college athletic recruiting and admissions. Many of us felt more confused as we asked one another questions like:

- *How do we help our kids get recruited?*
- *Should my kid play travel ball and high school sports?*
- *Is my daughter good enough to play Division I college sports?*
- *How do we get scholarship money and qualify for financial aid?*
- *When do our kids take the SAT?*
- *What is the difference between SAT and ACT?*
- *Are our kids taking the right courses to be an NCAA qualifier?*
- *Will college coaches find my kid?*
- *How do we get exposure for our kids to find the perfect fit for them academically and athletically?*
- *How do we help her choose a college?*
- *What are college coaches looking for?*
- *How do we contact coaches?*
- *Which college showcases do we pay good money for and which travel teams do we join?*

We sought out answers to these recurring questions and now want to share our research, our experiences, and our insights with other student-athletes and their parents.

After researching, interviewing, and learning about academic college preparation and athletic recruiting (to help our own kids find opportunities to play college sports), we could not find one book that covered both academics and athletics. Since we could not find **one book clearly explaining** the academic skills necessary for our teens to succeed in high school and meet NCAA requirements for college, with information on athletic recruiting and scholarship, we realized we had the skills and knowledge to compile all our resources and create **ONE** book with it all. One book with both the academic and athletic side of recruiting to help out parents in the same overwhelming situation that we were faced with.

While very challenging and arduous, we made it our goal to supply a parent, a coach, and the student-athlete or even the sports minded student with one overview resource to address the confusion. This book will help you navigate through the high school experience and into college with both an academic and athletic focus. The purpose is to bring clarity to the various organizations, rules, sites, and programs to help parents help their teens through high school and into college.

The key to success through high school and into college is **attitude, preparation, and hard work**. To prepare, a student athlete must plan.

Knowledge is Power Education is Leverage

Every single student-athlete we interviewed to write this book has emphatically stated, "I wish I had known to get better grades."

"**My number one supporter** is my family. Every minute of every day my family has always been by my side supporting me in every decision I make, whether it is golf or school related. After a few years of playing junior golf, I developed this dream of becoming a college and LPGA golfer; I fell in love with the sport and eventually saw much improvement in my game. I still have this dream and I believe that if I work hard and dedicate myself to this sport, it could become a reality a few years down the road."

–Paige Lee, Verbal Commitment for Golf to UC Davis

Each chapter is designed with a "Game Plan" and "Top Ten Plays" to help clarify the contents of the section. Student-athletes who are looking for specific information can go directly to the beginning of each chapter to find "Game Plan" for the topics covered in the chapter. Student-athletes who don't have time to read, will find helpful summaries called "Top Ten Plays" located at the end of each chapter. We have also included Highlights and Time-Outs throughout the book for special features and personal reflection, respectively.

If you only take one thing from this book, remember that your high school grades are incredibly important and that education is leverage if you plan on playing college—even professional sports.

This book is a tool for parents, guardians, and mentors, especially student-athletes. You can work through the chapters with your son or daughter, encouraging them to read and to set goals. The book will give you an opportunity to interact with your child and to spend quality time making decisions about his or her future.

Help your teen help himself or herself.

Ideally, a student would begin working through this book as a freshman. If this is not the case, you should make sure you are on track for your current grade level. An older student will need to "fast track" by using *The Academic Athlete Checklist* for sophomore and junior years, to make sure that all requirements have been met. If you don't read this until your senior year, it's not too late. You will need to read back through the checklist to make sure you are adequately prepared.

How do student-athletes balance academics and athletics? The key is to set priorities and make a schedule or a plan. Every individual and family is unique—use this planner, organizer, and resource to help you make the best decisions for your student-athlete and family. And keep in mind that high school is more than a stepping-stone for college. High school is also a place to be a kid and enjoy the moment.

High school is a challenging and exciting time. We hope that this book will help you see the big picture of what is needed for students to compete in our increasingly competitive college prep environment.

What this book is NOT

There are high school counselors, private college-prep advisors, life coaches, and educational consultants, who earn a living helping students prepare for college. We are not counselors or life coaches. We are experienced teachers, coaches, and parents with our own student-athlete children who went through the recruiting and college admissions process. Our goal is to provide an academic and athletic guide and planner to provide knowledge for student-athletes so they can make informed, educated life decisions.

College vs. University: We will use the words "school," "college," and "university" interchangeably throughout this book. According to askjeeves.com, "As a general rule, colleges tend to be smaller than universities and usually do not offer doctoral degrees, while a university offers a wide range of graduate programs, including doctoral degrees. Universities emphasize research as well as teaching (traditionally a strength of colleges), and universities that offer doctoral programs are usually referred to as research universities."

Insights for Student-Athletes

Success is a journey, not a destination. Be nice to your parents, and respect all that they do and sacrifice for you. Be kind to your brothers and sisters too even if they are annoying. Have a strong work ethic and good study habits.

"If I could do it over, I would absolutely have stayed in sports at the competitive level because it would have opened up so many more opportunities. I would have had a better chance getting into more of the top schools."

–Kendall Roth, UCLA Student

STUDENTS:
1. Earn the best grades you can
2. Work on sports skills
3. Improve fitness and nutrition
4. Develop a positive attitude
5. Set realistic goals and make a plan

Most student-athletes really don't know what they want to do until they are seniors in high school. There is no one set way to "do high school" and get into college because there are different paths for different kids. So, seek to open as many possible doors of opportunity. *You just don't know what will happen if you prepare.*

If you want to get the most benefit out of this book, we strongly encourage you to personalize it. Make it work for you.

Write in the book so you can refer back to important sections later:
- ‣ Take notes in the margin
- ‣ Ask questions in the margin
- ‣ Underline or highlight key ideas
- ‣ Use the templates in the book—make copies if necessary

6. Market yourself
7. Find your college fit
8. Prepare for the SAT/ACT
9. Meet college application deadlines
10. Apply for financial aid & scholarships

Insights for Parents

Again, our purpose as authors is to help you help your teen navigate through high school and into college academics and athletics...from a parent and teacher's first-hand experience and perspective. Parents, guardians, or mentors can make a difference by helping teens realize the importance of education in their athletic lives.

Make it work for you.
- • Write notes in the margin
- • Ask questions in the margin
- • Underline or highlight key ideas
- • Use the templates in the book

The journey through high school, as well as both the college preparation and application process can be complex and time-consuming, especially if you are not familiar with the high school system, the college application, or the athletic recruiting game. While teenagers can do this on their own, it will be less stressful if they have adults in their lives who guide and encourage them along the way. If you do not have the knowledge, the resources, the ability, or the time necessary to become highly involved with your teen's high school experience and the college application process, you can make a difference by offering positive support, especially when your teenager becomes overwhelmed, discouraged or confused.

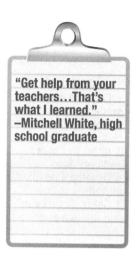

<blockquote>
"Get help from your teachers...That's what I learned."
—Mitchell White, high school graduate
</blockquote>

Many parents and coaches are not aware of the various organizations, websites, and programs available to help their child through high school and into college.

You can hire expensive recruiting services, educational consultants, or life coaches. You can find less expensive internet "connection and networking" services for both students and student-athletes. You can also do it yourself and use this book as a resource, which is designed to provide you and your student with the knowledge and tools to navigate through the process on your own.

"**I've been influenced by my parents** who have always supported and pushed me to succeed. They've encouraged me to not set limits, and lifted me up during challenges with soccer and school. Also, I've been impacted by my older brother, Nick. His academic and athletic success both in high school and college has driven me to achieve my goals."

—Caresse Little, Westminster College Soccer Player

As a parent, grandparent, guardian, coach, or mentor you can make a difference in the following ways:

1. Make a Difference in Academics

- **Attendance is key to excelling in school.** Be sure that your teenager is only absent if he or she is really sick. Schedule doctor and dentist appointments after school or during holiday breaks. If necessary, schedule appointments during elective classes rather than core academic classes, and schedule family vacations around school. If your teen is absent, it is his or her responsibility to see the teacher for make-up work, not the teacher's responsibility to seek out the student.
- As with absences, tardies also impact grades. Help your teen to get to school on time in the morning. Design effective consequences, such as taking away cell phones, for chronic tardies during the day.
- Help your teen dresses appropriately for school and exhibits polite behavior during the school day. Encourage your student to turn off his cell phone during class since most teachers view cell phone use during class as rude and inappropriate.
- Find challenging courses. What is challenging is different for each individual.
- Since most high schools offer honors or Advanced Placement (AP) or International Baccalaureate (IB) courses, your teen will make decisions about whether or not she should take college prep, honors, or AP/IB classes. For some students, playing year-round competitive sports and maintaining high grades in honors and advanced classes is easy. Some student-athletes will be able to maintain a demanding athletic schedule and a handful of advanced classes,

while other student-athletes will only be able to balance their athletic schedule with college prep classes. Encourage your student-athlete to take college prep classes in order to keep as many doors open as possible for college admissions. Some counselors will advise students to take more challenging AP/IB classes while others might advise students to take regular college prep classes where they could more easily earn an A. You need to help your student choose what is the best path for them.

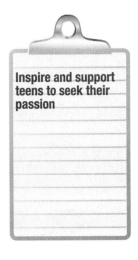

Inspire and support teens to seek their passion

‣ Encourage your student to take advantage of any on campus tutoring or learning centers operating before or after school or even during lunch. Often, students don't really need specific tutoring for a class, rather supervision to actually get them to sit down and do the homework.

‣ Ask to look at their class work and homework in their school binders. Many students say they don't have homework when they really do. Check that homework is complete, not just done. Many schools give teachers the ability to post homework, assignments, attendance, and grades online so that parents have access to this important information.

‣ Help as a tutor and use your pen wisely. Instead of writing the assignment for your teen, write suggestions in the margins, edit, help revise, or scribe your teen's own words.

‣ Some high school students need help with revising writing assignments. There is a fine line between editing a paper and taking over the process and writing it for your student. Make suggestions for revision, but allow them to do the writing.

‣ Monitor progress, grades, transcripts, and attendance using the high school website. Most high schools give parents a pin number to gain access to their student's records.

‣ Help your student arrange to take some kind of SAT/ACT preparation. Your high school's career center will have information on local preparation classes. Students have reported that the Princeton Review or Kaplan type classes are a bore and time consuming, yet helpful. We were able to get (bribe) our sons to prepare for the SAT by having them take practice tests together in exchange for Xbox time. Taking practice tests is very valuable and they are free at collegboard.org, or you can purchase the College Board or Barron's prep books at any bookstore. Starting freshman year, make flash cards for the high frequency vocabulary words on the SAT. Don't overload your teen with prep books. Let him or her pick out one book or apps to use. Parents often tend to buy too many prep books. (There are suggestions for test prep in Chapter 14.)

2. Make a Difference with Organization

- Help your teen use *The Academic Athlete Checklist.* It covers 8th through 12th grade academic and athletic progress. Realize many students struggle in 9th grade because of the overwhelming transition from junior high. Often by sophomore year, they figure it out, and study habits and grades improve. It's never too late to start to become a student.
- Monitor the academic and athletic schedule to help meet goals.
- Help your teen find balance because athletics and college prep academics are very demanding. Note that research has demonstrated that high school students involved in sports, performing arts, clubs, student government, or other activities do earn higher grades and are happier in high school. It is about belonging, having a sense of community, and pride.

Use our kitchen table model for homework. Monitor your student at the table with no distractions. No phone, TV, or games.

- Offer academic support for all types of students, whether they are underachievers or overachievers. Follow the "kitchen table" model: Sit at the kitchen table with your teenager and monitor, or even offer help, to keep them focused on schoolwork. This means that there needs to be no phone, TV, or distracting music during this time. Most teens just need someone to supervise them so that they actually stay on task.
- Help your teenager maintain a personal planner through the entire year by purchasing a day planner or using an app that they like and will use. They should write down the following:
  - » Homework
  - » Quiz and test dates
  - » Athletic practices & schedules
  - » Deadlines (PSAT, SAT, ACT, college applications, etc.)
  - » Social/recreational time (phone, TV, friends, etc.)
  - » Responsibilities/chores/commitments
- Help your teen with time management on long-term assignments. Help them set up a calendar since it is easy to procrastinate.
- When your teen is in his or her junior year and registers for the ACT/SAT college admissions tests, have your teen thoroughly complete the questionnaires in addition to the actual test registration. This will help your teen determine where he/she fits both academically and athletically.

3. Make a Difference in Athletics

▸ Check out your options so that you can find the right team or club for your student-athlete's. Look for stability, and research the history of programs and coaches. Observe the coach at a practice and in a game situation. Ask the coach or manager questions that are important to you and your teen about coaching philosophy, playing time, practice guidelines, and building athletic confidence. Ask the coach what tournaments and showcases the team is going to compete in. Try to meet other parents and get their views on the coach also. You can also go online and read blogs about programs and their coaches. Be careful with coaches who are overly focused on winning and not developing your student-athlete over the long term. Remember, teamwork skills are an important element of your teen's athletic development.

▸ If you are going to talk to the coach, follow the coach's parent/coach communication guidelines. Most coaches prefer that the athletes talk to them first before parents become involved. Communication is appropriate when the coach is not participating in a game and only after what is called a "cooling off" period, ideally 24 hours later. Arrange a time and place where you and your teen can meet the coach privately rather than in front of other players and parents, and ask the coach to explain his/her thought processes. Constructive criticism is appropriate sometimes, depending upon the coach. If you are going to ask the coach questions, don't be afraid of the answers or the coach's perspective.

▸ Let's be real; you, your teen, and your family will have to make many SACRIFICES to get your child prepared for college athletic recruiting. Families will have to make financial sacrifices, and also, time commitment sacrifices.

> The 24-hour rule means that you should wait 24 hours after a frustrating game to communicate with a coach so that you have a "cooling off" time.

"**Sacrifice is so huge**. Many students are not willing to do what it takes to play college ball. For every athlete being recruited, there is another one practicing 110 percent. Someone is practicing more than whatever you do. Sacrifice means you have to be consistent. You can't just show up on the athletic field; you have to do your homework. Athletes and parents must make sacrifices, to the point that they may even struggle financially. Parents pay thousands of dollars for private lessons, but if the kid does not practice the skills learned in the lesson on his own, with a teammate, friend, parent, or sibling, it won't make a difference. Athletes must work on their game beyond the lessons. Many parents hit a "wall" during their child's high school career—it may be financial issues, time, or athletic ability. They may not have the time or the athletic ability to work with their teens beyond paying for lessons. This becomes the WALL for the athlete—the obstacle for improving. Seek a teammate to work on your game. Be creative when you hit a wall or when your resources run out. No matter what, to enter the competitive world of youth sports, athletes must train in the off-season. They can't dust off the cobwebs when the season is going to start."

–Terry Smith
Club Softball Coach & Parent

- Be realistic about your student-athlete being recruited and playing DI sports. Less than 1% of high school student-athletes receive full DI scholarships. There are numerous affordable DII and DIII opportunities for your teen to get a good—even outstanding education, play college sports, and earn scholarships, grants, and/or financial aid.
- Resources are key. Some parents are athletic and can work with their teen on skills and training. Some parents have the academic abilities to help their teen with school work. Some parents or other relatives have more time to spend working on the different athletic and/or academic skills each individual teen needs. Other parents have the money to pay for private tutors, trainers, and coaches. Make the most of the resources available to you.
- For parents who pay for lessons, make the most of those lessons. Parents are needed to help their teen commit to practicing the skills learned from the instructor.

Student-athlete Billy Marsden advocates high school sports are essential to a successful high school career. "As an athlete, I feel like sports greatly contribute to my success because I learn valuable lessons, stay in good shape, have an outlet in my stressful life, and feel a sense of belonging and purpose."

4. Make a Difference with Support

Help your teen, but don't do it for him or her.

- Help your teen personalize this book. Encourage them to write in the book so that he or she can refer back to relevant sections later:
  » Write notes in the margin
  » Ask questions in the margin
  » Underline or highlight key ideas
  » Use the templates in the book or on our website
- Be supportive. Talk about school, and ask about your student's progress toward reaching academic and athletic goals.
- Praise your teen's strengths. Help him or her to find ways to improve weaknesses.
- Have your student write 2-3 positive affirmations about themselves, like:
  » I can pass my English test.
  » I can hit the ball down the line.
  » I can shave 2 seconds off my time.
  » I will be coachable or a leader. See Chapter 6 for details.
- Most importantly, be sure you are not a helicopter parent who takes on all responsibility and speaks for his or her student-athlete. By doing this, you could be detrimental to your teen's natural development in becoming responsible for his or her actions and coaches will avoid you. You will impact the empowering feelings of growth, independence, and responsibility. Find balance between being supportive instead of being pushy and living vicariously

through your kid's life. Use restraint and let your student-athlete live his or her life.

- Find out who your teen's friends are to see who they are being influenced by.
- Be a parent who plays the support role. Your role is to provide understanding and empathy while encouraging your teen to work hard and to learn from mistakes. Help your student-athlete focus on the task and not the outcome. At all times, refrain from doing anything to embarrass your teenager. Show your teen you love him or her no matter the outcome of any academic classes or athletic games.
- Realize that it is excruciatingly painful for some students to learn how to think and write down thoughts. Be supportive through your teen's frustrations and patient.
- Support your student in the process rather than doing work for him or her. Offer advice, but put the responsibility on your child.
- Establish lines of communication. We learned from counselor Linda Drever a great way to do this is to ask your teenager to rate his or her day on a 1 - 10 scale, 10 being the best. Have your teen give rationale for the rating to encourage dialogue. You could also rate your day. Another idea is for each family member to share the highlight of the day. This could happen at the dinner table if you are lucky to have this family time together. Usually, it's better not to prod or ask your teen about his or her day, but rather be patient and refrain from initiating conversation. Wait for them to divulge what is going on or use the rating and/or highlight activity.

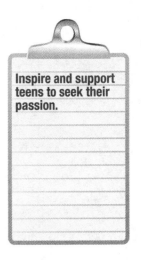

Inspire and support teens to seek their passion.

"**Let the coaches coach** and you root! It is probably the most important thing you can do for your son and his team. Stay positive when the boys have a tough inning; it's all for a purpose bigger than a trophy. We like to win too, but we like to develop even more. Have fun and play HARD."

- An Email to Parents from Competitive Baseball Club Director Rick Sundberg

Begin With The End in Mind

We know from experience that it is very challenging to be a parent. Help your teen advocate for himself or herself and offer unwavering emotional support whether they win or lose. Remember, **education is the leverage** in the college athletic recruiting process, negotiating scholarships, and even with the draft for the professional athletes.

You will find the time spent together on college prep to be invaluable. You can use this time to connect to your teen—especially if he or she participates in competitive sports outside of high school. This time will pass quickly, so try to enjoy every moment. Parenting and sacrificing is challenging but worth it.

1

GAINING LEVERAGE

Education provides leverage. Period.

BE A SUCCESSFUL COLLEGE PREP STUDENT-ATHLETE

The secret to success is simple: **education provides leverage**. Academically successful student-athletes will have more doors opened, options available to them after high school, and they will gain an edge in college recruiting. All teenagers who desire to play sports at the college level need to realize that academics are just as important as athletics.

Kyle concentrated on playing baseball throughout his youth and high school years. He figured he would earn a college baseball scholarship based on his athletic talents and baseball skills. He didn't think it was important to work at earning high grades and settled for C's. After high school, Kyle's only option was a local community college since he did not meet 4-year college admission requirements. He learned that a successful student-athlete is one who develops a work ethic in the athletic arena and in the classroom.

"I wish I got better grades in high school. I didn't care. If I knew then what I know now, I would have worked for better grades."
–Kyle Saukko, Former JUCO National Champion,
MLB Pittsburgh Pirates Minor League Player

Of course, becoming a successful student-athlete requires more than simply earning decent grades. A student-athlete must develop a work ethic both in the classroom and in the arena, as well as communication and leadership qualities. He or she also must develop peak performance (mental toughness) skills, which will allow him to compete at his best, both mentally and physically. All of these will contribute to a student-athlete's overall desirability in the eyes of recruiters and colleges.

Students who compete in athletics and who also earn high grades and high SAT/ACT scores have an advantage over similar academic students who did not complete in athletics. College coaches and recruiters know this; they understand that student-athletes with excellent grades will have many more options. Thus, college coaches will compete for and offer more incentives in order to recruit top student-athletes.

Scouts also recognize that they have to offer better draft deals to academically successful student-athletes, since going straight to the pros is a viable option over going to college for some sports.

Major League Baseball teams had to offer Derrek Lee (who eventually became a first baseman with the Chicago Cubs) a higher signing bonus because he excelled in not only baseball, but academics as well. As a result, the MLB had to offer him more to lure him away from an athletic scholarship to the University of North Carolina. Because he prepared himself academically and athletically, he was able to use his education as leverage to obtain a better offer from the MLB.

> **Gaining leverage means you are working hard each day, one day at a time, to get a little bit better in sports and school.**

Again, remember that education is leverage, and the college prep student
- ‣ Works hard to achieve challenging goals
- ‣ Takes responsibility for his/her education
- ‣ Understands the value of education

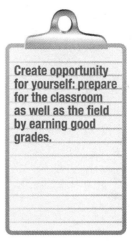

Create opportunity for yourself: prepare for the classroom as well as the field by earning good grades.

"I wish I would have set a high school goal of a 4.0 GPA instead of a 3.0 GPA because could have done better with higher goals."
–Mikela Olsen, Baseball Academy Coach and
Former California State University, Sacramento Baseball Player

Mikela believes that he would have had more college baseball offers if he had worked a little harder academically and earned a higher GPA. He realizes that he should have done his best, rather than settling for minimum standards.

So what about you? What kind of student-athlete do you want to be? How much are you willing to work? Do you want to open all possible academic and athletic doors for yourself? Do you want to be able to make choices about your college future?

How do you get recruited? Terry Battenberg spoke to our student-athletes, giving them excellent advice: "With good direction and a good high school education that you work at, you'll get there." He knows from experience being a high school coach, college coach, college recruiter, and basketball book author. He has found over the years that preparation, networking, and some lucky breaks make a difference in getting recruited. He also advises student-athletes, "Since you never know where you will end up, the journey is important—that you enjoy it and work at it."

You want to have dreams and reach for the stars, and you will need to have a plan to reach your goals. At the same time, you need to understand the reality of competitive sports and college sports.

When asked what advice would you give high school student-athletes, then Fresno State student-athlete Devon Wylie stated, "You have to make sacrifices. You have to sacrifice time with friends and spend your time in the gym working out to gain an edge and you have to spend time studying so you will do well in the classroom." Devon Wylie's sacrifice and hard work took him through high school and college football to the NFL. He was drafted in 2012 by the Kansas City Chiefs.

From Instruction to Evaluation and the Funnel Effect

As you move from competitive club/academy sports and enter high school, you will receive less and less instruction and more evaluation. Your objective should be to understand the desired qualities and performance expectations that colleges look for in student-athletes in regards to academics and in sports. You need to realize the reality of the "funnel effect"—the diminishing numbers of student-athletes who play sports as the intensity level increases.

To get an idea of the competitiveness of playing sports at the next level, look at the chart on the NCAA website, ncaa.org. Choose "Resources" and then click on "Chart on the Probability of a High School Student Going Pro." It reveals the funnel effect on the number of student-athletes who play a specific sport from high school all the way through to the pros. While large numbers of students play sports in high school, only a small percentage continue to the college level. Even a smaller number go pro. For example, of the approximately 1,000,000 boys who played high school football in 2011, only about 6.1% (61,000) will go on to play NCAA football. From those NCAA players, less than 2% (1,340) will make it to the professional level. The NCAA specifically reported that in 2011 only 0.08% of high school football players were estimated to make it to the professional level.

Academic and Athletic Evaluation

You will be evaluated both academically and athletically throughout the recruiting and college admission processes. College scouts look at your GPA and SAT/ACT scores when considering you for their school. In order to be eligible to play NCAA athletics, a student must meet the additional minimum GPA and SAT scores determined by the NCAA. These minimums are based on a sliding scale, which can be viewed in the *NCAA Guide* on their website. On this scale, the higher your grades are, the lower your SAT/ACT scores need to be for NCAA academic eligibility.

Rick Sundberg of Hard 90 Baseball Academy educates his competitive players to know that, they will be forever evaluated much more often than instructed as they compete in tournaments.

Listed are categories of how colleges and scouts evaluate the academic and performance ability of high school students.

Academic Evaluation
- ✓ GPA and strength of schedule (rigor of coursework)
- ✓ Standardized test scores: SAT/ACT
- ✓ Class rank
- ✓ Potential in college coursework/demands
- ✓ Awards/Honors

Athletic Evaluation

Physical Attributes:
- ✓ Height, weight, body type, strength, appearance
- ✓ Specific sport and position skills and talent

Technical Ability:
- ✓ Understanding of position and game strategies/situations
- ✓ Instinct
- ✓ Student of the game

Psychological Qualities:
- ✓ Mental approach to the game
- ✓ Ability to deal with adversity
- ✓ Passion for the game
- ✓ Ability to be part of a "team"
- ✓ Ability to be a leader

In terms of athletic evaluation, the physical attributes and technical ability are most important for recruiting. Psychological qualities and mental toughness are important in terms of getting playing time once on a college team, given that you have the grades to be eligible to compete.

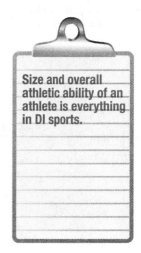

Size and overall athletic ability of an athlete is everything in DI sports.

Potential DI blue-chip athletes (the most highly recruited athletes) should not be considered "the norm" or the "typical kid" found in high schools across the nation. They are athletically gifted, physically dominant and talented primarily because of genetics. Many of these DI athletes are exceptions to the norm for their age groups. The good news is that non-blue-chip athletes can still play college sports. There are potential DII and DIII, as well as, NAIA athletes found in many high schools. There is a place for you to play if you are willing to work for it.

Now that you have been exposed to the reality of college sports and the funnel effect, you need to be realistic about evaluating your physical attributes and sport-specific talents so you can find the right college for you athletically. You also need to find an academic fit based upon the grades and SAT scores you earned.

To be a successful college prep student-athlete, you will need to develop essential academic skills and athletic fundamentals, as well as mental toughness. You will need to evaluate your academic and athletic skills and then set achievable goals. You also will need to take the time to research college sports and understand NCAA eligibility rules, so that you are able to achieve your goal of becoming a college athlete. Of course, to become one, you will first need to get college coaches' attention by marketing yourself. A smart student-athlete will also make unofficial and official college visits to find the right fit for him or her academically and athletically. In addition to this, you will also need to prepare for college admissions tests, stay on top of college applications, and negotiate scholarships and/or financial aid.

Find the right fit, both academically and athletically.

Roy Williams, then Kansas University,and current University of North Carolina Basketball Coach shared impressionable words with us high school basketball coaches at a Nike sponsored Las Vegas clinic: Play Hard, Play Smart.

Most student-athletes play sports because they are passionate about them. However, sports are only one part of a student-athlete's life and the college experience. College, for most, is about maturing, learning to make good decisions, being exposed to diversity, making lifelong friends, and finding a career path. Student-athletes should remember that sports participation is fairly short term; athletes can't play sports their whole lives and only a select few go pro. So, while high school success is important in getting recruited, consider making your high school experience more than a stepping-stone. Seek that difficult balance between preparing for college academically and athletically while enjoying still your high school years.

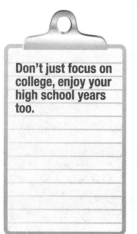

Don't just focus on college, enjoy your high school years too.

The rest of this book will actually guide you through your high school and college prep journey so that you gain the leverage you need to compete at the next level. The following chapter is about getting organized, followed by developing academic and athletic essentials and peak performance skills. The chapter after that will help you set goals. The remaining chapters are about considering college athletic opportunities, being an NCAA qualifier, determining the role of college sports for you, finding the right place to play, and understanding college recruiting. Then, the book will guide you through marketing yourself, making college visits, taking admissions tests, completing college applications, and researching college scholarships and financial aid.

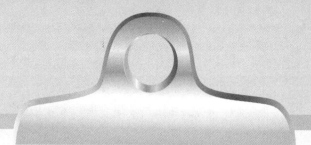

Chapter 1
Top 10 Plays

1. Successful athletes are students first

2. Academics are equally as important as athletics

3. Develop a strong work ethic

4. Be realistic about the "funnel effect"

5. Be realistic as you evaluate yourself academically

6. Be realistic as you evaluate yourself athletically

7. Create opportunities for yourself

8. Play hard

9. Play smart

10. Don't forget to enjoy your high school years while preparing for college

2 GETTING ORGANIZED

Chance favors the prepared mind.

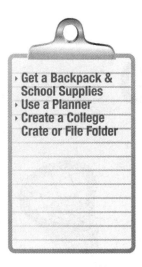

▸ Get a Backpack &
  School Supplies
▸ Use a Planner
▸ Create a College
  Crate or File Folder

FIRST STEPS TO GETTING ORGANIZED

The key to success in your high school classes, athletics and college preparation is to get and stay organized. It's easy to say, but takes effort to execute (just like it's easy to learn a play in sports but takes commitment and effort to execute). You will need a planner, school supplies, and a crate or a expandable file folder. You will also want to use *The Academic Athlete Checklist* (located in Chapter 3).

✓ Get a Backpack & School Supplies
✓ Use a Planner
✓ Create a College Crate or File Folder

Get a Backpack and School Supplies

Listed here are recommended supplies that you will need to bring to high school or have at home:

School:

✓ Backpack
✓ Binder (some teachers have specific requirements)
✓ Dividers w/tabs
✓ College ruled paper
✓ Calculator (scientific or graphing)
✓ Pencils
✓ Pens
✓ Colored pencils
✓ Highlighters
✓ White out
✓ Water
✓ Snacks (preferably not chips or candy)

Home

✓ A consistent, quiet place to study
✓ Internet access
✓ Computer
✓ Flash drive
✓ Printer paper
✓ Dictionary
✓ File folders to keep work from each subject
✓ Stapler
✓ Hole punch
✓ 3 X 5 Index cards, loose or spiral-bound (for flashcards or note cards)

Use a Planner

Using a planner will help you organize your academic, athletic, and personal life. Successful athletes know how important it is to prepare for a game and successful students know how important it is to prepare for academics. Successful student-athletes prepare for both by using a planner.

The first step is to get a planner or use a calendar application on your phone. Many schools offer student planners, but you can also purchase or make one. We provide examples of a weekly template for planners, which can be found in Chapter 7, as well as on our website. You can make copies for yourself and put them into your school notebook.

Also, many athletes keep a training log to make sure they are doing what it takes to meet their athletic goals each day. You can choose to combine your academic calendar with your athletic training log or maintain two separate time management organizers. We highly recommend that you use only one calendar/planner for everything, including school, sports, and personal life to avoid confusion.

The key is to write down all of your tasks, responsibilities, homework, sports, and personal schedule in your planner so that you can budget your limited time efficiently. When you write down what you want and need to do, you are more likely to get it done.

STAY ORGANIZED

Once you get organized, you need to stay organized. This is the commitment and execution part of being organized. Commit to checking your schedules and reviewing your daily athletic and academic commitments. Don't miss one day. All successful student-athletes write down their academic, as well as athletic activities, to keep their lives organized. They realize the importance of maintaining an academic calendar and a training log to keep them on track to prepare to compete at the college level. By doing so, you will be better able to avoid overbooking yourself or getting off track.

Use a File Folder for College Materials

In addition to keeping a planner, you will want to document all your communications with college admission and scholarship personnel, coaches, and scouts. No doubt, collecting, organizing, and recording college materials may become a challenging task and even a chore, but it will be very rewarding during the recruitment process. You will need to keep copies of official documents you send for NCAA eligibility, college admittance and financial aid, as well as scholarships.

Alex Diemer, a recruited volleyball athlete, found that during her junior year she had an overwhelming amount of college informational materials. Her dad thought the best way to keep the abundant materials organized was to use a plastic crate. He bought a box of manila folders, and included one folder for each college that Alex had been in contact with. Follow the steps below to create a filing system that will help you stay organized.

Organize and record college information in file folders

- **Step 1: Purchase or get a crate or box, several manila folders, and four colored folders (orange, blue, red, and green.)**
- **Step 2:** Label the orange folder "Personal & Family Data," label the blue folder "Athletics," label the red folder "Testing," and label the green folder "Scholarships & Financial Aid,"
- **Step 3:** Write the name of the potential college on the tab of each manila folder.
- **Step 4:** Staple your communication log to the inside left cover of the folder (see sample below) and complete a log every time there is interaction with a college.
- **Step 5:** As soon as you receive college materials, file them immediately into your file folders (procrastination will lead to piles of materials that you will lose or forget about.)
- **Step 6:** Later, when you are narrowing your choices, arrange the college folders in order of preference to help you decide which one you want to attend. Colleges that you are no longer considering can be moved to the back of the crate file, but don't throw anything away. You never know if you will reconsider a specific college.

Colored File Folders
- *Personal Information (Orange)*
- *Athletic Information (Blue)*
- *Academic Information (Red)*
- *Scholarships & Financial Aid (Green)*

Manila Folders
- *One for each college interested in*

Your orange colored folder will be the first folder in your crate. It will contain your personal data that most colleges will ask you for. You won't have much in here to begin with, but you will be continually adding and updating the information. You will start with a list of extracurricular and volunteer activities, your family background information, and academic honors. The blue folder will be your second folder and will contain all athletic information. The red folder, third, is used for SAT/ACT and AP/IB information and scores. The green folder will follow and contain financial information if you plan on applying for scholarships and/or financial aid.

📁 *Athletic Information (Blue)*

- ‣ Personal profile
- ‣ Athletic schedules (high school, club team, tournaments & camps)
- ‣ NCAA Eligibility Center pin number (register beginning of junior year)

📁 *Academic Information: (Red)*

- ‣ Keep passwords & usernames for SAT/ACT online login
- ‣ SAT/ACT scores
- ‣ AP or IB test scores
- ‣ Name of high school
- ‣ 4 or 6-year high school academic plan
- ‣ List of high school coursework/transcript
- ‣ Grades
- ‣ Class rank
- ‣ Academic honors/awards
- ‣ Make a list of 12-15 colleges you would like to attend

📁 *Scholarships & Financial Aid (Green)*

- ‣ SAR document
- ‣ FAFSA pin number and documents
- ‣ List of possible scholarships

📁 *Personal Information (Orange)*

Personal and Family Data
- ‣ Name
- ‣ Address
- ‣ Phone number
- ‣ Email
- ‣ Social Security number
- ‣ Parent information (occupation, educational level, ethnicity, etc.)

Extracurricular Activities during high school
- ‣ Committees
- ‣ Clubs/Student government
- ‣ Leadership positions
- ‣ Athletics—schedule for the year (high school, camps, tournaments)
- ‣ NCAA pin number

Work Experience/Volunteer Activities
- ‣ Work experience
- ‣ Community Service/Volunteer work
- ‣ Church/Youth groups

Personal Statement
- ‣ Highlights of activities
- ‣ What you want to promote about yourself

The information to the left will eventually be placed in your colored folders. You will continue to add to these folders through your senior year.

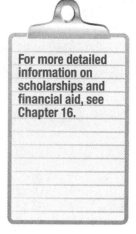

For more detailed information on scholarships and financial aid, see Chapter 16.

To keep track of activities use this log. Start writing down information your freshman year, and continue to update the log at the end of each semester. Make copies or download extras when you run out of room at dcipress. com. If you don't keep track of it now, you'll have to search through documents later on to log your college application activities, so it's better to start early and update often.

ACADEMIC, ATHLETIC, EXTRACURRICULAR & VOLUNTEER ACTIVITIES LOG

Use the Activity Log to record your participation in academic, athletic, and extra-curricular events throughout high school starting in your freshman year. You will refer to this information when you apply to colleges your senior year (see Chapter 15 and 16).

Activity	Year in school	Date	Time spent (hours)	Positions held	Awards

SAT/ACT TEST LOG

Tests	Registration	Test Date	Test Scores
PSAT 10th grade			Math _____ Critical Reading _____ Writing _____
PSAT 11th grade for NMSQT eligibility			Math _____ Critical Reading _____ Writing _____
PLAN 10th grade			Math _____ Science _____ Reading _____ English _____
SAT 11th grade fall			Math _____ Critical Reading _____ Writing _____ Total Score _____ Essay _____
SAT 11th grade spring			Math _____ Critical Reading _____ Writing _____ Total Score _____ Essay _____
SAT 12th grade fall, if necessary			Math _____ Critical Reading _____ Writing _____ Total Score _____ Essay _____
SAT Subject Test Subject: _____			#1: _____
SAT Subject Test Subject: _____			#2: _____
SAT Subject Test Subject: _____			#3: _____
ACT 11th grade fall			Math _____ Science _____ Reading _____ English _____ Composition _____ Writing _____
ACT 11th grade spring			Math _____ Science _____ Reading _____ English _____ Composition _____ Writing _____

Keep a list of any Advanced Placement (AP) or International Baccalaureate (IB) courses, and keep a log of the test scores if you take the exams in the spring. We recommend you take at least one AP or IB course while in high school. Challenge yourself.

AP/IB LOG	
AP/IB courses	Scores (if test taken)

You may want to add more colored folders, or simply use one folder for all four categories, depending on how you like to organize the information you gather. If the crate concept does not work for you, accordion files might be a better fit. Regardless of how you keep track of the information, it is absolutely essential that you remain organized. Having a system when you receive your initial college information will keep you from getting overwhelmed. Try to keep up with the filing and recording on your logs at least weekly, if not daily.

📁 *Manila Folders*

In addition to your four colored folders, you will need a manila folder for every college you visit, contact or receive materials from.

You will be constantly receiving and sending materials to and from schools, as well as answering phone calls, making college visits, and exchanging information at tournaments or competitions with coaches, recruiters, and other student-athletes. Some of the items you will want to file in the manila folders in your crate are:
- Brochures
- Letters
- Phone call records
- Copy of emails
- Notes from your unofficial and official visits

Communication Log

Keep track of all communications you have by filling in the communication log you have stapled to the inside of your college manila file folder. Write down the date, type of communication, who initiated contact, name of the person you talked to, and a summary of the content of the communication.

Also write down what you send out to colleges and coaches, such as emails with your profile and links to athletic highlights, and perhaps a cover letter to accompany a DVD requested by a college coach.

Almost all contact today between parents/athletes and coaches/admissions personnel is done by email. It is important to keep all emails brief but specific. College coaches are known to delete emails that are too lengthy without reading them.

COMMUNICATION LOG FOR COLLEGE 1: _____

Date	Email or phone?	Initiated by	Name & Position:	What did you talk about?

COMMUNICATION LOG FOR COLLEGE 2: _____

Date	Email or phone?	Initiated by	Name & Position:	What did you talk about?

COMMUNICATION LOG FOR COLLEGE 3: _____

Date	Email or phone?	Initiated by	Name & Position:	What did you talk about?

Bottom line…

Use the ideas in this chapter to get yourself organized with a method that works for you. At the minimum, keep all of your college documents in a box so they are in one place when you need to find them. Many files can be stored digitally, but you will need some sort of organization plan to collect brochures, letters and other documents, especially if you are being recruited by many colleges or plan on applying to multiple schools.

Get organized; find a method that works for you and stick with it.

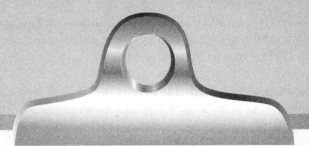

Chapter 2
Top 10 Plays

1. Get organized

2. Keep necessary school supplies in your backpack

3. Use a planner

4. Collect college materials in folders or in one box

5. Keep record of awards and volunteer activities

6. Keep track of all testing dates and results

7. Stay on top of scholarships

8. Document financial aid information

9. Create a communication log with coaches

10. Stay organized

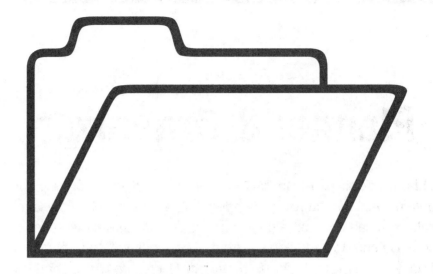

What should you keep for your college application?

We recommend that you keep all of your important documents in one college bin with a few folders. Keep track of your awards and achievements from the beginning of high school, maintain a list of SAT/ACT website login usernames and passwords, keep all AP, PSAT/PLAN, SAT/ACT and other official test scores, and log all community service hours as you complete them.

Colored File Folders

🗁 *Personal Information (Orange)*

🗁 *Athletic Information (Blue)*

🗁 *Academic Information (Red)*

🗁 *Scholarships & Financial Aid (Green)*

Manila Folders

🗀 *One for each college interested in*

Planner & Organizer

This Academic & Athletic Checklist will help you keep track of both necessary and recommended academic and athletic essentials. You can print extra copies of this checklist from dcipress. com. Be sure to keep it in the front of your college crate or file folder. Always refer to the *Summary of Recruiting Rules* chart on ncaa.org, because rules are constantly changing and vary depending on the division.

☑ ACADEMIC   ☑ ATHLETIC

☐ The left column describes academic responsibilities for all students.	☐ The right column lists recommendations for student-athletes specifically.

If you are currently a high school junior or senior and you just purchased this planner, then you need to "fast track" yourself, going back to the preceding years and making sure you have met all the recommendations and requirements. We recommend that you read through the checklist until senior year, no matter what grade you are currently in, so that you are prepared from the beginning.

3

Using The
ACADEMIC ATHLETE CHECKLIST

If you fail to plan,
plan to fail.

☑ ACADEMIC

- ☐ Parents: Be proactive in supporting your student
  - › See "Insights for Parents" in Purpose

- ☐ Take foreign language, Algebra I, keyboardng, computer qpplications, and study skills, if available

- ☐ Investigate options of attending private or prep high schools for rigorous academic preparation

- ☐ If you struggle academically, get the necessary academic support
  - › Tutors, parental monitoring, progress reports, weekly checks, contact with parents, course and teacher selection, counseling, homework centers, on-site assistance

- ☐ In Spring: complete a 4-year plan and 9th grade course selection for high school with the goal of meeting admissions requirements for the most desirable colleges

- ☐ Volunteer & Charity Work: church, school, hospital, Goodwill, environmental organizations, or clubs

☑ ATHLETIC

- ☐ Download a current copy of *NCAA Guide for the College-Bound Student-Athlete* at ncaa.org

- ☐ The NCAA guide defines what core courses are needed for eligibility for college athletes
  - › *Note:* There are special circumstances and situations for home school, GED, independent study students, foreign, special needs, transfer students, and eligibility waivers
  - › **The regulations in the guide change yearly; make sure to go online for most current information and guidelines**

- ☐ Investigate options of attending private or prep high schools for athletic development and exposure

- ☐ Research opportunities for sports specific training such as local competitive clubs and academies if not already participating

- ☐ Develop your athletic potential (fitness, strength, speed, conditioning, agility, nutrition) and participate in sport specific training

- ☐ Start filling in DI & DII worksheets for NCAA eligibility qualifier status

- ☐ Set summer goals and priorities

- ☐ Maintain a summer planner

☑ ACADEMIC

- ☐ Organize high school required materials and books

- ☐ Set academic goals
  - ‣ Short/long term
  - ‣ Use the **SMART** goal-template
  - ‣ Take course work that makes you a desirable college-bound student (advanced courses, foreign languages, etc.)

- ☐ Take the initiative to schedule a meeting with your high school counselor with your parents—let them know your college plans

- ☐ Know that colleges look at
  - ‣ GPA
  - ‣ Rigor of schedule/AP or IB coursework
  - ‣ SAT scores
  - ‣ Extra-curricular activities
  - ‣ Volunteer work

- ☐ "Open doors" by creating opportunities and completing the most rigorous course work and earning the best grades you can. (No D's or F's)

- ☐ Attend any parent/student informational workshops

- ☐ Start to think about the kind of college environment you want to be a part of (private, public, big, small, etc.)

- ☐ Make a list of potential colleges you'd like to attend

- ☐ Develop Academic Skills
  - ‣ Organization
  - ‣ Note-taking
    - » Cornell Notes
  - ‣ Study Skills
  - ‣ Test-taking strategies

☑ ATHLETIC

- ☐ Download a current copy of *NCAA Guide for the College-Bound Student-Athlete* at ncaa.org

- ☐ Set athletic goals
  - ‣ Note desired athletic qualities

- ☐ Set peak performance goals
  - ‣ Write positive self-affirmations

- ☐ Practice good communication skills between students, teachers, and coaches

- ☐ Create your personal profile/resume
  - ‣ Include both academic and athletic accomplishments

- ☐ Get a physical examination and bring your school's athletic forms—turn paperwork into your school office

- ☐ Meet with your counselor in fall and inform him/her that you want to play college sports

- ☐ Read and understand NCAA recruiting process and rules (academic eligibility requirements)

- ☐ Complete DI and DII worksheets located in the *NCAA Guide*

- ☐ Read about the differences between DI, DII, DIII, NAIA, and community colleges.

- ☐ Read about the NCAA DI GPA/SAT sliding scale and requirements to be a qualifier (DII and DIII do not have a sliding scale)

- ☐ Maintain qualifier status. Meet with your counselor again to insure that you are a NCAA qualifier

College coaches cannot admit you if you do not qualify academically

9TH GRADE

☑ ACADEMIC

- › Positive mental preparation
- ☐ Improve Academic Literacy
  - › Reading
    - » Textbook
    - » Active
    - » Reciprocal
  - › Writing
    - » Essay structure
  - › Vocabulary
    - » Flashcards
- ☐ Develop essential math skills
- ☐ Create opportunities by taking initiative
- ☐ In spring, update your 4-year plan and review high school transcripts
  - › AP/IB/Honors courses
  - › A–G course selection
  - › Graduation requirements
- ☐ Get involved in summer activities that are interesting to you and admissions counselors, such as volunteer or charity work
- ☐ Look into college scholarships and applications just to become familiar with the process

☑ ATHLETIC

NCAA academic regulations are becoming more rigorous

- ☐ Do sports specific training
- ☐ Work on fitness and nutrition

No contact off campus (in person or via phone) from college coach to you or to parents

- ☐ Communicate with high school/club coach
- ☐ Investigate summer camp opportunities
  - › Attend summer camps at colleges you are considering
- ☐ On your computer, create an Excel table or Word document to keep track of your contacts
- ☐ Consider attending key events/tournaments to be seen by scouts
- ☐ Notify college coaches of tournament play via email
- ☐ Update DI & DII worksheets for NCAA eligibility qualifier status
- ☐ Set summer goals and priorities
- ☐ Maintain a summer planner

10TH GRADE

☑ ACADEMIC

- ☐ Update academic goals
- ☐ List potential colleges
- ☐ College Search Resources
  - ‣ Online resources
  - ‣ High school career center
  - ‣ High school counselor
- ☐ Create a file for letters, brochures, and other college mail
- ☐ Visit your high school counselor with your parents—let them know your college plans
- ☐ Earn the best grades you can get
- ☐ Develop peak performance skills
- ☐ Register for PSAT/PLAN in August or September
- ☐ Register with the College Board website and take advantage of their resources
- ☐ Take PSAT/PLAN in October
- ☐ Begin SAT/ACT prep
  - ‣ Vocabulary
  - ‣ Timed writing—expository
  - ‣ Reading comprehension
  - ‣ Math review
- ☐ Register for AP tests, if taking any AP courses
- ☐ Practice good reading skills
  - ‣ Annotate/highlight
- ☐ Practice Writing
  - ‣ SAT/ACT prompts
  - ‣ AP/IB/FRQ/DBQ structure
- ☐ Take AP/IB tests in May
- ☐ Review high school transcript

☑ ATHLETIC

- ☐ Download a current copy of *NCAA Guide for the College-Bound Student-Athlete* at ncaa.org
- ☐ Inform your varsity high school coach that you want to play college sports
- ☐ Learn how college recruiting works (Chapter 11)
- ☐ List potential colleges with playing sports as a goal
- ☐ Create a file to collect emails, letters, camp information, etc. from schools, coaches & admissions staff
- ☐ Update athletic goals and personal profile/resume for colleges
- ☐ Purchase a video camera and tripod. Begin to create a highlight DVD
- ☐ Email college coaches your profile with a YouTube link to your highlight film
- ☐ Develop peak performance skills
  - ‣ Imagery scripts (Chapter 6)
- ☐ Initiate coach contact
  - ‣ See sample email template (Chapter 12)
  - ‣ Read through call scripts (Chapter 12)
- ☐ You may receive questionnaires and camp brochures
- ☐ Research colleges to build your potential college list. Make unofficial visits
- ☐ Attend day camps or mini-camps at colleges
  - ‣ Many are invitational and low-cost
- ☐ Coaches cannot talk to you or your parents in person

☑ ACADEMIC

☐ Update 4-year plan

  ‣ Remain a qualifier

  ‣ Meet graduation requirements

  ‣ Fill out DI & DII worksheets

☐ If the colleges you are applying to require or recommend the SAT II subject test, register and take subject tests immediately after completing course work (Biology, World History, World Language, etc.)

SUMMER AFTER 10TH GRADE

☐ Consider making visits to colleges (Chapter 13)

  ‣ Make appointments with admissions officers

  ‣ Tour campus

☐ Research information online at collegeboard.org

☐ Start studying for the ACT/SAT

☑ ATHLETIC

☐ Meet with counselor in spring to plan junior courses and to review transcript

  ‣ Keep focused on being a qualifier

☐ Develop your athletic potential (strength, conditioning, agility, nutrition) and participate in sport specific training

☐ Update Excel document for contacts

☐ Consider attending key events/tournaments to be seen by scouts

☐ Email college coaches your tournament information so they can see you play

☐ Read college team rosters to note types of physical attributes and positions of current players

SUMMER AFTER 10TH GRADE

☐ Calls can be made at your expense at the end of 10th grade, **after** school is out (refer to the NCAA recruiting chart)

☐ Consider making **unofficial** visits to colleges

  ‣ Make appointment with admissions officers

  ‣ Meet coaches

  ‣ Tour campus

  ‣ Observe a practice or game

☐ Set summer goals and priorities

☐ Maintain a summer planner

11TH GRADE

☑ ACADEMIC

- ☐ Revise academic goals

- ☐ Refine list of colleges

- ☐ Send letters to request information packets from all the colleges you are interested in

- ☐ Visit your high school counselor with your parents—let them know your college plans and ask for any guidance

- ☐ Talk to older friends who are at college about their experiences

- ☐ Research scholarships, financial aid, grants (online and career center)

- ☐ Earn the best grades you can

- ☐ Take the PSAT in October. It will qualify you for National Merit Scholarships

- ☐ Prepare for the SAT/ACT

- ☐ Consider applying for early decision or early action
  - ‣ These applications are due in the fall

- ☐ Register and take SAT/ACT in winter
  - ‣ Be sure to check the websites for current registration deadlines and testing dates

- ☐ Register and take the SAT/ACT in spring, preferably in March and June
  - ‣ Be sure to mark the Eligibility Center Code 9999 and the codes of schools you are interested in
  - ‣ Take the tests twice to try to improve your score

- ☐ If you are applying to highly selective colleges, consider taking SAT II subject tests immediately after completing course work (eg. U.S. History, Spanish, etc.)

- ☐ File all test results

☑ ATHLETIC

- ☐ Download a current copy of *NCAA Guide for the College-Bound Student-Athlete* at ncaa.org

- ☐ Register online at ncaa.org for a small fee with the Eligibility Center at the beginning of the junior year if you intend to play college athletics
  - ‣ You are not eligible for DI or DII without this certification. You will be assigned a PIN number
  - ‣ Designate colleges you want notified of your eligibility

- ☐ Update athletic goals

- ☐ Inform your high school varsity coach that you plan on playing college sports

- ☐ Consider your capacity to play multiple high school sports and/or club teams

- ☐ Evaluate your athletic abilities to determine where you can play

- ☐ Revise college lists with sports and without sports

- ☐ Begin recruiting actions

You may receive recruiting materials

- ☐ Promote and market yourself to colleges
  - ‣ Return questionnaires
  - ‣ Send your profile to 30-50 college
  - ‣ Send your DVD, if requested
  - ‣ Send your game schedules
  - ‣ Send thank you notes and always follow-up

- ☐ Email coaches your profile with a YouTube link to your highlight film and, if requested, game film

- ☐ Talk to older friends who are at college about their experiences

☑ ACADEMIC

☐ Register for spring AP/IB tests

☐ Practice your speaking skills

☐ Develop writing skills
- Expository writing for SAT/ACT
- College application essay

☐ Research colleges and majors online at collegeboard.org

☐ Attend your school's college/career night

☐ Update a list of desired colleges (at least 10-15 including dream and backup) with academic and athletic fit

☐ Visit your high school counselor to make sure you're on the right track. Review your schedule with him or her

☐ Take AP/IB tests in May

☐ Update 4-year plan
- Retake courses to improve your GPA
- Meet graduation requirements
- Consider AP/IB courses for senior year

☐ Take a leadership class as well as advanced academic course

☑ ATHLETIC

☐ Make **unofficial** visits to colleges
- Make appointment with admissions officers
- Meet coaches
- Tour campus
- Observe a practice or game

No official visits are allowed until senior year

☐ Save formal evaluations by coaches/scouts/recruiters

☐ Update your personal profile and think about how to promote yourself
- Coaches may not find you, even if you are a top player, if you don't put yourself out there

☐ Remain a qualifier and update DI & DII worksheets

☐ Research scouting services before committing. They are not NCAA endorsed

☐ Coaches can make limited phone calls starting in the spring and summer. The exact date varies depending on the specific sport and division. See *Summary of Recruiting Rules* chart on ncaa.org

☐ Continue researching athletic programs and coaches

☐ Send athletic schedule of your high school games, club tournaments, and any camps to coaches

☐ Ask your high school counselor to send an official transcript to the Eligibility Center after finishing your junior year (fax is not accepted)
- If you attended more than one high school, send transcripts from all high schools

11TH GRADE

☑ ACADEMIC

SUMMER AFTER 11TH GRADE

☐ Make visits to colleges

- ‣ Make appointment with admissions officers
- ‣ Tour campus
- ‣ Observe practice

☐ Make a list of teachers and coaches to write letters of recommendation (ask the first week of school your senior year)

☐ Draft essay for college application

☐ Update your personal profile

☐ Continue preparing for SAT/ACT exams in fall

- ‣ Take practice tests
- ‣ Study online with YouTube and other free resources
- ‣ Check out SAT/ACT prep books from your local library

☐ Explore scholarship opportunities

☐ Order or print out college applications

☐ Register for a FAFSA PIN so you can begin applying for scholarships

☑ ATHLETIC

☐ Research scholarships, financial aid, and grants

SUMMER AFTER 11TH GRADE

☐ For most sports, after July 1st you can have face-to-face contact with the coach off the college campus

☐ Develop your athletic potential (strength, conditioning, agility, nutrition) and participate in sport specific training

☐ Read a mental toughness or peak performance book and apply it to your sport

☐ Attend tournaments, academic showcases, or combines

☐ Attend summer camps at colleges you hope to attend

☐ Set summer goals and priorities

☐ Maintain a summer planner

12TH GRADE

☑ ACADEMIC

- ☐ Revise goals and update college lists

- ☐ Avoid "senioritis" to prepare for college academics

- ☐ Take rigorous academic classes. Continue in math or science classes if you want to attend prestigious institutions

- ☐ Update your profile

- ☐ Visit your high school counselor with your parents and let them know your college plans

- ☐ Take a leadership or public speaking class

- ☐ **Earn the best grades you can**

- ☐ Ask teachers, coaches, and counselors to write letters of recommendation for you a month before you need to send them
  - ‣ Remind them of the deadline

- ☐ Edit your personal essay for admissions
  - ‣ Review with a teacher who will help you edit

- ☐ Make **official** and **unofficial** visits to colleges
  - ‣ Make an appointment with admissions officers
  - ‣ Tour campus
  - ‣ Check if the college has overnight or weekend visits

- ☐ Continue preparing for the SAT/ACT

- ☐ Register and take the SAT/ACT in fall

DECEMBER IS THE LAST SAT/ACT TEST DATE FOR SENIORS

☑ ATHLETIC

- ☐ Download a current copy of *NCAA Guide for the College-Bound Student-Athlete* at ncaa.org

- ☐ Develop your athletic potential (strength, conditioning, agility, nutrition) and participate in sport-specific training

- ☐ Update your personal profile

- ☐ Email coaches an updated profile with a YouTube link to your highlight film

- ☐ Continue to maintain your qualifier status
  - ‣ Meet NCAA academic eligibility requirements
  - ‣ Make sure you fulfill university, state, and private college entrance requirements
  - ‣ In addition, double-check your high school graduation requirements

- ☐ Take rigorous classes senior year rather than coasting through
  - ‣ Deal with "senioritis" and continue your learning so that you will be prepared for college academics

- ☐ Make **unofficial** visits to colleges (dependent on your sport season)
  - ‣ Make appointment with admissions
  - ‣ Meet coaches
  - ‣ Tour campus
  - ‣ Observe a practice or game

- ☐ Take official visits to DI & DII schools you are interested in (up to 5 visits, only 1 visit per school)

- ☐ Ask to meet with your coach to get advice on playing college sports
  - ‣ Ask coaches for college recommendations

12TH GRADE

☑ ACADEMIC

- ☐ Take the SAT/ACT until you have achieved your best score or the necessary score for a specific college. Send scores to each of the colleges you are applying to

- ☐ Check in with your high school counselor to find about research financial aid, scholarships, grants, etc.

- ☐ Complete the applications for your targeted colleges

- ☐ Write your college application essay

- ☐ File the FAFSA (Free Application for Federal Student Aid) beginning January 1
  - ‣ Many colleges have January deadlines. For some schools, you must apply before you can receive any merit money
  - ‣ Apply even if you don't think you qualify for need-based money

- ☐ Verify your FAFSA online. Mark section G of the form to denote which colleges you want forms sent to

- ☐ Apply for grants, loans, and scholarships
  - ‣ Research institutional grants in the scholarship section of college catalogs

- ☐ Call and ask if the application fee can be deferred until after being admitted

- ☐ Complete the CSS Profile if colleges require it

- ☐ Review the Student Aid Report (SAR) for accuracy
  - ‣ Call for another free copy of SAR report at 319-337-5665
  - ‣ Make a copy of SAR form for every recruiter and visit, even if you think they received it with your FAFSA

☑ ATHLETIC

- ☐ Note that college coaches have limited contact/evaluation yet there are plenty of opportunities to meet coaches
  - ‣ Continually consult NCAA recruiting regulations

- ☐ Initiate calls to college coaches
  - ‣ Have questions ready and use phone etiquette

- ☐ Send your athletic schedules to colleges so they can watch you compete

- ☐ Compete in the significant sport-specific events if you can afford them
  - ‣ These are helpful ways to be seen but not necessary

- ☐ Check NCAA for rules regarding all-star contests

- ☐ Ask college coaches where you are on their "depth chart"

- ☐ Read rosters to see what the team needs in the near future and look for patterns in the roster and note where players are from (high school or community college)

- ☐ Go to the National Letter of Intent section of the NCAA website for early and regular signing deadlines

- ☐ Send follow-up emails to coaches and send a thank you note if you signed early

- ☐ Research scholarship possibilities

- ☐ Observe a college practice or game

☑ ACADEMIC

- ☐ Note the Expected Family Contribution (EFC)—this is a calculation of what you are believed to be able to pay

- ☐ Complete the optional, yet beneficial, Financial Aid Estimator (FAE), which is an estimation of what college financial aid is needed to attend

- ☐ Complete the Institutional Financial Aid Application Form
  - ‣ For private colleges and research specialized scholarships and special circumstances such as alumni, department, or religious scholarships

- ☐ Follow-up on letters of recommendations from teachers and coaches to make sure letters were sent, and send thank you notes

- ☐ Request transcripts to be sent to colleges by either your high school registrar or high school counselor
  - ‣ Final transcripts are sent after graduation

- ☐ Work on improving your writing:
  - ‣ Expository essays
  - ‣ Literary analysis
  - ‣ AP/IB essays

- ☐ College acceptance letters are usually sent out by the end of April. Go to collegeconfidential.com to see if other students from your school have received acceptances

- ☐ Visit colleges after receiving acceptances to help you decide. Try to schedule overnight visits

- ☐ Attend admitted student days in spring

- ☐ If placed on a wait list, consider your options

☑ ATHLETIC

- ☐ Some colleges offer the opportunity for seniors to meet the minimum SAT/ACT score after the deadline, during the summer before fall admittance (if they really want you for their sports program)

- ☐ Continue to visit colleges
  - ‣ Focus on colleges that are interested in you (if they pay for your trip, they are interested)

- ☐ Make a second visit if necessary

- ☐ Narrow down your list. Weigh the pros and cons of college possibilities with and without sports

- ☐ Stay in contact with coaches. Send performance updates

- ☐ Discuss financial aid packages and calculate if additional scholarships or loans are needed

- ☐ Negotiate financial aid packages, especially with DIII and private colleges

- ☐ Sign National Letter of Intent and "athletic tender" simultaneously. Return them by the deadline

- ☐ Request your final high school transcript to be sent to the NCAA Eligibility Center

SUMMER AFTER 12TH GRADE

- ☐ Participate in competitive summer athletics

- ☐ Continue your athletic training and conditioning—most colleges will send you a summer workout program

- ☐ Read a peak performance or leadership book

☑ ACADEMIC

- ☐ Complete appeal letters if you did not gain admittance or financial aid
- ☐ Weigh pros and cons of college possibilities (PMI charts)
- ☐ Officially commit to the college of your choice. Decline offers of admission from remaining colleges in early May
- ☐ Take AP/IB exams in May
  - ‣ Make sure scores are sent to your selected college
- ☐ Send required deposits to your selected college, including housing deposit
  - ‣ Fill out housing-preference forms early to guarantee housing
- ☐ Inform your counselor and career center of your decision
- ☐ If you are wait listed, expect information about your status
- ☐ Request final grades and transcript to be sent to the college
- ☐ Send thank you notes to teachers, coaches, and counselors for helping
  - ‣ Also send thank you notes to college personnel who assisted with visits

SUMMER AFTER 12TH GRADE

- ☐ Attend orientation
  - ‣ Register for college courses at orientation
- ☐ Continue working on academic skills prep (essay writing, reading comprehension)
- ☐ Read, read, read!

☑ ATHLETIC

- ☐ Investigate your health insurance options while you are playing sports in college
- ☐ Set summer goals and priorities for your first year at college
- ☐ Maintain a summer planner

4

Developing
ACADEMIC
ESSENTIALS

Learning is not a spectator sport.

BE AN ACADEMIC STUDENT-ATHLETE

There are fundamental academic skills that apply to all subjects and can help you be successful in high school and in college, just as there are fundamentals in sports that help you compete successfully in all aspects of the game. This chapter outlines the necessary skills including building vocabulary, reading, note-taking, writing, speaking, listening, solving math problems, studying, test-taking, researching, and using technology.

"Show me a kid who is a good student and there is a chance he will be a better player on the field because a coach will only have to tell him once what to do instead of annoyingly and exhaustingly explaining something day in and day out. A college player has mental discipline because he is also a good student academically."

–Jim Barr, Former MLB Pitcher and
California State University, Sacramento Baseball Coach

It's never too late to learn how to be an academic student. A difference maker will be the attitude you choose—whether you choose to work hard and get help or whether you choose to continue to get by with lower grades.

Education experts claim that reading is the key to academic success. Successful students spend their free time (especially summers and vacations) doing different activities to keep their minds engaged. Download some fun and motivational educational apps that can help you stay sharp during vacations.

Take Rigorous High School Courses

Since education is leverage for student-athletes, make the most of your high school years by taking the most rigorous college prep classes you are able to. Just like good athletes work hard by practicing fundamental skills and developing knowledge of the game, good students need to work hard to do well in rigorous classes. You need to understand and practice the essential academic skills to be a contender in the competitive world of high school academics and college admissions.

"If students want to play sports in college, the first thing I would tell them to do is to get good grades. When I go to high schools to recruit, there are so many kids who could play for different schools, but they don't have the grades or the SAT scores. Everybody thinks that their grades are going to improve by their junior or senior year, and that they will have plenty of time to boost their GPA. But in the end, they don't have the grades and they can't get in to play anywhere."

-Dallas Sartz, Former University of Southern California Linebacker
and Current Assistant Football Coach at UC Davis

Meet High School Graduation Requirements

Every high school has specific graduation requirements that vary between districts and states. There will be a minimum amount of classes and specific subjects you must take and pass. In addition to meeting these high school requirements, students need to be aware of specific expectations for college admission, and meet NCAA academic course requirements. We advise that you take the most challenging classes that you can manage while competing in sports. This means that you want to consider enrolling in Honors and Advanced Placement (AP) or International Baccalaureate (IB) courses. Some may be appropriate for you; some may not. If you are a strong writer, you may want to take Honors English and AP Language or Literature. If your strengths are in math and science, you might want to enroll in Pre-Calculus, AP Chemistry, or AP Biology. Talk with other students to find out the typical homework load, expectations for the course, and the instructor's style. Talk to your high school counselor if you need help planning your schedule.

Meet College Entrance Requirements

In addition to your graduation requirements, you will have to meet the specific college entrance requirements of each institution. Aspire to meet the standards of the most rigorous and impacted school you intend to apply to. For example, in California, students must meet what are known as the A-G requirements to attend any college in the University of California or California State system. Be sure you make yourself a strong candidate for college admission, by making sure you are taking the appropriate classes.

Meet NCAA Academic Eligibility Requirements

Besides keeping track of high school graduation and college requirements, athletes must also meet NCAA academic eligibility requirements for both DI and DII colleges. The NCAA publishes a yearly *Guide for the College-Bound Student-Athlete* which can be found at eligibilitycenter.org. See Chapter 9 for more information.

"I still wish I had educational direction when I was in high school. I earned only a 2.99 GPA but easily could have done better if I would have been told it would make a difference in my options for college baseball recruiting. I regret not earning higher grades and never having the opportunity to play beyond high school."

-Cliff Hinkle, High School Baseball Athlete

Be a Participant, Not a Spectator

You need to develop homework and study habits, think critically, and communicate effectively to be an active participant in your education.

The college prep student-athlete is an academic participant, not a spectator. Practice these behaviors to make yourself an academic participant:

- Be active and ask questions
- Collaborate with peers
- Take responsibility for your own learning
- Take advantage of academic resources and tutoring

Also, positive rapport between teachers and students impacts student success. Since it is challenging for a teacher to make connections with all of the students, students who approach their teachers and initiate a connection, will impact their learning in a powerful way.

In your senior year, avoid "senioritis" and continue to take rigorous academic classes including math and science. Prestigious universities and colleges want high school students to continue taking a high-caliber classes throughout their senior year. If you stop taking math, you will lose those skills, just as you lose muscles if you don't use them in training. As many as 40% of college students drop out of school since many were not prepared academically partially because they coasted through high school. Keep developing your critical thinking skills throughout your four years of high school to best prepare yourself for college success!

GET TUTORING BEFORE IT'S TOO LATE

Some students struggle more than others in academics. If you find yourself having difficulty keeping up, get help before it's too late. Most high schools offer tutors, counselors, and other resources to help you. A student who needs to strengthen academic skills or develop specific social or communication skills should ask for help as soon as possible. Talk to your teacher or send in a request to see your counselor. Learn how to improve your study habits, organization skills, time management, and test-taking skills. Some coaches even help student-athletes by requiring weekly academic and behavioral progress reports completed by teachers, or a study hall period. Don't be embarrassed by this potentially valuable tool—even some junior and state college coaches require this of their athletes.

Teens who struggle in high school would improve significantly if they asked for help. It is available, so ask a teacher, counselor, or librarian for resources.

Additionally, students need to be able to learn from their mistakes. Parents should allow their children to make mistakes in a safe environment. Students will ultimately be much more resilient and have a better understanding if they have experiences where they can learn from their mistakes. Parents need to find a balance between being the hovering helicopter parent and helping their student-athletes be successful.

Identify your Learning Style

Students have individual strengths and weaknesses, as well as preferences regarding their learning styles. Some students are better at listening, some are visual learners, and some need to learn by being actively involved kinesthetically. Researchers believe that learning styles do not affect an individual's ability to learn, but rather influence the varying study habits that work better for different learners.

You need to know how you learn best so that you can adapt to any teacher's style. You can also study at home, employing strategies that work best for you. A successful student-athlete does not use a teacher's instructing style as an excuse for not doing well, but works to strengthen weaknesses and to develop strengths.

There are numerous websites available for you to identify your learning styles, strengths and weaknesses, including:

- powermylearning.com
- learning-styles-online.com
- collegeboard.org

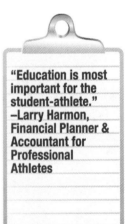

"Education is most important for the student-athlete."
–Larry Harmon, Financial Planner & Accountant for Professional Athletes

Once you determine your learning style, use that knowledge to become a better student. For example, if you know you are not a strong auditory learner, you need to learn how to ask questions to clarify lectures. If you are a kinesthetic learner, take notes, and if you are a visual learner, make diagrams and flashcards to see the information. Ask other students in class for help and compare notes after school. Find ways to focus and to listen better.

DEVELOP ESSENTIAL ACADEMIC SKILLS

Students need to develop and practice a number of academic skills to be successful throughout high school and to prepare for college. Over the next few years, most schools will adopt the Common Core State Standards, which will apply a more cohesive standard curriculum across nation. In addition to those standards, below is an overview of those skills, which will be described in detail later in the chapter.

ESSENTIAL ACADEMIC SKILLS

Vocabulary	Academic and high frequency SAT words
Reading Strategies	‣ Read actively ‣ Develop critical reading strategies ‣ Annotate and highlight ‣ Paraphrase and summarize key ideas ‣ Understand how to read for learning ‣ Read both literature & non-fiction ‣ Navigate a textbook
Note Taking	‣ Annotate and highlight ‣ Use Cornell Notes to analyze and summarize text ‣ Personalize and create interactive notebooks ‣ Use graphic organizers
Writing Strategies	‣ Practice and revise paragraphs and essays ‣ Practice timed writing ‣ Write expository & literary analysis essays ‣ Practice writing conventions (See SAT chapter)
Speaking/ Listening	Practice speaking and listening skills
Studying	Develop habits & time management with homework
Test-Taking	Develop and practice strategies
Solving Mathematic Problems	Review Pre-Algebra, Algebra, Statistics and Probability, Geometry and Measurement, introductory Trigonometry
Research-ing & Technology Literacy	Use library and Internet research skills and evaluate web sources

Note about Common Core Academic Standards

In the past, education and learning standards have been left up to individual states to decide upon and implement as they have seen fit. However, with the adoption of the Common Core State Standards, educational expectations for K-12 grade learning have been redefined to include the entirety of the United States. The initiative has been adopted by 45 states so far, and gives educational expectations to be met in the English language arts and mathematics departments by all schools involved. In English, the standards uphold that a greater emphasis will be placed on reading, writing, and analysis of texts, as well as creating arguments and supporting them with evidence from provided sources. In mathematics, lessons will be structured around integrated material and the goal of preparing students to be successful in Algebra I, and balancing skill with understanding of the information. In math, students will be required to apply their knowledge of math skills. They will also be asked to argue a point based on information they are given. Within the next few years, the principles of the Common Core State Standards will be implemented in every grade in all public schools that have signed on to the initiative.

Understand Academic Vocabulary

It is essential that you begin building your vocabulary because these words will repeatedly show up in your textbooks, teacher lectures, tests (including SAT/ACT), and in classroom discussions. Be sure to study the vocabulary words your teachers give you, and even research websites with academic word lists.

Build your SAT/ACT Vocabulary

Make flashcards for the most common SAT/ACT vocabulary words and begin to learn and use them in your daily discussions. If you really want to learn these words, you need to review 10-20 flashcards a day. You should not only know the meaning, but be able to use the word in your writing and in discussions.

Google "SAT words" and you will find tons of free sites with common SAT vocabulary words. The word lists are free, but you can pay for strategies on how to learn them.

Learn to be a Good Reader: Read Actively

Reading to learn requires active engagement. There are specific activities that good readers do in order to make sense of and understand what they read. Good readers are active readers when they read, including predicting, clarifying, and making connections before, during, and after reading.

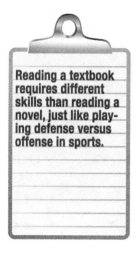

Good readers do most of these actions:

- **ANNOTATE**
  - » Write in the margins any unknown words; ask questions; look at organization of text; paraphrase key ideas; write mini-summaries; draw mini-graphics

- **PREDICT**
  - » Look at the title of the book or chapter and any pictures included. Make an educated guess about what you think the topic or purpose or outcome will be

- **CLARIFY**
  - » Define unknown vocabulary; ask questions about the main point or purpose

- **CONNECT**
  - » Make connections to other background knowledge and/or personal experiences

- **PARAPHRASE**
  - » Write what you think the author says in your own words

- **SUMMARIZE**
  - » Write little picture summaries along the way and a big picture summary at the end of the reading, even draw like in the game Pictionary to help you remember

Try Reciprocal Reading

Reciprocal reading is another critical reading activity that will help you with your reading comprehension. You will work with a partner, a tutor, or family member who wants to help you achieve greater understanding of the reading assignment. Try the following steps to see if reciprocal reading works for you:

1. Divide the reading into short paragraphs.
2. Both of you read the first chunk silently.
3. Both annotate. Circle unknown words and look them up (unless you can figure out the meaning in context), underline key ideas, and write thoughts, questions, paraphrases, and/or personal connections in the margin.
4. Partner #1 summarizes the passage out loud.
5. Talk together. Clarify the meaning and investigate questions together.
6. Repeat process with next passage—read, annotate and have Partner #2 summarize this time. Continue switching off with the following passages.
7. Just like training to perfect sport skills, this academic skill must be practiced over and over so that it becomes internalized with everything you read. Remember that reading actively will greatly improve your comprehension and is well worth the effort to practice.

Reading a Textbook for Comprehension

To get the most out of reading your text, you need to engage your brain so it is ready to answer questions. Try this technique as described below:

PARTRR—HOW TO READ AND STUDY A TEXTBOOK
Preview Ask Questions Read Take Notes Review Reflect

PREVIEW—before reading
- Skim chapter headings and sub-headings
- What are key words?
- Look at the following and read the captions: illustrations, charts, tables, pictures, graphs, maps

ASK QUESTIONS
- Turn chapter and sub-headings into questions
- Read the section to help answer the question—now you have a purpose in reading
- What is the main point?
- What are important supporting details?
- Does this example make the point clear? How?
- Can you think of another example?

READ
- Read the assignment carefully in order to understand the main ideas as well as the details

TAKE NOTES
- After reading, write the main idea for each paragraph
- Look for supporting information
- Look for examples
- Make an outline or visual diagram, chart or graph
- Use abbreviations to increase note-taking speed
- Use highlighting, underlining or symbols to make sense of key ideas

REVIEW YOUR NOTES
- Review to help with quizzes and tests
- Do you understand the main points? If not, ask for clarification
- Answer chapter questions as part of your review

REFLECTION
- Focus on the author's purpose
- Think about the main idea and its relevance to class
- Think about what you just read and the content
- Think about the course or subject
- What did the author want you to learn?
- Does this reading help you better understand the topics covered in class?
- What questions do you still have?

Practice Note-taking Skills

In addition to critical reading skills, you will need to employ note-taking skills while you read, listen to lectures, collaborate on projects, watch videos, or work on labs in class. This will help you learn the content and prepare for quizzes and tests.

Now that you understand the importance of taking notes, there are many different ways to record and organize them. The following pages will offer you some different strategies.

Cornell Notes is one popular method of recording your ideas, thoughts and questions about material. Cornell Notes are designed to help you engage or think actively about the content, and help you organize and reflect on your notes.

CORNELL NOTES

Copy this Cornell Notes template or visit dcipress.com to print a template. You can also create this template on binder paper or Google "Cornell notes" to find lots of note paper options.

Class Notes/Textbook Notes

Name _____

Date _____

Memory Key

Title: _____

Notes:

Write key words or draw stick figures and symbols to help you remember your notes

Main ideas and supporting ideas
_____
_____
_____
_____
_____
_____
_____
_____
_____
_____
_____
_____
_____
_____
_____

Summary or Reflection: _____
_____

Why else take notes?

Another reason to take good notes is because many students don't like or have difficulty reading and find that taking good class notes makes a difference. Write down everything you hear in class and tape record your notes in your own voice. One of the best ways to learn is to hear your own voice. Play the tape over and over until you understand the information.

Use Graphic Organizers

Graphic organizers are another way of taking notes. Graphic organizers help you understand content and organize information from textbooks and lectures. There are all kinds of graphic organizers including Venn diagrams, flow charts, lists, outlines, cluster or web diagrams, and matrices. You have probably seen many styles of organizers in your school textbooks.

- ‣ **Venn Diagram**: to show similarities and differences or to compare and contrast
- ‣ **Flow Chart**: shows timing or hierarchy
- ‣ **List**: sequence of ideas, brainstorming ideas
- ‣ **Outline**: information in a logical order—main ideas & details
- ‣ **Cluster**: brainstorming and grouping of ideas without a lot of structure
- ‣ **Matrix**: formal relationships, organizing parts of a document
- ‣ **Cause and Effect**: sequencing events in a causal order

Google "graphic organizer" to find a variety of other organizer ideas.

Develop Writing Skills

Beyond reading and note taking, you need some foundational writing skills to be successful throughout high school and college. Most of your high school and college writing will be either expository/persuasive essays or literary analysis essays. You will find that your writing skills will benefit you throughout your life in whatever career you select, so you should be able to respond appropriately to writing prompts, organize your ideas, and to write essays effectively.

"Writing is a core skill that is used in every step of the learning process, from note-taking to study questions to analysis to essay writing." (Jacobson 32)

–Mary Swanson, Founder of AVID

How to Write an Expository Essay

Expository essays are commonly seen on the SAT/ACT, and the AP tests. Expository essays will ask you to develop your point of view on a topic, issue, or abstract concept with reasoning and examples taken from your reading, studies, experience, or observations.

Venn Diagram

Flow Chart

Cluster

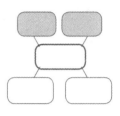

Matrix

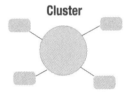

HOW TO WRITE AN EXPOSITORY OR PERSUASIVE ESSAY

Carefully read the directions

Essay Essentials

- Respond to Prompt
- Intro
- Thesis
- Topic Sentence
- Body
- Evidence
- Analysis
- Conclusion

Directions: You will have 35-50 minutes to plan and to write an essay on the topic assigned. Before you begin writing, read the passage carefully and plan what you will say. Your essay should be as well organized and as carefully written as you can make it.

1. UNPACK THE PROMPT: Circle, box, underline, or highlight keywords that tell you what to do as you read the prompt.
Many athletes take performance-enhancing substances, such as steroids, to gain the edge they need to play at the highest possible level of performance in their sport and stay competitive. The consumption of banned performance enhancing substances is evident across the world, from high school to professional sports. The athletes who use performance-enhancing drugs do not see themselves as cheaters or lacking moral character, rather view consuming these substances as a sacrifice to doing whatever it takes to be the best.

Plan and write an essay in which you agree or disagree with the statement above. Support your position with reasoning and evidence from your reading, studies, experiences, or observations.

2. Specifically, explain the argument and discuss the extent to which you agree or disagree with the argument
Support your position, providing examples from literature, history, current events, personal experiences or observations, or media (TV and movies).

Make sure you pick a side to the argument. Either disagree, or agree, but don't do both!

How do you effectively summarize the argument in an expository essay?
- Summarize the argument in a sentence or two at most
- Do not spend an entire paragraph explaining the author's opinion on the subject
- Place the brief summary in the introduction (possibly in the commentary connecting the hook to the thesis)

3. Outline the essay
- Brainstorm and outline your essay using an organizing technique that works for you. This could be a brief outline, web, table or bubble cluster.

You can use the following sources for evidence:
- Preferred—reading from literature, history, current events
- Acceptable—observations from or about friends, family, movies/TV
- Last Resort—personal experiences
- Provide enough evidence, and have 2-3 body paragraphs that include specific examples. You could have 2 or 3 examples in one body paragraph or 1 extended example throughout the entire essay.
- Structure your essay with an introduction, 2-3 body paragraphs, and a conclusion.

- Introduction with a thesis
    - »Thesis is clear, specific, deliberate and focuses the paper
    - »Don't use the second person (you)
- Make body paragraphs focused and purposeful
    - »Have clear topic sentences that focus the paragraph and support the thesis
    - » Use specific and precise evidence
    - » Analysis of evidence is deliberate and controlled
- Conclusion
    - »Summarize your argument
    - »Connects back to the thesis without repeating it
    - »Have a final thought and a finished feel

Below are some sample prompts that you can practice with. The SAT website also has a variety of sample prompts available.

SAMPLE PROMPT: ENGLISH

Money! Nothing worse
In our lives, so current, rampant, so corrupting.
Money—you demolish cities, root men from their homes,
You train and twist good minds and set them on
To the most atrocious schemes. No limit,
You make them adept at every kind of outrage,
Every godless crime—money!
    –Sophocles' *Antigone*

In a well-developed essay, explain Sophocles' argument, and discuss the extent to which you agree or disagree with his analysis. Support your position, providing reasons and examples from you own experience, observations, or reading.

Remember—a strong essay:
- Contains a clear, focused thesis statement
- Begins body paragraphs with clear topic sentences that make a point relevant to the thesis
- Incorporates specific examples to support the thesis
- Analyzes the examples to show how they support the thesis
- Ends with a conclusion that draws the essay together
- Reads clearly and easily with a minimal number of errors

SAMPLE PROMPT: SOCIAL STUDIES

An essay for an AP US history, World history or European history follows the same basic structure of an English essay. There are two types of essays: Free Response Question (FRQ) and Document Based Questions (DBQ). The free response requires you to use information that you have learned in the course, while the document-based question provides you with a number of primary sources to analyze, synthesize and use as evidence for your thesis. However, the DBQ does encourage outside supplemental information. It is vital to have a clear thesis and brief outline to keep you organized for both types.

How to Write Literary Analysis

Suppose that your teacher assigns you a text, poem, short story, essay, speech, or book to read and then asks you to write about the techniques and structures used in the work. This kind of writing is called literary analysis. Sometimes you are given a specific prompt to respond to and other times you will be asked to analyze the literature and develop your own ideas and thesis. Usually when you analyze the literature, you will be asked to write on one of the following topics:

- Character motivation (dynamic vs. static characters)
- Themes (main idea/ message)
- Style analysis of literary devices (what is the effect of the language the writer chooses for the piece?)

If your teacher gives you an unclear prompt, you need to "unpack the prompt" just as you would with expository writing. (See "Unpacking the Prompt" in *How to Write an Expository Essay*.)

Practice Speaking Skills

Public Speaking: There are important fundamentals involved in giving a speech or presentation in class.

- Determine the purpose of the speech. Is it to inform, persuade or entertain?
- Understand your audience
- Choose a topic that is interesting to you or research the topic you were given
- Organize your speech—it will be structured similar to an expository essay
  - » Introduction or opening with a hook to get your audience's attention
  - » Introduce your topic, talk about it, then review what you talked about
  - » Have a purpose – either to inform, entertain, or persuade
  - » Use stories or anecdotes to make your speech interesting
  - » Be clear on your main points
  - » Summarize
  - » Close

Practice your speaking skills: Volunteer to give a pre-game speech to your team

- Delivery of speech
  - » Confidence—look at audience and pause before beginning
  - » Eye contact—look at everyone in the room, don't read directly from notes
  - » Voice— speak loudly and clearly; vary your pace and avoid talking in monotone, project your voice to the person the furthest away
  - » Use academic discourse. Speak intelligently to make your speech sound more credible and yourself sound smarter
  - » Posture, movement, gestures—remember to breathe, stand tall, avoid fidgeting, use appropriate gestures (do not move your arms over your head or below your knees)
  - » Dress appropriately
- Practice your speech in front of your mirror, or friends and family
- Visualize yourself giving an excellent presentation

If you can, take a speech, debate, or drama class to help you with verbal and physical communication.

Practice Listening Skills

Active listening in class will help you learn the material better and asking questions of the teacher will help you to understand and clarify information.

Here are some fundamentals for good listening:
- Stop talking! You can't listen when you are talking
- Show your teachers and classmates that you want to listen by looking and acting interested. Don't be disrespectful by doing other activities like texting or drawing while they speak
- Try to understand other people's perspectives
- Don't interrupt
- Hold your temper
- Avoid argument and criticism
- Ask questions
- Be open. Hear more than what you WANT to hear

"Are you listening or just hearing? When someone is speaking to you, you might hear her attitude but you won't understand her words. To understand her words, you have to listen. Ask questions to clarify before you respond to validate what the speaker is saying. Don't let your interpretation override her intentions.
—Rita Prichard, English teacher and Nationally-Recognized Speech & Debate Advisor

---

Solving Mathematics Problems

It is important that you gain a foundation in math and learn how to solve algebra and geometry problems. This book does not cover all the details of math foundations; rather it is an overview of the math concepts and skills you will need to do well in your math classes (and eventually on the SAT/ACT). You can find a variety of interesting and very informative websites to help you learn and review math. YouTube has become a desirable site for students to learn how to do anything, even math fundamentals. At the minimum, you need to understand what aspects of Algebra and Geometry you are more comfortable with, and those you need to work on. Studying and doing extra work in areas you are less familiar with could make a huge difference in your math grades and overall success. Most four-year colleges require three years of high school math.

Use the practice problems below to gauge what you know and what you still need to work on. If you need more instruction, your teachers or the internet are great resources.

ALGEBRA I REVIEW

Solve.

1. $x + 3 - 4x = 6$

2. $\frac{3}{2}(4x + 2) = -9$

3. $2x - (x - 3) = 3x + 9$

4. $\frac{x+4}{48} = \frac{5}{2}$

5. Solve for P.
   $M = 4N - 4P$

6. What is the value of $4x^2 - 3$ when $x = -2$?

7. Mrs. Wilkinson charges a flat fee of \$210 plus an extra \$20 *per hour* to fix your television. Write an equation that could be used to solve for the number of hours Mrs. Wilkinson worked on your television, h, if the total bill is \$287.50. Then solve the equation.

8. Find the slope.
   $(-2, 10) \ (1, 8)$

9. Evaluate when $x = 3.5$
   $f(x) = -5x$

10. Identify the slope and y-intercept.
    $y = 2x - 6$

Graph.

11. $y = -\frac{3}{2}x + 1$

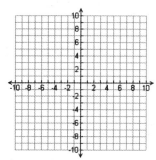

12.   x-intercept: -3
       y-intercept: 2

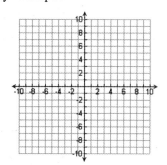

13. $y = -2$

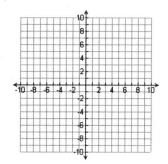

Write the equations:
14.   Standard form:

15.   Slope-intercept:

16.   Point slope:

Using the given information, write an equation in standard form:
17. $P(-2, -2)\ m = 3$

18. $(-3, 0)\ (2, 2)$

Using the given information, write an equation in slope-intercept form:
19. $P(1, -3)\ m = -2$

20. $(2,1)$ $(-1,0)$

Using the given information, write an equation in point slope form:

21. $P(4,-1)$ $m=1$

22. $(-3,2)$ $(0,1)$

23.   Find the x-intercept.
       $-2x + 2y = 8$

24.   What is the slope of the equation $x=4$?

25.   Write the equation of the line and find the slope.

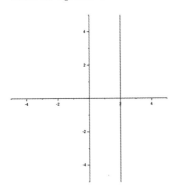

26.   Find the equation of the line below.

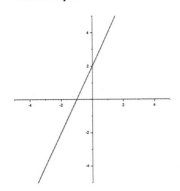

Write the equation of the line in slope intercept form with the given information.

27.   Parallel to $y = -3x - 2$ and goes through $(2,0)$

28.   Perpendicular to $y = \frac{1}{2}x - 2$ and goes through $(1,2)$

Solve and graph.

29. $-2x + 4 > 20$

30.　　$-3(x + 1) \geq 1 - 2x$

31.　　$-9 \leq 2x - 5 \leq 1$

Solve.

32.　　$3|x - 2| + 2 = 8$

Solve the linear system using substitution.

33.　　$2x + 4y = 8$
　　　　$x - y = 5$

Solve the linear system using elimination.

34.　　$10x - 5y = -2$
　　　　$5x + 3y = 3$

Graph the system of inequalities.

35.　　$y < x + 3$
　　　　$y \geq -2x - 2$

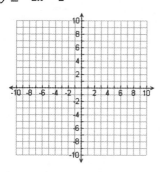

Graph and find the solution by estimating the point of intersection.

36.　　$y = 2x + 1$
　　　　$y = -3x + 6$

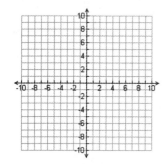

Simplify the expression. Write your answer using only positive elements.

37. $\frac{(-2)^5}{(-2)^2}$

38. $\left(\frac{2x^3}{y^2}\right)^3$

39. $(-9x^2)^0$

40. 2^{-3}

41. $x^0 * (4x^3y^{-2})^{-1}$

42. $2^3 * 2^0 * 2^2$

43. $(4x^2y)^2$

44. $\frac{1}{y^3} * y^4$

Which expression is a polynomial? Name the leading coefficient and degree.

45.   a. $8x - 3x^{-3} + x^2$
     b. $\frac{12}{x^2}$
     c. $3^x + 24 - 8x$
     d. $-8x^5 - 2x^2 + 3$

Find the difference.

46. $(4x^2 + 3x^3 - 2x) - (3x^2 - 3x^3 - 4x)$

Find the product.

47. $-5x^2(-3x^4 + 2x + 2)$

48. $(2x - 3)(8x - 2)$

49. $(x + 3)(x^2 - 2x + 3)$

50. $(x + 3)^2$

51. $(3x - 2)(3x + 2)$

Factor the polynomial completely.

52. $x^2 - 12x + 36$

53. $m^2 - m - 20$

54. $6x^2 + 5x - 6$

55. $54x^2 - 18$

56. $8x^2 - 10y^2$

Solve the equation.

57. $(x - 3)(4x - 2) = 0$

58. $(2x - 3)(x - 1) = 0$

59. $x^3 - 10x^2 + 25x = 0$

Solve the equation using the square root method.

60. $4x^2 - 16 = 0$

61. $2(x - 3)^2 = 8$

Solve the equation by using completing the square.

62. $x^2 - 10x \qquad = 36$

Write the Quadratic Formula.

63. $x = \frac{-b \pm \sqrt{b^2 - 4ac}}{2a}$

Solve the equation by using the quadratic formula.

64. $6x^2 + 5x - 25 = 0$

Use the discriminant to tell how many solutions.

65. $x^2 + 3x - 14 = 0$

66. $3x^2 + 6x + 3 = 0$

67. $12x^2 + 3x + 10 = 0$

Graph the following functions in parabolic form.

68. $y = (x - 2)^2 + 1$

69. $y = -\frac{2}{3}(x + 2)^2 - 1$

Find the line of symmetry and vertex and then graph.

70. $y = x^2 + 4x + 3$

Tell whether the function has a minimum or maximum value. Then find the min or max value.

71. $f(x) = -3x^2 - 6x + 5$

For the following function, answer all the questions and graph.

72. $y = x^2 + 6x + 8$

Max or min? _____

Line of Symmetry _____

Vertex _____

X & Y-intercepts _____

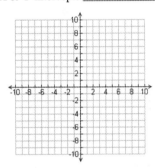

Graph the following square root functions. Identify the domain and range.

73. $y = -\sqrt{x+1} + 1$

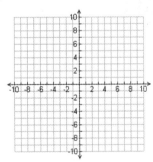

Simplify the expressions.

74. $\sqrt{90}$

75. $4\sqrt{32x^3}$

76. $2\sqrt{12x^2y^3} * \sqrt{3xy}$

ALGEBRA I ANSWER KEY

1. $x = -1$
2. $x = -2$
3. $x = -3$
4. $x = 116$
5. $P = N - \frac{M}{4}$
6. 13
7. $210 + 20h = 287.50$
   $h = 3.875$
8. $-\frac{2}{3}$
9. $f(3.5) = -17.5$
10. Slope = 2
    y-intercept = -6
11.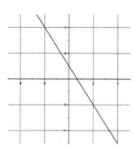

12.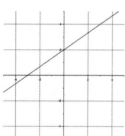

13.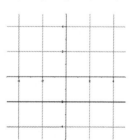

14. $ax + by = c$
15. $y = mx + b$
16. $y - y_1 = m(x - x_1)$
17. $-3x + y = 4$
18. $-\frac{2}{5}x + y = \frac{6}{5}$
19. $y + 3 = -2(x - 1)$
20. $y - 1 = \frac{1}{3}(x - 2)$
21. $y = x - 5$
22. $y = -\frac{1}{3}x + 1$
23. $x = -4$
24. $m = 0$
25. $x = 2$, slope is undefined
26. $y = 2x + 2$
27. $y = -3x + 6$
28. $y = -2x + 4$
29. $x < -8$
30. $x \leq -4$
31. $-2 \leq x \leq 3$
32. $x = 4, -4$
33. $x = \frac{11}{3}, \; y = -\frac{1}{3}$
34. $x = -\frac{9}{4}, \; y = 4$
35.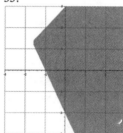

36. $x = 1, \; y = 3$
37. -8
38. $\frac{8x^9}{y^6}$
39. 1
40. $\frac{1}{8}$
41. $y^2/4x^3$
42. 32
43. $16x^4y^2$
44. y
45. $d, -8, 5$
46. $6x^3 + x^2 + 2x$
47. $15x^6 - 10x^3 - 10x^2$
48. $16x^2 - 28x + 6$
49. $x^3 + x^2 - 3x + 9$
50. $x^2 + 6x + 9$
51. $9x^2 - 4$

52. $(x - 6)(x - 6)$
53. $(m - 5)(m + 4)$
54. $(2x + 3)(3x - 2)$
55. $18(3x^2 - 1)$
56. $2(4x^2 - 5y^2)$
57. $x = 3, \frac{1}{2}$
58. $x = -\frac{3}{2}, 1$
59. $x = 0, 5$
60. $x = 2, -2$
61. $x = -1$
62. $x = 11$
63. $x = \frac{-b \pm \sqrt{b^2 - 4ac}}{2a}$
64. $x = -\frac{5}{2}, \frac{5}{3}$
65. Two solutions
66. One solution
67. Zero solutions
68.

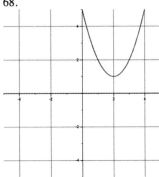

69.

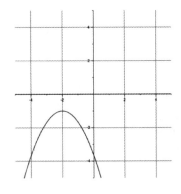

70. Line of symmetry: $x = -2$
Vertex: $(-2, -1)$

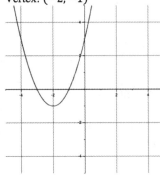

71. Minimum. $(-1, 8)$
72. Max, $x = -3$, $(-3, -1)$, $(-4, 0)(-2, 0)$, $(0, 8)$

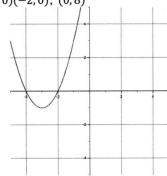

73. Domain: $x \geq -1$ \quad Range: $y \leq 1$

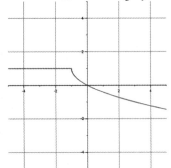

74. $3\sqrt{10}$
75. $16x\sqrt{2x}$
76. $12xy^2\sqrt{x}$

ALGEBRA II REVIEW

For all the Algebra II skills below, line through skills that you feel you are proficient in. Then use the boxes next to the left to check off subjects that you think might need some more work. Use the practice problems below each set of skills, to see how you do. If you need more instruction, your teachers or the internet are both great resources.

1. What is the value of $4^{\frac{3}{2}}$?

2. What does x equal if $4x^5 = -128$?

3. Simplify $\sqrt[4]{\dfrac{x^{10}}{y^{12}}}$

4. If $f(x) = x^2 + x - 2$ and $g(x) = x - 2$, what is $f\big(g(x)\big)$?

5. What is the inverse function of $f(x) = 2x - 8$?

6. Are the following functions inverses of each other?
   $f(x) = \sqrt[3]{12x}$ and $g(x) = \dfrac{x^2}{3}$

7. Graph the function $y = \sqrt{x - 2} + 3$

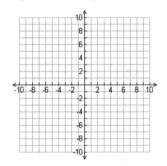

8. What is the solution of the equation $\sqrt{3x + 4} - 4 = 3$?

9. What is the solution of the equation $\sqrt[4]{42 - 3x} = \sqrt[4]{70 - x}$?

10. What is the mean of $2, 4.2, 4.5, 5, 6, 7, 9.8, 11, 13$?

11. What is the standard deviation of $9, 2, 11, 12, 2, 7, 4$?

12. Which of the following is an exponential growth function?

    a. $f(x) = 3(4)^{-x}$
    b. $f(x) = 4\left(\dfrac{3}{2}\right)^{x}$
    c. $f(x) = 2\left(\dfrac{1}{2}\right)^{x}$
    d. $f(x) = 8\left(\dfrac{4}{9}\right)^{-x}$

13. What is the simplified form of $4e^4 * (2e)^{-2}$?

14. What is the simplified form of $(-6e^{-4x})^2$?

15. Which of the following is equivalent to $\log_3 27 = x$?

    a. $3^x = 27$

    b. $27(x) = 3$

    c. $x^3 = 27$

    d. $327x = 27$

16. What is the inverse of the function $y = \ln(x + 7)$?

17. What is the expanded expression for $\log \frac{4x^2}{y^3}$?

18. What is the condensed expression of $3 \log x + 2 \log 5$?

19. What is the solution of $4^{3x} = 64^{2x-1}$?

20. What is the solution of $\log_3(2x + 5) = 3$?

21. What is the extraneous solution found in solving the equation

    $\log_4 x + \log_4(x + 6) = 2$?

22. Which of the following is a function whose domain and range are all nonzero

    real numbers?

    a. $f(x) = \frac{5}{3x+2}$

    b. $f(x) = \frac{x+7}{x-3}$

    c. $f(x) = \frac{3x-5}{x}$

    d. None of these.

23. What are the asymptotes of the graph $f(x) = \frac{x^2}{4x^2-2}$?

24. What is the quotient $\frac{x^2+x-12}{x^2-9} \div \frac{x^2+6x+8}{x^2+5x+6}$?

25. What is the sum of $\frac{9}{2x^2} + \frac{x}{4x^2-2x}$?

26. What is the simplified form of the following complex rational number?

$$\frac{\dfrac{x-6}{2}}{\dfrac{1}{2} - \dfrac{3}{x-2}}$$

27. What is the solution of the equation $\frac{-4-x}{3} = x + 2$?

28. What are all the solutions of the equation $\frac{x+6}{2} = \frac{-1}{x+1}$?

29. In how many ways can 12 runners finish a race first, second, or third?

30. How many different license plates are possible if three digits are followed by

    three letters?

31. How many distinguishable permutations of the letters in TENNESSEE are

    there?

32. In how many ways can a 6 person committee be chosen from a group of 10 people?

33. A drive-in theater has 8 different movies showing. If you want to attend no more than 4 of the movies during the weekend, how many different combinations of movies can you attend (where viewing order matters)?

34. What is the coefficient of x^3 in the expansion of $(2x - 1)^5$?

35. What is the probability of drawing a face card or an ace from a standard deck of 52 cards?

36. A regular six-sided dice is rolled. What is the probability of rolling a prime number?

37. If $P(A) = 0.2, P(B) = 0.6$, and $P(A \text{ and } B) = 0.1$, what is $P(A \text{ or } B)$?

38. Solve the following: $(4x + 5)^{1/3} - 2 = -1$

39. Simplify the following: $\sqrt[3]{8x^3y^6}$

40. Find the inverse of $f(x) = 6x - 1$

41. Evaluate the following: $\log_5 125 =$

42. Condense the following: $\log 6 - 2 \log x$

43. Simplify the following: $-12x * (2x^2)^{-2}$

44. Solve the following: $\log_3(5x + 7) = 3$

45. Simplify the following:

$$\frac{\dfrac{5}{x^2 - 9}}{\dfrac{10}{x - 3}}$$

ALGEBRA II ANSWER KEY

ALGEBRA II ANSWER KEY

1. 8
2. $x = -2$
3. $x^2y^3\sqrt{x^2}$
4. $f(g(x)) = x^2 - 3x$
5. $f(x) = \frac{1}{2}x + 4$
6. No
7.

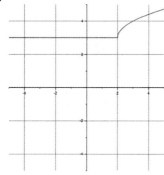

8. $x = 15$
9. $x = -14$
10. 6.94
11. 4.15
12. b
13. e^2
14. $\frac{36}{e^{8x}}$
15. a
16. $y = e^x - 7$
17. $2\log(2x) - 3\log y$
18. $\log(25x^3)$
19. $x = 1$
20. $x = 11$
21. $x = -8$
22. d
23. $x = \pm\frac{1}{\sqrt{2}},\ y = \frac{1}{4}$

24. 1
25. $\frac{x^2+18x-9}{4x^3-2x^2}$
26. $x - 2$
27. $x = -2$
28. $x = -3$
29. 1320 ways
30. 17,576,000
31. 3780
32. 151,200
33. 1680
34. 80
35. $\frac{4}{13}$
36. $\frac{1}{2}$
37. 0.7
38. $x = -1$
39. $2xy^2$
40. $f(x) = \frac{1}{6}x + \frac{1}{6}$
41. 3
42. $\log 6x^2$
43. $-\frac{3}{x^3}$
44. $x = 4$
45. $\frac{1}{2x+6}$

GEOMETRY REVIEW

For all the Geometry skills below, line through skills that you feel you are proficient in. Then use the boxes next to the left to check off subjects that you think might need some more work. Use the practice problems below each set of skills, to see how you do. If you need more instruction, your teachers or the internet are both great resources.

1. What are the three undefined terms in geometry?
2. What is the difference between a postulate and a theorem?
3. If M is the midpoint of $\overline{NP}$, then _____?
4. What is the converse of the statement: If two lines do not intersect, then they are parallel.
5. Is the argument valid: If there aren't clouds, the stargazers are happy.

   The sky is cloudy.

   The stargazers are not happy.
6. What conclusion can you make: If it is 3:00 pm your class is over.

   It is 2:30 pm.

   _____

7. Write as a bi-conditional: If a quadrilateral has 4 equal sides then it is a square.

   If a quadrilateral is a square then it has 4 equal sides.

_____

Consider the following diagram.

Give an example of the following:
   8. Linear pairs
   9. Vertical angles
   10. Alternate interior angles
   11. Corresponding angles

12. Find the midpoint of $\overline{BC}$: A(-4, 2) and B(2, 0).
13. Find the length of $\overline{BC}$: A(-4, 2) and B(2, 0).
14. If MN is the perpendicular bisector of PQ, list what you know to be true.
15. Find the slope of the line $\overline{CD}$: C(-4, 4) and D(-2, 0)
16. If the slope of $\overline{BD}$ is 1/2, what is the slope of a line parallel to $\overline{BD}$?
17. If the slope of $\overline{BD}$ is 1/2, what is the slope of a line perpendicular to $\overline{BD}$?
18. Find an equation of the line through the points A(-4, 3) and B(-3, 2).
19. For $\triangle ABC$, $m\angle A = 7x$, $m\angle B = x$, and $m\angle C = 20°$. Find $m\angle B$.

20. Find x:

21. If x is an even number, then $2x > 4$. Find a counter-example.

22. A triangle with three equal sides is a(n) _____ triangle.

23. Give the congruence postulate that proves the triangles are congruent.

24. Given $\triangle ABC \cong \triangle FGH$, then by CPCTC:

$\overline{AB} = 10$, then _____ = 10; $\angle F = 25°$, then _____ = 35°

25. Consider the following triangle:

List the sides in order from largest to smallest.

26. Are the following triangles similar?

27. Find x: vertical lines are parallel.

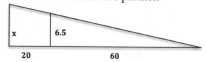

28. Find the geometric mean between 5 and 20.

29. Is a triangle with sides $1, 4, 4.5$ a right triangle?

30. Find the length of the diagonal of a square with side length 10.

31. Find the altitude of an equilateral triangle with side 12.

32. Find the sin A, cos A, and tan A for the triangle:

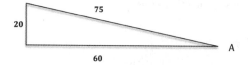

33. Find cos 50°

34. Given the right triangle, use trigonometry to find x:

35. The diagonals of a rectangle are _____.

36. The diagonals of a rhombus are _____.

37. The sum of the interior angles of a pentagon is _____.

38. Each interior angle of a regular hexagon is _____.

39. Each exterior angle of a regular nonagon is _____.

40. The sum of the interior angles of a polygon is 1080°. What is the figure?

41. Name a letter that has rotational symmetry.

42. Translate the point (-2, 3) by the mapping: $(x, y) \rightarrow (x - 1, y + 2)$

43. If the point P (3, -4) is reflected over the y-axis, then A' is _____.

44. If the point P (3, -4) is rotated 180°, then A' is _____.

45. How many degrees do the hands of a clock at 2:00 make?

46. The standard equation of a circle with center (4, 2) and radius 5 is

_____.

47. Find $\angle BAC$

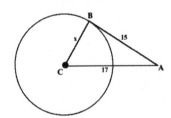

48. OC = 12; AO = 5; BO = 10; DO = _____

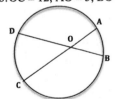

49. Find the area of the shaded region.

Inner circle diameter is 5m. Outer circle diameter is 8m.

50. Find the area.

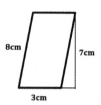

8cm   7cm

3cm

51. Find the area.

8

5

20

52. What is the area of a regular hexagon with side length 8cm?

53. What is the area of a square inscribed in a circle with a radius of 5cm?

54. What is the length of an arc of 12°, if the circle's radius measures 5?

55. If the ratio of sides of two similar squares 4:5, then what is the ratio of their volumes?

56. Find the area of a rhombus with diagonals 5 and 6.

57. Find the surface area and volume of a sphere with diameter of 12.

58. Michael's favorite radio station plays music for 40 minutes each hour, weather for 5 minutes each hour, and commercials for 15 minutes each hour. If he turns on the radio at a random time, what is the probability he will turn it on during the weather?

59. Find the area.

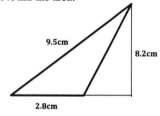

9.5cm   8.2cm

2.8cm

60. How many faces, vertices, and edges?

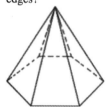

61. Find the volume of a cone with height 7m and base radius 3m.

62. Use special right triangles to find the missing side:

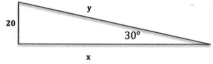

y

20

30°

x

GEOMETRY ANSWER KEY

1. Point, line, and plane
2. A postulate is something assumed to be true, and a theorem is something that we can discern to be true based on our set of postulates.
3. $\overline{NM} = \overline{MP}$
4. If two lines are parallel then they do not intersect.
5. Yes
6. Your class is not over.
7. A quadrilateral is a square if and only if it has 4 equal sides.
8. 6 and 8
9. 2 and 3
10. 4 and 6
11. 1 and 5
12. $(-1, 1)$
13. $\sqrt{40}$
14. Lines are perpendicular, creates two 90 degree angles.
15. $m = -2$
16. $m = \frac{1}{2}$
17. $m = -2$
18. $y = -x - 1$
19. $20°$
20. $100°$
21. $x = 2$
22. equilateral
23. SAS (Side-Angle-Side)
24. $\overline{FG}, \angle A$
25. $\overline{PQ}, \overline{PM}, \overline{MQ}$
26. Yes
27. $x = \frac{13}{6}$
28. 10
29. No
30. $\sqrt{200}$
31. $\sqrt{108}$
32. $\sin A = \frac{4}{15}, \cos A = \frac{12}{15}, \tan A = \frac{1}{3}$
33. 0.64
34. 10.3
35. congruent
36. perpendicular
37. $540°$
38. $120°$
39. $40°$
40. Octagon
41. O
42. $(-3, 5)$
43. $(3, 4)$
44. $(-3, 4)$
45. $60°$
46. $(x - 4)^2 + (y - 2)^2 = 25$
47. $28°$
48. $\overline{DO} = 24$
49. 39π
50. $21 cm^2$
51. $70\ units^2$
52. $166.3 cm^2$
53. $50 cm^2$
54. 1.05cm
55. 64:125
56. $15 units^2$
57. $SA = 144\pi; Area = 288\pi$
58. $\frac{1}{12}$
59. $11.48 cm^2$
60. 7 faces, 7 vertices, 12 edges
61. $A = 21\pi\ m^3$
62. $x = \sqrt{60}, y = 40$

Now that you've reviewed math topics from Algebra I, Geometry and Algebra II, and discovered what you need to focus on, there are several resources available to help you review these areas. Google the specific math topic and you will find anything you need that your teacher has not explained (or did but you weren't listening). YouTube is also a great help for some students.

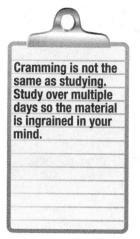

Cramming is not the same as studying. Study over multiple days so the material is ingrained in your mind.

Understand Studying

Many students do not understand HOW to study. Just looking over your notes from a class or looking through a chapter doesn't count. There are a few things that a student-athlete can do to really improve his/her understanding of class material.

Studying is not Homework

Homework is when you have a specific teacher-assigned task to complete, whereas studying is reviewing your work in various subjects without a particular assignment. On the nights when you don't have homework, take advantage of that time to review and study.

Develop Study Habits

First, you need to develop study habits involving when, where and how you study. Find a quiet place in your house where you will not be distracted and establish this as your study location. Keep the radio, stereo, and TV turned off, and avoid using your phone. (When our teens were in grades 7-10, we had them complete homework and study at the kitchen table where we could help. Then when our teens became responsible for homework and studying, they worked in their bedrooms.)

How to Study

- Make a schedule of your responsibilities, then plan studying time
- Have a regular time and place to study
- Don't wait until you feel like studying.
- Turn off distracting electronics.
- Be in a properly lit room
- Read the lesson to get a view of the whole before studying details
- Make your own illustrations, examples, and cases
- Identify the main points
- Take notes with clear headings
- Hearing your own voice is a great help in studying, so record your notes and play back the tape
- Don't cram the night before
- Review frequently
- Work hard
- Don't expect the teacher or your parents or your friends to do the work for you

Tips

Flashcards

▸ If using flashcards works for you, they can almost be considered a secret to success. You can make flashcards for any subject, from words for a unit, to math and science formulas to historical information. In chemistry, you might need to memorize the Periodic Table of Elements, which can also be studied with the aid of flashcards. Since they are portable, you can study from them on a bus, the bleachers, the sidelines, or on the way to a tournament. If you have 10-15 minutes of spare time, you can get out your flashcards and study by yourself and or have somebody quiz you. They are much easier to study from than notes in a binder or a textbook.

Review

▸ A great way to help remember the information on your flashcards is to review them every night for 10-15 minutes before you go to sleep. Your brain will continue to process the information all night while you sleep.

Memory

▸ Studying is more effective when you review material in parts over an extended time period. This is called chunking memory where your mind can digest material if it is in smaller chunks. Creating mnemonics is also a very effective device to help you remember class content.

Get Help

▸ We have learned that to have a successful homework and/or study session, parents need to sit with their students and actively monitor, facilitate, and assist the student. Even if the parent does not know the material, parents can ask questions to help clarify, read through the text for the information, and help students find information on the web. Oftentimes study materials are available to students online for numerous subject areas and literary works. In addition, many high school teachers put study guides, tutorials and PowerPoint presentations on their websites.

Manage Your Time

If a student is playing sports, time for studying is often limited. It is imperative to schedule time every day for completing homework and reviewing. Some days the study time may be immediately after school if practice or competitions are in the evening. If practice is right after school, student-athletes need to make sure they set aside time after practice to do homework or study. Even if you are busy, you can always find time to fit studying in throughout the day. Many freshman and sophomore athletes are required to attend varsity games. If so, you can review vocabulary words, read and review notes, or do other assignments for classes while sitting in the bleachers and watching.

Since you have an athletic schedule that details your practices and competitions, you will need to plan your homework/study time around those commitments. If you know that you have 3 days of practice and 2 games, for example, then you may have to do more homework than is assigned some nights to make up for nights you won't get home until late. If you are assigned reading in a novel, you may have to read more than the assignment one night, since you know that another two nights you won't have time to read. You must always be thinking ahead and instead of "catching up," you want to be getting ahead.

As a student-athlete, you will have to face the reality that you will not have a large amount of social time. If you want to excel in academics and athletics, you must make homework/studying a daily priority. Just take it one day at a time as you take one game at a time in sports.

Learn Test-taking Strategies

Doing your homework and studying consistently will give you a great foundation to be successful when taking tests.

Keeping a positive frame of mind by using positive self-talk will also help you do well while taking tests. What this means is that the conversations you have in your head begin with "I can….," "I will….," "I am able….," and " I am prepared to…." Focus on your strengths, your hard work and what you know, and don't worry or focus on what you forgot to study.

Tell yourself:

I can.
I will.
I am able.
I am prepared.

The night before a test, review your notes before going to sleep and remind yourself of your strengths. On the way to school, continue the positive self-talk. Successful people put in the hard work (game and test preparation) to earn the right to have this positive self-talk.

How to Take a Test
- Read and follow instructions carefully
- Quickly preview the entire test. Budget your time
- Jot down any formulas or items you memorized
- Answer the questions you know first, then go back and answer all the others if there is no penalty for guessing. If you guess, put a faint question mark in the margin, so you can go back and check those questions if you have time later on
- Use process of elimination on multiple-choice questions. Eliminate obviously incorrect answers, then narrow down the answers and select the best one
- For timed-writing essays, be sure to allot time to unpack the prompt, quickly organize, write, and edit the essay

Researching and Technology Literacy

Students are asked to research and use technology daily. The key to researching is to find multiple sources and evaluate them for credibility and purpose. Is the author of the website or article credible? Is he an authority on the subject? What is the purpose of the website and the author? Who is the intended audience?

When a teacher asks you to do research, be sure to find and compare lots of sources and DO NOT plagiarize. As technology improves, the temptation to plagiarize becomes greater, but don't do it. When reporting your research, you want to use your paraphrasing and summarizing skills, and not steal the ideas and or written works of others.

Students also need to know how to cite their sources when doing research. This may be in the form of a bibliography, works cited, or works consulted. There are a variety of formats for citing sources including, MLA (Modern Language Association) and APA (American Psychological Association).

Basically, you will be citing the author's name, title of work, and publishing information in order to give them credit for the information you are using, and you can automatically format your bibliography by using a website tool like easybib.com.

Financial Literacy

Financial literacy is when you develop money management skills and understand credit so that you can make informed decisions and set personal financial goals, including how you will pay for college.

RIGOROUS COURSES, ACADEMIC SKILLS & GRADES

Colleges look at your coursework and GPA. While it is important to develop good fundamental academic skills and take rigorous classes, students must also focus on their grades. Be aware of your school's grade policy about making up course work and also GPA calculation. Be sure to carefully read the policy and if you have any questions, check with your high school counselor. Sometimes a grade can be replaced by taking the course over, and other times both grades remain on the transcript. This difference could result in different GPA calculation. Some districts do not allow students to repeat courses where you received a C or higher. One district has a policy where if you make up a D grade, the new grade is averaged with the D. However, if you had received an F, the new grade would replace the F. This could work to your advantage. Again, please verify the grading policies for your school before making up course work. Getting all A's and B's would eliminate any worrying about this, so work hard.

Once you get to your last year in high school, you want to avoid "senioritis." Do not look at it as a year to take it easy. You want your senior year to be rigorous and to prepare you for college. Think of your senior year as a critical year to continue building your academic skills necessary to be successful in college. You want to be able to compete with other college freshmen who worked hard during their senior year and did not take a "break." Many college freshmen (about 25%) do not make it to their sophomore year in college because they find themselves academically unprepared for college expectations. You can avoid this by working hard to prepare yourself for the demands of college during your high school senior year.

Also, you will be required to take entrance exams at many colleges and you want to qualify for freshman level courses, not remedial courses. Most importantly, you want to make sure you maintain your acceptance status since college admission personnel pay attention to your senior schedule and grades. Many colleges require a mid-year grade report from high school counselors. If you are accepted, it is contingent on your final grades. Colleges may deny you admissions if your grades drop.

Morgan Ragan was a successful high school student-athlete who was recruited at nine colleges to play basketball. She was very excited about her decision to go to a state university in Southern California. Unfortunately, when she let her grade slip to a "D" in one elective course in the spring of her senior year, the university retracted her admission. Morgan felt the other colleges weren't a fit for her and so decided to stay home to attend her local community college. While she was disappointed, she enjoyed a season at Sierra College—especially when her team won second in state. Unfortunately, Morgan had to undergo shoulder surgery, she left college basketball and moved to Los Angeles to take TV broadcasting classes and work. After two years, she moved back home and returned to Sierra College to earn her AA degree and also decided to use her second year of eligibility to play basketball. Her long-term plan was to continue and finish her basketball career at a DII school but she had to stop playing because of her reoccurring shoulder injury and several concussion injuries. Morgan will focus on her broadcast journalism degree—maybe we will see her on ESPN one day.

Parting Shot...

Be an academic student-athlete. You can't play college sports unless you are a student first. Your GPA is gold. Take notes. Make time to do your homework daily so you prepare yourself for tests. Doing your homework is like going to practice and taking tests is like playing the game. Do what you are capable of. Education is leverage.

In addition to the academic information in this chapter, there are numerous websites with excellent tools including the high school college-prep program called AVID at avidonline.org.

Chapter 4
Top 10 Plays

1. Be an active learner and engage in your education

2. Take rigorous courses and meet high school graduation, NCAA, and college prep requirements

3. Build vocabulary, especially high frequency SAT words

4. Read actively: highlight, annotate and take notes

5. Take notes and create personal interactive notebooks, using graphic organizers or Cornell Notes

6. Become a better writer by revising and editing your paragraphs and essays

7. Practice listening and speaking clearly. Think and ask questions

8. Work at understanding math foundations and practice solving problems in Algebra, Geometry, and introductory Trigonometry

9. Do your homework, and develop good study habits

10. Learn test-taking strategies

Tilford's Math Tips

How To Succeed In Any Math Class

1. At the start of any test, plan out how much time to take for each problem or section. Recognizze what strategies you have at your disposal and make a strategy for the test. Leaving blank problems at the end because you ran out of time can often ruin any chances of a good grade.

2. Be sure to understand the more complex problems from your homework. That one you skipped because it seemed too hard to end up on the test will likely show up on the test.

3. If you're expected to know a lot of equations for an upcoming test, always make flashcards. No matter how well you think you know them, the pressure of an important test could make you forget some crucial equations, but not if you've been practicing your flashcards often enough!

4. Don't stress out—ever! A single math test doesn't make or break your academic career. Just do your best to be well-prepared, and the good grades are sure to follow.

5. If you hit an academic wall and just can't seem to grasp a particular concept or two, then personal one-to-one tutoring is a great option. First try free tutoring if your school offers it. If that doesn't work out, look for student tutors that have already taken the class you're in, particularly those that had the same teacher as you—the best advice comes from those that have been through exactly what you're going through.

6. You've heard this one before: stay healthy before a big test! Get a good amount of sleep the night before, and be sure to eat breakfast and bring some snacks with you the day of the test. Don't pull an all-nighter studying because you will be far too physically and mentally exhausted come test-time.

7. Study as often as possible, not for the longest durations possible! Sitting down for an hour every weekday is better than 5 straight hours of nothing but math at the end of the week. This keeps your mind fresh and keeps you on track with the material you need to study. More importantly, it helps you truly learn the material instead of cramming for the test and then forgetting it.

8. After you do really well on a test, think back to the actions that helped you earn that good grade. Do your absolute best to mimic those same habits for every future test, because clearly they worked!

Developing ATHLETIC ESSENTIALS

*Play forward.
Forget your mistakes and move on
to play better in each game.*

OVERVIEW

Just like good students learn school subjects and practice reading and writing skills, good athletes need to understand and practice the necessary set of skills and have the knowledge to compete successfully in their sport. Today's fast-paced and powerful sports require players to be more than players – they need to be athletes with speed, power, and agility. Successful athletes are gym rats, the first to arrive to practice and the last to leave. They are committed to working hard and improving their speed, power, strength, and agility to gain advantage over other athletes working just as hard.

Student-athletes need to train for fitness and athleticism, and develop core strength, power, speed, agility, reaction time, and footwork. In addition, athletes will spend much of their time training specifically for their sport.

"I do something everyday to improve my game."
–Max Stassi, USA National Baseball Team, UCLA 2008-09
Drafted by MLB Oakland A's

Some sport coaches provide and even supervise year round conditioning and sport-specific workouts for their athletes. However, some athletes are on their own for off-season fitness and sport training. In addition to what your high school coach offers (or requires), there are many options for athletes desiring sport-specific training from personal coaches, trainers, parents, and friends, in private training centers and gyms, or even in their own backyard. The Internet offers an abundance of workouts, training, technique and skill sets - all you have to do is look for them. There are many "how to" instruction clips on YouTube.

Note that the world of personal athletic and sport trainers is a business. Many high school coaches and club coaches are turning over their athletes to the regimen (and costly fees) of personal trainers. Some of this training is good, but it can be overdone for high school athletes. Teens must have a balance in training and be careful not to over train or spend too many resources on it. An athlete can work out at a park for free, running a mile, doing ten 100-yard sprints, then doing push ups, pull-ups, dips, and sit ups. This simple, yet effective workout is a great addition to the specific-sport training an athlete will get from his coach.

Refer to The Academic-Athlete Checklist in Chapter 3 to make sure you are on target for developing athletic qualities and getting the desired exposure. Always do something! Note that the older you get, the less instruction and the more evaluation by coaches there will be. Pay attention to what college coaches look for when recruiting student-athletes.

The key to athletic prowess, sport-specific skills, and individual position skills is to train smart. It is important to train in a well-rounded regimen, eat healthy, train correctly and consistently, and get plenty of rest. It is also recommended that athletes take time off from their sport at an appropriate time during the year to avoid burn out or injury. We suggest using a training log so that you recognize what you are actually doing and not doing for your body.

Before we talk about training, note the desired qualities coaches and scouts look for in student-athletes.

☑ DESIRED QUALITIES IN STUDENT-ATHLETES

College recruiters and scouts look for sport-specific talent and athletic prowess. The following are qualities that high school and college coaches deem desirable:

- ☐ Sport-Specific Talent & Skills (Technique)
- ☐ Athletic Ability
- ☐ Size
- ☐ Speed
- ☐ Strength
- ☐ Agility
- ☐ Works Hard
- ☐ Coachable
- ☐ Committed (to training & player development)
- ☐ Game Performer/Competitor ("Gamer")
- ☐ Hustles
- ☐ Performance under Pressure
- ☐ Handles Adversity
- ☐ Mental Toughness
- ☐ Respect of Authority and Teammates
- ☐ Initiates Communication with Coaches
- ☐ Confident
- ☐ Disciplined
- ☐ Focused
- ☐ Responsible for Actions
- ☐ Good grades

Athletic ability is important to giving players an edge. Basketball players must set a pick, lead a fast break, pull up for a sweet jump shot, and be tough on defense. Baseball and softball players must get a jump to steal, beat out a throw home, turn a double play, and show power at the plate. Football players must make quick cuts, hit hard, and explode off the line. Hockey players must find a stride pattern on the ice and withstand hits.

Players must train to develop lower body strength, speed, agility, balance, and quickness to be athletes in all these sports.

Most importantly, coaches look for sport-specific and position-specific skills and talents. Athletes must execute skills and sport-specific techniques in addition to the related physical abilities. You can research the qualities required of your sport that coaches are looking for on the internet, and find information on desired physical attributes, as well as important mental qualities that coaches look for.

Commit yourself to practice, and you will develop the skills you desire. Think about it – why are you a good walker? You are because you have done it every day since you were one year old. Just think of how much you would improve if you made the commitment to shoot free-throws and jumpers, practice ball handling, hit golf balls, field ground balls, take batting practice, or practice flip turns in your free time. Imagine how great you could become.

PLAYER DEVELOPMENT

Athletes need to maintain a training regimen to be healthy and fit, minimize injuries, and develop their athleticism and skills. Your body is everything. Know that successful student-athletes are gym rats and work before and after practice doing strength, agility, and power training with weights, plyometric boxes, jump ropes, fitness balls, and ladders. Flexibility is more important than most high school student-athletes realize, and so it is also important to focus on. Whatever you are doing, there is someone else doing more in this competitive youth sports world. The following are essential components for player development.

Fitness and Athleticism

Athletes must train correctly by working out in all areas of fitness and athleticism. Many athletic trainers are focusing on sport-specific training for optimal sports performance. All athletes need to be fit and athletic. You want to design or follow a fitness program that includes:

- Flexibility
- Conditioning (Cardio)
- Strength
- Power
- Speed
- Quickness
- Agility
- Reaction Time

An athlete will want to develop a training program and consider the following elements dependent upon your specific sport. Be careful how you train as proper body mechanics are very crucial when doing exercises. Understand how to move your body in the most efficient manner, so you will maximize your results and reduce the risk of injury.

Typical Sports Performance Training Includes:

- Dynamic warm-up with active stretching and movement to activate muscle groups
- Running technique and movements for speed, agility, strength, and power
  - » Proper body mechanics including proper arm swing, knee drive, and foot placement for better 40 yard dash and start speeds (0-20 yard speed) and also for more explosive ability
- Running workouts including distance, sprints, and interval training
- Agility skills to improve foot speed, reaction time, quickness, and lateral movement (ladders, cone drills for change in directional speed)
- Weight lifting for muscle strength and muscle endurance
- Olympic style lifting for power and total body strength
- Plyometrics for explosive power and quickness
- Daily core abdominal routine, possibly using a physioball/stability or medicine ball
- Jump rope workouts
- Static stretching and cool down
- Sport-specific training to develop sport specific fundamentals and skills

Many student-athletes follow a basic fitness and athletic routine consisting of dynamic warm up, push ups, sit ups, pull ups, sprints, and 2 mile runs. Others start lifting weights and doing plyometric exercises in high school. We suggest that you have a PE teacher, coach or a competent personal fitness trainer teach you the correct technique and form for all exercises to avoid potentially serious injury. There are also websites and DVDs on all types of training, including ladder training for agility and core work on stability balls, which can be purchased at local sporting goods and discount stores, or online.

There are many free resources online as well. Google "workouts" for your specific sport and for core training, flexibility, cardio, strength, and endurance training. You will find lots of great training ideas from these sites.

Search online for workout ideas.

Look at:
1. Nike's SPARQ Athletic Training
2. MidWestFit.com

Group fitness and personal trainer Dede Walker suggests MidwestFit.com for a free daily online workout.

Nike has developed a training and assessment program called SPARQ (Speed, Power, Agility, Reaction, and Quickness) for six specific sports as well as for general athletics. Athletes can use the results of the assessments to train targeted areas of weaknesses. Visit Nike's SPARQ Training website for details.

If you have trouble training on your own and if you have the resources to pay for it, there are several individual or group training programs available. For example, Pure Athletics Human Performance Center, located in El Dorado Hills, CA trains people with a focus on fitness and athleticism. A personal trainer at your local gym could also be a viable option for you.

Patrick Gallagher, a former University of Oregon football quarterback, and certified performance trainer ATC, CSCS is the owner and head coach at Pure Athletics. He defines the complete athlete as one with natural talent, including strength, power, speed, and, one with a training regimen that develops an explosive functional movement base, mental strength, while emphasizing nutrition, rest, balance, and rhythm. His motto at the performance center is "train movements, not muscles." Muscles like to move with each other, not alone and building big muscles means nothing if you don't know how to move them. He says that kids who don't grasp this concept usually get injured, and very few reach their true potential because of it.

Gallagher explains that muscles fundamentally serve three purposes. First, they put the limb in a position to move (loading) and/or they create power (unloading). If they are not involved in the motion then they are called on to stabilize the rest of the body during the movement. In sports, the quads are called on to stabilize the knee and allow the hip to transfer explosive power to the ground, which is why training a muscle in a sitting position with the feet off the ground makes no sense. He warns against work out programs that train all the muscles and joints to be movers and not stabilizers. The knee extension machine is telling the knee to move when it really needs to be stable. This is why isolated movement can actually set the body up for injury.

The best exercises are ground-based, meaning the feet or hands are planted on the ground and the body moves around them (push-ups instead of bench press, squats instead of leg curls, etc.).

Training should be a 1-2 year investment, not a quick fix. Build a functional movement base, then work on speed, agility, quickness, and power, and lastly, on athletic abilities. Do correct ladder form. Work on having quiet feet. Eat a high protein and carbohydrate diet 30 minutes after your workout for recovery, and be sure to give your body rest. There is no such thing as can't. Don't just survive your work out; own it.

–Patrick Gallagher
Pure Athletics Human Performance Center

Knowledge of the Game, Student of the Game, Respect for the Game

In many team sports, coaches look for individual athletes who actually understand the strategies of the game and know what to do in game situations. It is visualizing and seeing things before they happen. This allows the athlete to anticipate, instead of react, to the game situation. In basketball it is seeing all four of your teammates and predicting where the ball will rebound; in baseball it is automatically wanting the ball to be hit to you and knowing what you are going to do with the ball before it comes to you, depending upon how many runners are on base and the score; and in soccer it is anticipating a run your teammate will make once you receive the ball. Successful competitors know that one of the keys to winning is to exploit the weaknesses of their competitors.

"All my groundwork of my knowledge of football was so much better than other freshmen when I went to college. I was taught to understand football and coached so well that I continued to be a student of the game. It's not just basic X's and O's: you go here, you go there. My high school coach made it into, 'You go here because they did this.' There's a lot of places where the coach would just draw up on the board: 'Here's the play, you do this.' However, Coach Cooper says, 'Here's the play. You do this, but if they do that, this is what we do.' My coach prepared athletes to react to situations, not just do what they were told. As a high school athlete, I was fortunate to have been given the in-depth look at football that prepared me to compete in college and helped me get to where I am now with coaching football myself."

–Jared Vanderbeek, University of Hawaii Graduate Assistant

If you want to grow as an athlete, you should become a student of the game. The difference between kids who go on and play college sports and those who don't is that the former work on the mental, as well as physical, part of the sport.

While warming up with his opponent, David Luther, a former James Madison University competitive tennis player, hits to all spots on the court to determine his opponent's weakness. He is then able to exploit that weakness during the match to increase his chances of winning. This strategic play has helped David beat many of his opponents.

Practice Behavior and Training Purpose

> "Let's get it done fellas. Let's get a little bit better today."
> —Ernie Cooper, Granite Bay High School Head Football Coach

Coaches want an athlete who continually works to improve and is coachable. Athletes improve by taking sport-specific lessons and/or practicing the required fundamental skills for their sport. Videotaping yourself is critical to improving your skills, because then you can see yourself and visualize the changes in technique that will make you better. Many athletes today join clubs, academies, or travel teams to get the high quality practice and game situation experience. Successful athletes practice skills on their own as well as in the garage, in the front yard, at the park, at school, or wherever they can find a suitable spot. Attend camps and clinics to get instruction also.

Athletes must have a purpose not only in games but also in all practices. Walt Rouse, a Seton Hall University basketball player who has played and coached reminds his athletes that you play how you practice. No pain, no gain is also part of the toughness training that successful athletes realize. Put your mind to something and do it. **Do it well, do it right, and work hard.**

"Practice does not make perfect. Perfect practice makes perfect."

—Walt Rouse
Former Grant High School Basketball Coach

Off-Season Training

It is necessary in today's competitive world of high school sports to train year-round. You either need to play multiple sports or train for your sport in the off-season. To remain in the best shape possible, you will need to continue athletic and fitness training including: speed, agility, strength, endurance, power, and running form, as well as sport-specific movements and fundamental skills.

Madison Wallace spent her youth playing multiple sports because she liked trying new activities, enjoyed being very active, and wanted to stay fit. However, during her senior year, she realized it was necessary to focus on one sport only to best prepare for a college athletic opportunity. She chose track and attended a summer camp to improve her technique, learn from other coaches, visit the college, and get exposure. She believes a track experience will help her get into college. Her plan is to apply to several colleges and see where track takes her.

Again, there are numerous free websites with conditioning programs where you can get daily exercises and workouts. Google general fitness workouts and sport specific workouts. If you can afford a gym membership, attend group strength and training classes or use the facility to work out on your own. If you can invest in a personal trainer, be sure he or she is certified and competent.

Play Hard, Play Smart

Many gifted high school athletes don't have to play as hard as their teammates because they have a natural talent that their peers don't have. However, with hard work, your teammates may catch up. Both types of athletes should work hard on their athletic skills, as well as work on their mental toughness as many college coaches comment on the lack of mental toughness of high school athletes today.

"**I was a 'gymmer.'** I would sneak into my high school and try every single key and door to get in, and go to the local community college every weekend to use its gym. If you want to succeed, do it full speed, do it a 100%. If that's what you really want to do in life then that's the next step to college to play football or whatever sport you choose. If you are going to do it do it 100% you have to buckle down and you have to focus if you want to go to college and play football."

–Dallas Sartz, Former University of Southern California Linebacker and Current Assistant Football Coach at UC Davis

Pre-Game Routine and Game Plan

Athletes must have a pre-game routine to get ready to play, both physically and mentally. Athletes need to find a routine that works best for them. Some like to listen to their music, others visualize the whole game or picture themselves executing fundamentals. It is important that you run, stretch, and practice fundamentals in warm-up drills so that you are prepared for anything during the game. For example in baseball, it is important to have a hitting plan long before stepping up to the plate, or in golf, you need to have a routine you go to each time you strike the ball.

Competition and Exposure

Today, athletes help themselves improve their game and get exposed to college coaches and scouts by participating in tournaments and competitions. For most student-athletes, it is not enough to play on high school teams only, and while college coaches ask high school coaches about the work ethic and character of athletes, most recruiting takes place at club tournaments and showcases.

Both high school and club sports offer valuable athletic opportunities for student-athletes.

This competitive experience gives athletes the opportunity to compete against the top performers in the field and maximum exposure to college recruiting. So the club and high school sports opportunities meet different needs. Football is the exception, with college coaches visiting winning local high school programs with athletic talent. Since there is not club football, combines and camps are important exposure venues. College tennis recruiting has become international, thus tennis players must play beyond high school tennis in state and local tournaments for maximum exposure.

Max Vogt, a California state ranked tennis player, found it too difficult to play competitive and high school tennis simultaneously. Without breaks, he suffered from back and knee problems, and other injuries. It was also difficult to get excellent high school grades, AND compete for his high school tennis team, AND compete in travel tournaments. He gave up high school tennis so that he could find time to earn good grades and better compete for recruiting and scholarship opportunities. Max believes, part of being a teen athlete is being a good student. Max received a full-ride scholarship to Bryant University.

In addition to gaining this high level competitive experience, tournaments offer the opportunity to be seen by college coaches and scouts. In terms of exposure, football is an exception since many college coaches visit high schools that have winning programs and blue-chip athletes. Football combines have become very popular for college coaches to attend to see many potential football athletes in one spot at one time. While Nike football combines are widely considered the best for blue-chip athletes, there are many combines across the nation.

For other team sports, private clubs or academies offer opportunities for athletes to train and travel to showcase tournaments. Research different clubs, communicate with coaches, and network with parents. Ask the right questions about the philosophy and goals of the clubs before joining to make sure it fits your needs, especially if you want to travel to key national showcases. (See Chapter 12 on details of getting exposure and marketing yourself.)

Nutrition

Sports enthusiasts argue that a huge difference between athletes who make it to the next level and those who don't comes down to nutrition. Serious athletes looking for an edge focus intently on their diets. High school athletes need to drink less soda and eat less sugar while eating clean, meaning eating fruits, vegetables, lean meat and fish, and drinking lots of water.

There are basic, simple, common truths about nutrition, including the following:
  ‣ Athletes must drink plenty of water to stay hydrated (drink at least 8 glasses of water daily), eat proteins to replenish energy (calories) burned, eat 4-5 smaller meals a day rather than 2 or 3 big meals

  ‣ Eat healthy

  ‣ Eating right means matching your calorie intake to calorie burning

  ‣ Consuming all food groups, including low fat meats (such as turkey) and fish, vegetables, fruits, and complex carbohydrates, such as whole wheat

- Smoothies are great options as long as you aren't drinking the ones loaded with sugar. Various frozen fruits, including blueberries, low sugar juices, and plain yogurt are healthy and convenient smoothie ingredients

- Eat healthy snacks like nuts (especially almonds), fruits, and sports bars without a lot of sugar

- Enjoy sodas, candy, and greasy foods sparingly

- Choose sports drinks that have less sugar and no caffeine. Stay away from energy drinks because they are full of calories and caffeine. Athletes need sports drinks with electrolytes if playing for more than two hours or in extreme heat or high humidity. If you drink sports drinks, get the lower sugar product

- It has even been suggested that athletes drink low-fat chocolate milk, rather than sports drinks, within 30 minutes after a workout to help build muscles, and speed up recovery

- Serious athletes wanting to build more muscle need to eat protein within 30 minutes after their workout for maximum benefits. Good protein powder supplements made with whey are also sometimes beneficial. Check for calorie content whether you want to lose, maintain, or gain weight

During off-season training, Jameel Ziadeh, training before his senior year in college eats healthy meals several times a day to put on muscle. For breakfast, he eats oatmeal, egg whites (and sometimes adds one egg into four egg whites for flavor), fruit, and drinks orange juice. For lunch he eats string beans, potatoes, and turkey, and for dinner he eats chicken breasts, wheat pasta, and vegetables. He knows that his nutrition gives him an edge when working out to build power, strength, and endurance.

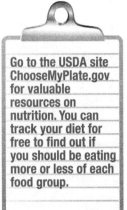
Go to the USDA site ChooseMyPlate.gov for valuable resources on nutrition. You can track your diet for free to find out if you should be eating more or less of each food group.

The United States Department of Agriculture (USDA) has revised its iconic food pyramid, and created a food plate to help children, teens, and adults make healthy choices. Visit ChooseMyPlate.gov for valuable resources and lots of great tips about eating for a healthy lifestyle. There is a super tracker feature where you can track your diet and analyze your deficiencies. And for tips on eating healthy, check out their *10 Tips Nutrition Education Series*, including: "Eating on a Budget," "Eating More Fish," and "Eating More Vegetables."

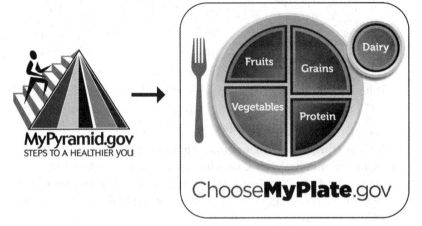

It's never too late to change your eating habits. Former USC football linebacker and captain Dallas Sartz, realized the value of good nutrition after modifying his college diet which previously consisted mostly of hamburgers. His football agent sponsored a meal plan for him during his pre-draft football combine training, and with six healthy meals a day, Dallas noted the extreme difference in his body composition, strength, and energy level. Dallas was drafted by NFL's Washington Redskins, but an injury during his first pre-season ended his NFL career. He is currently a college assistant coach at UC Davis.

Preventing sports injuries

Taking care of your body by eating a nutritionally balanced diet is one way to help prevent sports-related injuries. Athletes must also warm-up and cool down from exercise properly. For some athletes, preventive taping and icing muscles is important. Repetition of the same training movements overuses muscles, and doesn't strengthen other key muscle groups, which leads to most common injuries among teens. If you feel pain, pay attention, and don't ignore your symptoms. We can't emphasize enough how your health and being injury-free is imperative to your player development and ability to be recruited. Take care of your body!

Concussions in Sports

Concussions occur when the brain is violently rocked back and forth inside of the skull due to a blow to the head. If they are not managed properly, they can cause prolonged or permanent neurological and cognitive problems.

FACTS & STATISTICS: CONCUSSIONS

- Concussions are BRAIN INJURIES
- Most concussions do NOT involve any loss of consciousness
- 10% of all contact sport athletes sustain concussions each year
- An athlete who sustains a concussion is 4-6 times more likely to sustain a second concussion
- "Bell ringers" are mild concussions
- Mild concussions account for most of all concussive injuries
- Effects of concussions are cumulative in athletes who return to play before they completely recover
- The best way to prevent problems from concussions is to manage them effectively when they occur
- Don't return to play while experiencing symptoms of a concussion
- Some athletes are reluctant to tell coaches about a concussion because they may be afraid of losing playing time or being viewed as weak by their peers, but returning to play could cause permanent brain damage

---

Athletes with mild concussions might not realize that the injury they suffered is actually a concussion, or that a concussion is a **brain injury**.

When an athlete suffers a concussion he/she may experience any of the following symptoms:

- Has a headache
- Seems dazed or stunned
- Appears clumsy
- Is confused about an assignment
- Is unsure of game, score, or opponent
- Answers questions slowly
- Shows behavior or personality changes
- Forgets some events that occurred immediately prior to hitting head
- Loses consciousness (*this is rare*)

If an athlete exhibits *ANY* of these symptoms following a hit to the head or body, he/she should immediately be removed from athletic participation, and evaluated (preferably by a doctor.)

Minutes, hours, or even days after a concussion, an athlete may experience *one or more* of the following symptoms:

- Irritability
- Easily frustrated
- Headache
- Nausea
- Balance problems
- Double vision
- Sensitivity to bright light
- Depressed mood
- Feeling foggy
- Changes in sleep pattern
- Problems concentrating
- Dizziness
- Fatigue
- Feeling sluggish

-Craig Garabedian "Concussions" Powerpoint

If concussions are managed properly, most athletes can return to competition soon after their injury and avoid any significant long-term consequences. The NCAA has information about concussions on its website also.

Rest, Recovery and Healthy Sleep

Student-athletes lead demanding, fast-paced lives, so it's important to get plenty of sleep to allow your body to recover physically. Pay attention to warning signs of being over-extended or of being over-worked. Although it is difficult to make sleeping a priority with all the commitments you may have, doctors recommend that teenagers get 8-10 hours of sleep every night or they will experience sleep deprivation. You will need to monitor your time well so you can get the sleep your body needs to repair itself.

Unfortunately, technology like phones and computers are culprits in stealing sleep away from teenage student-athletes. It is very important that you don't overuse technology including your cell phone, video games, computer, and TV. Sleep deprivation leads to the inability to focus and concentrate in school and can even contribute to migraine headaches. You must form healthy sleep habits such as not eating or exercising before bed, maintaining consistent sleeping and wake times, and turning off noise and lights (cell phones, computers, and video games especially) so that you can get the necessary sleep for a healthy and restful life.

Time Management

Remember to manage your time and prioritize your athletic workouts and sport practices. You have to make time to work out and stay committed to a schedule. Include conditioning, strength training, and sport-specific skill workouts outside of practices and games. Some student-athletes like to use a training log to set goals and keep track of their workouts and competitions. (See Chapter 7 on goal setting and calendars to manage your athletic commitments along with your academic and social commitments.)

VALUE OF HIGH SCHOOL SPORTS BEYOND THE GAME

High school sports allow for competition and a way for athletes to practice their skills outside of their clubs, but they also contribute something more. High school sports allow for camaraderie between students who work together to represent their school. Being a member of a high school team teaches student-athletes to have pride in the way they play and conduct themselves because as long as they are wearing their school uniform, they are representatives of the school and have the opportunity to act and play in a manner that reflects positively on the school.

"Students who participate in sports, as well as any other program on campus, gain more than other students who aren't involved with the school. Athletics provide a more tangible connection to high school and to other people. Being a high school student-athlete helps teens to become more complete individuals. They develop confidence, and learn that failure is simply an important part of growth. Students in the athletics program learn they are responsible for their own improvement, which allows them to grow and mature both physically and mentally. They learn about effective and ineffective leadership by being exposed to different coaches. Well-coached teams have a shared vision, and when athletes subject their own needs to the goal of team, they recognize that being part of the organization or team is even better and more rewarding than fulfilling your individual needs. Students grow socially from the athletic programs as they learn to work with other people. Athletes in any sport realize how important camaraderie and teamwork are, and push themselves to work together as a team."

–Tim Healy, High School Athletic Director

Last Words...

You need to find what works for you and your family in terms of balancing priorities in your life. You will have to make decisions about budget, time, resources, goals, and family values. Families with multiple student-athletes must make decisions about how to manage the various sports and competitions. Some athletes will be able to spend more time and money on athletic fitness and sports-specific training, while others will have to make do with limited resources. Everyone needs fitness, training, skill development, and nutrition for a healthy life style, yet sports development and participation are unique processes in regards to each sport, individual, and family.

Chapter 5
Top 10 Plays

1. Get fit

2. Develop sport specific skills

3. Be a "student of the game"

4. Establish a practice mentality

5. Train in the off-season

6. Establish a pre-game routine

7. Compete to get better

8. Eat well

9. Rest and recover

10. Manage your time the best you can

 # Time out!

Take a break and use this space to reflect.

What is important to you? What do you need to do?

Developing
PEAK PERFORMANCE SKILLS

6

Confidence comes from being prepared.

PEAK PERFORMANCE DEFINED

The idea of the student-athlete comes from the Greek philosophy of a sound mind in a sound body. The Greeks realized that you need both physical and mental attributes to be successful and content. Today, we can call this philosophy peak performance. Peak performance is when the mental and physical aspects of the sport mesh together, which allows athletes to perform at their absolute best. They are "in the zone." Karen Scarborough, a former California State University, Sacramento sport psychology professor, reports that many athletes describe peak performance as

- Effortless performance—not forcing it
- Total immersion in the activity
- No analysis of performance
- Feeling confident
- Sense of calmness
- Feeling of complete control
- Narrow focus of attention
- No fear of failure
- Can do anything feeling

Student-athletes can work to develop peak performance skills so they can experience these qualities in athletics and in the classroom. Life coaches, self-help counselors, academic tutors, college prep advisors, sports coaches and sports psychologists all help student-athletes perform at their best by working on their mental game, as well as their communication and leadership skills.

Working on test-taking and interviewing strategies are just as important as fitness training and nutrition.

Peak performance involves all areas of a student-athlete's life, mentally and physically. The peak performance journey is the pursuit of success, fulfillment, and excellence in all areas of your life including sports, performing arts, test-taking, interviews, and communication performance. Peak performance is a journey and a result.

The peak performance result is like achieving your personal best because you were prepared, skilled, and focused. Peak performance is when student-athletes reach or perform their personal best in a game or in the classroom on a specific day.

Sports psychologists and coaches specializing in peak performance work on mental toughness, the mind over matter belief and ability for athletes to tell themselves that they can do it, that they can achieve excellence in competition. Many college coaches believe high school athletes are not mentally tough, so a great goal would be for you to work on your confidence each day. Those who take small steps toward improving their performance end up realizing those goals.

Academic tutors, college advisors, and life coaches also use peak performance training as a way to help students perform better on tests, job interviews, and interpersonal situations.

Athletic and personal sport trainers, coaches, nutritionists, sports medicine doctors, sport scientists, and researchers help student-athletes perform at their best by working on their physical fitness involving strength, agility, flexibility, speed, endurance, nutrition, and preventive sports injury. There are some amazing human performance sports labs that work with athletes to achieve the ultimate performance at the professional, college, high school, and youth levels. Lance Armstrong worked in this type of lab to improve his speed and endurance using physics principles and improved wind resistant clothing designs for his racing jersey. Nike also has a state-of-the-art laboratory in Oregon that is used to develop the ultimate performance clothing and equipment.

Helpful resources:

- **Academic Tutors**
- **College Prep Advisors**
- **Sports Psychologists**

Of course, the average student-athlete does not have access to all of these resources. Building mental toughness and peak performance is something you will have to do on your own. We will walk you through some techniques in this chapter to help you do so. Improving mental toughness is a commitment that you will have to work at every day.

YOU CAN BUILD PEAK PERFORMANCE SKILLS

The important elements of peak performance are made up of attitudes and mental skills that athletes must learn and practice, including:

Confidence
- I CAN Attitude
- Controllables vs. Uncontrollables
- Stretch your Comfort Zone
- Positive Self-Talk & Affirmations
- Visualization & Imagery
- Imagery Scripts

Pre-Game
- Have a Routine
- Relaxation
- Control your Breathing
- Be in the Present

Mental Toughness
- Learn from Mistakes
- Minimize Fear of Failure (FEAR)
- Avoid Pressure to Win
- Lower your Anxiety
- Overcome Adversity

Peak performance is achieved through having a positive attitude that can be developed by practicing these skills. Successful athletes do not acquire these skills without putting in the practice, and the effort, just like students do not acquire academic success without dedication and hard work. Be disciplined, determined, take responsibility, commit, make sacrifices, and work hard to achieve your mental toughness goals.

Making this kind of effort is not easy. You need to ask yourself: What am I willing to do to perform at my best and how am I going to get it done?

MLB Rick Rodriguez's Mental Keys:

1. Believe in yourself—most think it but don't believe it.
2. Be willing to change and try something new.
3. Be a 'Rock-head' to stay mentally tough once you make a team.
4. Have a routine.
5. Recover and make adjustments—which shows mental maturity gained from experience.
6. It's a learning process, so learn from your mistakes to become a better player.

The most important element of peak performance is developing confidence. Confidence comes from having a positive attitude, talking to yourself in a positive manner and visualizing success. You can't gain true confidence without putting in the real hard work and continual practice.

Confidence

Self-confidence begins with attitude. Athletes must have a positive "I Can" attitude and positive expectations for themselves. There are some mental skills that can help you build and maintain confidence. These skills are:

Being the best takes:

- **Hard Work**
- **Discipline**
- **Determination**
- **Responsibility**
- **Commitment**
- **Sacrifice**

1. Positive self-talk and positive affirmations
2. Focus on what you can control
3. Preparation

There are some negative feelings and behaviors that can shake your confidence, like the pressure to win and the fear of failure. Knowing how to minimize these distractions will help you stay in the zone and focused on your game. Having a pre-game routine and a mental and strategic plan during competition will also help build and maintain your confidence.

Your positive view of your self-worth will lead to positive athletic and academic expectations, which will in turn bring about successful experiences. That success will spiral you to a higher level with an improved self-worth, which leads you again to more success in athletics and athletics. In contrast, viewing yourself in a negative light will lead to negative expectations, which can lead to failure in your sport.

Athletes can be under- or over-confident, or their confidence can be only on the surface. These athletes are not confident internally, have self-doubt, are worried about failing, and may exhibit this false confidence through cocky behavior. The key to gaining confidence is to base it on past success, practice, and ability.

There are several skills you need to work on and practice when developing confidence, just like you do when practicing skills for your specific sport.

"I CAN" Attitude

A student-athlete gains true self-confidence by starting with an "I CAN" attitude. With this "I CAN" attitude comes drive, the ability to push yourself to be your absolute best. This drive is often motivated by having a goal, like being a starter or perfecting a move, so practicing good goal setting skills and doing your best to achieve your goals can work wonders for your confidence. The athlete needs to have a positive outlook on life, not a negative one. In order to gain an "I CAN" attitude, you first need to determine what you can and cannot control in your life.

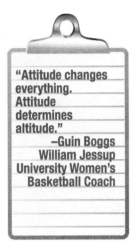

"Attitude changes everything. Attitude determines altitude."
–Guin Boggs
William Jessup University Women's Basketball Coach

Adam Jennings was recruited to play football at Fresno State University even though he was small in size. Adam admits he was not big and fast, and certainly not the best player. His high school coach told him to let it all hang out and that is what he did. Adam let it go when he played; he played with no fear, and Adam went 100% in practice and in games. He played different positions in high school and in college—until he found where there was a need and an opportunity to fill it. While at Fresno State, his new offensive coordinator told him he would never start as a receiver because he was too small. So, even after being recruited at the college level, he was told he couldn't do it. However, Adam made a place for himself on the field and earned a role on special teams because he did such a good job blocking and hitting defensive backs while on offense. Adam successfully returned many punts for Fresno State. He went on to play for the Atlanta Falcons and Detroit Lions before retiring from the NFL. He is a successful businessman with a "CAN DO IT" attitude and intense work ethic.

Controllables vs. Uncontrollables

A student-athlete needs to realize what he or she can and cannot control in order to avoid wasting his or her time, thoughts, and energy focusing on things he or she cannot do anything about. What can you control? What is out of your control? You can control your attitude and performance, but you cannot control your coach, teammates, officials or the outcome of the game. Focus on your own performance, not on the weather conditions, officials, other team, your coach's decisions and actions, or the desired outcome of the game. Don't worry about a starting position or playing time –only about your individual performance.

You can control: your attitude, your positive thinking, your reactions (especially to adverse situations), your behavior, and your performance.

You cannot control: people around you (other players, coaches, spectators, referees, judges, umpires, scouts), weather conditions, surface conditions, your opponent, or any other distractions.

Don't waste your energy on thoughts that serve no purpose but to frustrate you. Decide on what you can do to perform at your best and focus only on the controllable.

Now that you know that you need a positive outlook and a "CAN DO" attitude, and that you are aware of what you can and cannot control, you need to start working on building your self-confidence. There are a couple of skills that you must continually work on in order to do this. We will explain how you can use positive self-talk and affirmations, and how having a goal and the drive to reach it will help you to perform at your highest level.

Stretch Your Comfort Zone

You have to push the edges of your comfort zone to grow and improve. Without real challenges, you will remain stagnant, or the same, while your classmates and teammates pass you by. Your muscles get stronger when you stress them, and your mind grows when you stretch it with challenges.

"Live on the edge of your comfort zone."
–Lain Hensley, Odyssey Performance Enhancement Network

Positive Self-Talk and Affirmations

Positive self-talk and affirmations are both tools to build your confidence. Positive self-talk is that silent voice in your head, like giving yourself a pep talk to boost your confidence. To make your pep talk more effective, use cue words. For example, a softball player might say to herself, "see the ball" or "hit hard" or "stay down." These are just simple reminders, phrased positively, to help you focus.

I use the negative in a positive way. When athletes do it wrong, I focus on how to do it the right way rather than critiquing the error.

–Jim Barr, former MLB Pitcher and
California State University, Sacramento Baseball Coach

Positive affirmations help you build self-worth and lead to real self-confidence. These are best if written down on 3 x 5 index cards. Post them on your bathroom mirror, your bedroom walls, your school binder, the dashboard of your car, or in your wallet. They can be one word or one sentence reminders of what your strengths are. These could be phrased as "I am a leader," "I can score a PK," "I can throw a pitch on the outside corner," "I can catch a bullet pass," "I can make free throws," "I can tackle," or "I can make a perfect flip turn." (Turn the page for actual examples.)

These are simple reminders of what you can do and they remind you of your self-worth. Write these down and say them aloud or in your head whenever you see them. This helps you build confidence, especially in times of adversity. Conjure up your positive affirmations when things start going wrong. These will become a self-fulfilling prophecy. You have to believe you can perform these skills well, and continually hear positive messages in your head and they will come true.

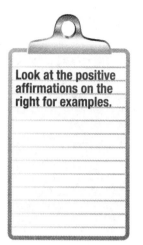

Look at the positive affirmations on the right for examples.

Be sure these positive affirmations are words or phrases you can visualize during competition. Do not carry on a conversation in your head—only repeat the one word or phrase to get you focused and confident.

Here are some positive affirmation sentence starters that you can use:
- I am proud that I am ......
- I have accomplished .....
- I am in control of......
- I am good at......
- I can...
- I will....
- I learn from mistake
- I learn from my experiences
- I get a little bit better every day
- I choose to win

Former MLB baseball player and high school guest speaker, Steve Sax of the Los Angeles Dodgers, warns high school students about phrasing actions in the negative: "If you tell yourself, 'Don't see the elephants,' your brain will automatically visualize elephants. Your brain processes an action, so you need to frame your comments positively. For example, instead of saying, 'Don't drop the ball,' you must say to yourself, 'I will catch the ball.' You control your thoughts. Your thoughts will direct your focus. If you think you will fail, you will become anxious. If you think about making errors, you will. You must focus on your strengths, which will make you strong."

Visualization and Imagery

Along with repeating positive self-talk and affirmations in your head, using positive visualization and imagery is another way to boost your confidence. Use it daily. Imagine what you want to happen during your events. Great athletes have excellent imagery skills, and can see themselves succeeding BEFORE they go out and compete.

While visualization has been described as a still picture or snapshot in your head and imagery as a movie played out in your head, they can be used almost synonymously.

When trying a new move or technique, imagine a picture or video you've seen of an athlete performing that move. Then visualize yourself executing that move perfectly. Create a movie in your head or mental scenes of you doing, feeling, and experiencing the desired skill, performance, or competition.

You might visualize yourself making a play, a flawless entry on a dive, crossing the finish line first, or completing a perfect putt. See yourself competing perfectly, and you are more likely to compete perfectly.

POSITIVE AFFIRMATIONS

The following are actual sample positive affirmations from our high school student-athletes in various sports and academic classes. We had our student-athletes put a statement on an index card the size of a credit card so it would fit perfectly in a wallet and be available at anytime. The initials are from the students who wrote these affirmations in our high school classes.

• I am confident • I can make this putt • I have trust in myself • I can get it out of the bunker **MA**	• I can go out fast, and come back stronger • I can do this • I deserve it **MC**	• I can hit the spot • I will succeed • I will not think negatively • I will always be positive **JW**	• I am the best defender in the country • I will get the ball • I will make the field goal **AA**
• I RUN with anyone • I can be the BEST **CZ**	• I am smart • I can read the pitcher's next pitch • I am confident **MG**	• I will conquer my fear • I am not scared • I will take the pain **XD**	• I can shoot free-throws • I will make the shot • I am strong **JH**
• I will run fast • I will make the play • I will be strong • I will tackle you **JD**	• I will show them I can • I will do it • I will be strong • I will lead by example **DH**	• I am focused • I am calm • I will sink the shot • I will be victorious **TC**	• I have momentum • Nothing can slow me down • I am fast • I will be first **AG**
• I am smart • I will get A's • I am accurate • I will make the shot **MG**	• I am confident • I will pass the ball accurately and quickly • Nothing will stop me **RS**	• Anyone CAN do it, but I WILL • Anyone CAN be the best but I WILL **MB**	• I WILL hit the target • I WILL succeed **DH**
• I am determined • I will stop you • I am calm • I will make the shot **DP**	• I am rebuilding myself • I will pitch again • I am regaining strength **CK**	• I am explosive • Nothing is going to stop me • I am powerful • I will get the take-down **RW**	• I can make the shot down the line • I can get my serves in • I can win the game **MP**

Imagine what you're going to do before you do it.

Imagery is not a bird's-eye view of you doing something. It is as if are actually living it, doing it, live in your brain. This allows your brain to integrate what skills you need to keep practicing and perfecting.

You need to completely envision what you are going to do. If you are a swimmer, picture yourself on the blocks. Hear, smell, feel everything around you. Focus and feel your feet on the rough blocks. You feel the sun on your shoulders, and see the water before you. Envision yourself making a perfect dive into the water, swimming the laps of the pool, and finishing first before all your competitors. Feel yourself touching the timer pad. You have to see yourself being successful. Practice this envisioning a couple of times a day, especially before bed, because your brain will continue to perfect the skills while you sleep.

When learning how to envision, you might need to include movement. Stand up, and pretend to be at bat, or kick an imaginary soccer ball. In time, you will be able to visualize yourself successfully completing these actions while you are sitting on the coach or relaxed in your bed.

Many athletes video record their performances so they can view themselves later for skill correction. They also watch videos of other athletes and then imagine themselves performing similarly. Watch film and break down every detail of their actions, then visualize yourself doing the same thing over and over until you can go out and imitate the skill. Try going beyond watching the players, and put yourself in their body, feeling and executing the correct form and technique that you are trying to imitate. SEE and FEEL yourself excelling.

Use these imagery scripts as models to build your own personal script. Then go over your script until you have it memorized so that you can use it. The value of your script is that you already saw it in your mind and thus know you can do it. This continues to build true confidence in your game.

IMAGERY SCRIPTS

Here are some of our favorite imagery scripts from a teacher and high school student-athletes:

Driving a Golf Ball

As I walk up to the teeing area I feel the moist soft grass beneath my feet. Reaching into my bag I grab my soft fuzzy driver head cover. Pulling the head cover off the driver, I throw it to the ground as I glance down the fairway and choose the ideal position to land the ball. While I reach into my pocket for a golf ball, I survey the teeing area to find a good flat spot to tee my ball. I find a great spot, just right of the center. I take my Titleist #4 and a white tee and plant it firmly into the ground. Standing behind the ball I quickly imagine the perfect flight and landing of the ball in my desired area. I approach the ball and square the clubface to the back of the ball. My feet begin to make short choppy movements as I waggle the golf club. Glancing down the fairway, I continue this movement until I feel comfortable. Once comfortable, I forward press my hands and take the club away low and slow. I feel my weight transfer to the inside of my back foot as my left arm remains somewhat straight across my body. At the top of the swing my eyes are looking over my left shoulder at the ball, my back is toward the target and my body is coiled. As I start to release forward, I stay on an inside path with my hands well ahead of the golf head. My weight begins to transfer to the front leg as the club head becomes square to the ball. I feel a great deal of power and control as I strike the ball and release the club forward. My head is down and stays down until the club is fully released and my hands are near my left ear. At this point I see the ball take off and its flight is perfect as the ball lands and rolls to the ideal spot in the fairway.

– Brian Hewitt, High School Counselor & Golf Instructor

Baseball

I hear the cheers of the crowd, the smell of hot dogs on the grill, and see the fresh green grass that extends all the way to the warning track. As I'm sitting, waiting in the on-deck circle, I scrutinize every little detail about the pitcher. I'm checking the signs like which arm clot he's throwing at and where the catcher is setting up. As I take my position at the plate, I check where the outfielders and infielders are setting up. I close my eyes and picture that meaty pitch coming right down the middle. As I swing my arms across my body, the bat makes perfect contact with the ball, placing it precisely between the left and centerfielders. As the other team races toward the ball, I take off at a sprint, unscathed as I round the bases. Opening my eyes, I step up to the plate. I dig and wait for the first pitch. I notice how tense my muscles are and relax my grip on the bat. The pitch is delivered and I realize it's the same pitch I had imagined when I closed my eyes. With the identical reaction, I swing with all the strength in my body. Hearing the sweet crack of the bat, I hit it to same place, between left and center field. It was like an instant replay of what I had envisioned. Immediately, I start a sprint toward first base. Gliding past it, I head for second, seeing that the center fielder isn't even to the ball yet. As I step over second, I tell myself that no one can touch me, I'm going home, no one is going to stop me. Now I see my third base coach waving me home. I'm rounding third when the center fielder hits his cut-off man. He rifles it to the catcher. This is it. I accelerate, pumping my arms as fast as I can, and dive.

Creating a cloud of dust all around me, I stretch toward home base. Feeling a tag right after I touch the plate, I look up and see the umpire waving his arms as he yells "Safe!" Wiping the dirt off my chest, I get up and high-five all of my teammates as I head back into the dugout.

Track

I breathe steadily into the chill air. I hear the announcer repeat "All runners to the track." I gather my shoes and find a quiet spot to lace up, sit, and think. As I tie my shoelaces, I feel the tightness of my shoestrings engulf my feet and toes, and feel the cool pavement beneath me. I close my eyes and picture the cool wind blowing upon my face as I glide past everyone on the track. I'm just across the finish line when the sound of the officials brings me back to reality and I see the runners now gathering at the start line. I take one last deep breath of air. Then the gun goes off. As I take off, the ringing of the shot still echoes in my ears. I keep a close distance with the other runners. I stay with the pack. I steadily and calmly inhale and exhale the oxygen throughout my lungs. A steady rhythm emerges as I repeat to myself, in and out, in and out. I keep my hands loose, low to my hips. I pass one runner at a time. One by one, I get to the finish line and quicken my pace. 100 meters, 50 meters. No one passes me; it's just me competing to win. No one is between me and the finish line. Sprint! Heart pounding, muscles tense, I thrust my body forward as I pass over the line. The race is over. I won. I let all the stress out and become filled with the exhilaration of first place. I tell myself there is only more of this to come.

Soccer

As I see the man moving toward the goal, I get ready. I yell out to my teammates, as the mud under my feet causes me to sink slightly. I stay ready on my toes, slightly bouncing. He dribbles closer and closer to the goal. Everyone is yelling, screaming; then everything goes quiet. The man with the ball is moving slower and slower, dirt flying off his shoes. I look straight into his eyes, still bouncing, still moving, still on my toes, I lean forward. I'm thinking about the possibilities of his shot. Left? Right? Straight? Is he left footed or right footed? Maybe both? A million questions race through my mind. Still bouncing on my toes I take a step slightly forward, my heart pounding in anticipation. As he advances even closer, he leans somewhat right, planting his left foot down. Right footed shot. I move slightly to the left, sinking even further into the ground. As his leg moves across his body, I'm already moving toward the right. Side stepping, I hear the sound of his foot making contact with the ball. Grass flings through the air like shrapnel up after the ball. Everything is silent. I take a deep breath and relax, take a step forward and jump. I try to imagine myself diving toward the corner as I lunge and stretch for the ball. It's a long shot, but I'm able to grip the ball with my fingers and cradle it into my chest. Perfect save, now just have to make that actually happen. Jumping up, I feel the pressure lifting from my quads as I soar through the air. My eyes on the ball, everything seems slow, quiet. I extend my arm out, reaching for the ball. I feel it brush the tips of my fingers, then hear a loud ringing as the ball ricochets off the cross bar. Everything around me once again erupts into a commotion of screaming, yelling, and movement. I fall to the ground with a loud thud and feel the impact smash my ribs into the mud as I see the ball bounce out of play. We're still in the game and there's still time for me to make that perfect save.

The following is a very valuable and helpful activity to guide you to write your own imagery script. Once you write your script, record your voice reading the script so you can play it over and over until it is ingrained in your head and you can recall if at any moment while you are competing.

IMAGERY SCRIPTING INSTRUCTIONS

Now it's time to make your own imagery script. This imagery script activity was developed by former California State University, Sacramento sport psychology professor, Karen Scarborough. Select an activity that you know very well and that is fairly short in duration. Choose an activity that has body movement, sounds, tactile sensations, colors, smells, etc. In short, try to choose an activity that is rich in sensation. If you are not presently involved in a sport, choose a different activity.

Activity: _____

List lots of words that describe the performance of the activity

Examples:
Names of equipment, colors, sounds, muscular feelings, emotional feelings, people, environmental factors, objects that you see, tactile feelings, words that describe movement.

_____	_____
_____	_____
_____	_____
_____	_____
_____	_____
_____	_____
_____	_____
_____	_____

List, in correct order, the procedures or movements associated with the activity. Do not break the movement down into too many precise mechanical parts. You want to think of the movement as a whole act that FLOWS from beginning to end.

_____	_____
_____	_____
_____	_____
_____	_____
_____	_____
_____	_____
_____	_____

PRE-GAME

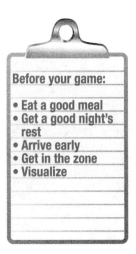

Before your game:

- Eat a good meal
- Get a good night's rest
- Arrive early
- Get in the zone
- Visualize

Focus on the task at hand, not the outcome. Focus on what you can control, and get yourself in the present. A consistent pre-game routine will give you the necessary confidence and focus.

Many athletes have designed a specific routine to help them prepare for competition. This may entail eating your pre-game meal, packing your athletic bag, putting on your uniform, doing physical warm-ups, and using mental toughness qualities.

The advantage of a pre-game routine is that you are getting ready, not only athletically, but also mentally for your peak performance. Remember, focus on the task, not the outcome, because you can control your actions but not the outcome of your actions. Make use of your positive self-affirmations, such as "I can perform today" to start your competition with a winning mindset.

Have a Routine

While it is normal for athletes to experience nervousness in pressure situations, it is critical to learn how to overcome those nerves so you can perform at your best. There are things you can do to assist you in overcoming nerves and self-doubt.

As well as having a routine the night before competition, it is critical to establish a routine during your competition. Your routine and how you step up to the ball is essential in overcoming your nerves. You need a step-up routine at the plate, on the first tee, on the starting block, for a penalty kick, for a field goal, at the free throw line, or any other pressure situation.

In golf, for example, how you step up to the ball and taking a practice swing is essential in being able to overcome your nerves so you have something to go to every time then its easier to get into a rhythm.

"**Harness your anxiety** and make it powerful. Balance your emotions. Slow your breathing, get locked in, run through the game in your head, form positive images, and just do, don't think.

–Brian Hewitt,
High School Counselor & Golf Instructor

Relaxation

Many student-athletes are unable to reach their goals because of high levels of stress, which can cause nervousness, shakiness, sweaty palms, a sick feeling in their stomach, and other symptoms. High levels of stress and anxiety symptoms can even be debilitating. The goal is to be able to relax enough to perform at your optimal ability, at a high intensity. Terry Orlick, a prominent sports psychologist, explains in his book, *In Pursuit of Excellence*, how intensity and relaxation work together:

Intensity and relaxation are not necessarily opposites; they can work together in complementary ways to bring out the best in you and your performance. You need an optimal amount of intensity to perform your best—not too much and not too little....Trying too hard or pushing too much can work against you....You go after your goal with full focus, you push your limits, and at the same time you relax enough to free your body to perform in a powerful yet flowing way.

Orlick suggests that you need to find your "sweet spot" or an intensity level that is just right:

You can enter your ideal intensity zone by trusting yourself to do what you are capable of doing, by relaxing your breathing and your body, and by connecting fully with the doing part of your performance. Turning down the intensity a little when it is too high frees you to be powerful and fluid, but not forced. You become less rigid, less tense, more supple, more flowing, and more focused on the step in front of you.

Relaxation Scripts

In order to be able to relax when you need it during a performance, you need to practice the techniques in isolation, practice, and competition. There are a variety of free relaxation scripts online. Find one that works best for you and have someone read it to you, or record yourself saying them and play them back.

Included are two relaxation scripts from sports psychology professor Karen Scarborough. They were used successfully with our high school students. In addition, use the Centering technique to relax yourself quickly at home or even during competition.

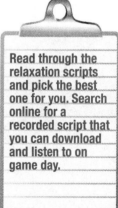

Read through the relaxation scripts and pick the best one for you. Search online for a recorded script that you can download and listen to on game day.

Relaxation Scripts: Active Progressive

The dots (...) represent pauses that give you time to follow the directions.

Lie down in a comfortable position with your eyes closed...Bring your attention to your breathing...Feel the gentle rise and fall of your chest... As you exhale, feel the warm air as it exists your nostrils...Gently let your focus become completely internal...You are becoming increasingly aware of how your body feels...If your attention wanders, gently bring it back to focus on the voice and on your body...Draw your attention to your feet... Gently draw your toes back toward your knee and hold the tension for a moment... Notice the tightness in your feet and legs... Let the tension go...Feel the relaxation in your feet... Tense the muscles of your calves by gently pointing the toes... Hold the tension for a few seconds, feeling the tightness...you release the muscles, feel the relaxation in those muscles... Now lift your foot up an inch or two, feeling the tension in the muscles of your thighs... Hold... Relax... Contract your buttocks muscles tight enough to feel the tension... Hold the tension... Relax the muscles and notice the different feelings in tension and relaxation... Tighten the muscles in your abdomen and lower back by pulling in your abdominal muscles... Hold them tightly for a few seconds... As you slowly let go of all the tension, pay attention to what it feels like for the muscles to be completely loose... Tense the muscles of your chest and shoulders by shrugging your shoulders tightly, tensing the muscles of your shoulders and neck... Hold... Release... Now shrug your shoulders again but only slightly... Notice what only a small amount of tension feels like... Relax... Remember how a small amount of tension feels in your shoulders and neck... Make a fist and tense the muscles of your arms and hands... Hold... Release... Be aware of the feeling of relaxation... Now scrunch all the muscles in your face... Knit your eyebrows... Press your lips together... Tense the muscles of your chin, eyes, throat, nose, forehead, and mouth... Hold... Let it all go... Press your tongue to the roof of your mouth... Hold... Now relax... Make sure your jaw, forehead and mouth are completely loose... Your mouth may even hang open just a little as it relaxes...

Scan your body, starting with your feet, moving from one part to another... If you feel any tension, remember what the muscle group felt like when relaxed and let it go... You are beginning to feel completely relaxed... You will remember this awareness about your body and can recall the feelings whenever you need...

Continue scanning and relaxing until you feel that your body is relaxed... As you gently bring your focus back to the room, you are filled with peace, calm and contentment... Slowly begin to open your eyes and stretch out... Sit up very slowly, concentrating on remaining relaxed.

Relaxation Scripts: Imagery

Lie down in a comfortable position with your eyes closed... Bring your attention inward and centered on your breathing... Feel the gentle rise and fall of your chest... Breathe deeply...you exhale, feel the warm air as it exits your nostrils... Breathe in relaxation and peace... Breathe out tension and stress... Gently let your focus become completely internal... Scan your body, releasing all the muscle tension... Feel the relaxation wash down from your head to your face, neck and shoulders... Down your arms to your hands... Down your chest to your abdomen... And down your thighs to your feet...

As your lie here, content and relaxed, you're become aware of a bright light... you become accustomed to this light you realize this light is coming from the sun... You begin to feel the sun warm you...It's the perfect temperature... Not too hot and not too cool... You feel a slight breeze blow across your skin cooling it... The breeze is so light you can feel it stir the hairs on your arms... You also notice that this slight breeze has brought with it the light smell of salt air... You realize that you must be near the ocean... You begin to look around... You are on top of a large dune, sitting in the warm, soft sand with beach grass surrounding you...No one else is around... You have this place to yourself...You sit here, you feel completely relaxed and at peace... You notice you are overlooking the calm blue of the ocean... And you notice the blue of the sky and the soft white clouds... You watch the waves, gently lapping on the shore... Your body and mind feel completely free... You notice the birds gliding on the air currents... You haven't felt quite as relaxed in a long time...You continue to sit there and reflect on your daily activities, you begin to feel a confidence growing inside you... Makes you feel like you can accomplish anything... You continue to feel the warmth of the sun... You feel this warmth spreading through every fiber in your body... You feel very relaxed and content... You know that, at any time, you can come to this special, private place... You have the power to bring that peace to yourself whenever you need it...

With that in mind, you begin to feel comfortable in returning your attention to the room... Scan your body to maintain relaxation... When ready, slowly become more alert... Stretching your arms and your legs... And when ready, open your eyes and sit up.

Relaxation Technique: Centering

Think of a word or phrase and of a color that you can associate with peacefulness, contentment and relaxation. You will use these as cues to relax yourself.

What is your relaxation word or phrase? _____

What is your relaxation color? _____

Get into a comfortable position and close your eyes. Take several deep breaths through your nose, hold each breath for 5-6 seconds, and slowly exhale through your mouth. As you inhale, imagine filling your lungs completely from the bottom up. Concentrate on each breath, in and out, then on the breathing out. Now focus on the word or color that reminds you of relaxation. Return to normal breathing, maintaining your concentration on the breathing in and out. Each time you breathe, think of your word/phrase/color and feel yourself relaxing.

Control Your Breathing

Successful athletes have learned it is so important to practice controlling their breathing. Controlled breathing will help you perform in high-pressure situations. Take deep breaths, while counting to ten. Do whatever it takes to slow your breathing and heart rate so that you feel in complete control of the situation.

"**I kicked a winning field goal** against Army. I felt my nerves coming on when the coach called a time out for a field goal. I tried not to get nervous by using mechanisms to control my breathing. I calmed myself by slowing my breathing. I would have been extra nervous in that pressure situation if I didn't slow my breathing. When the game is on the line, how do you handle the pressure? Have you prepared mentally? Have you played the scenario out in your head?"
–Scotty Enos, University of Hawaii Kicker,
Semi-Pro Football Player

Be in the Present

The challenge for student-athletes is to compete and stay in the present. You need to constantly talk to yourself and tell yourself to focus on the moment at hand, which will keep you from feeling pressure and stress. Take one shot, or at bat, or race at a time.

Many athletes struggle with focusing on the present because they get caught up in what happened in the past, like a bad play or a strike out, rather than focusing on the current task. Or they might become distracted by the necessity to win this game in order to go to playoffs or to move to the next level, rather than focusing on the task at hand. You must stay focused on the present task and not become distracted by anything. Once the competition begins, take it one play at a time.

All athletes, even pro athletes, get distracted during competition. There are a few techniques that student-athletes can use in order to minimize distractions during a game. One great technique is to have a word or phrase to say to yourself to get you back in focus. Don't carry on a conversation with your self, but stick to a word or phrase. Another technique is to imagine a huge red stop sign the moment you realize you are daydreaming, which will signal your brain to stop spacing out and to focus on the present. Another problem athletes face is when they worry about their competitor's strengths or previous records. Again, don't waste your energy by focusing on outcomes, but focus on the task at hand.

MENTAL TOUGHNESS

Mental toughness is the ability to bounce back from adversity. When playing sports, sometimes your biggest opponent is not the other team, but yourself. You walk up to the plate, with the game on the line and strike out. Is this one at-bat going to define your career, or will you take what you learned from the experience to become a stronger player mentally so that the next time you are put in a pressure situation you will know what to expect? You should be able to enjoy every second of playing, and a large part of that comes from knowing how to tame your emotions. The most important thing to remember is that you need to play sports for you, not your parents or anybody else.

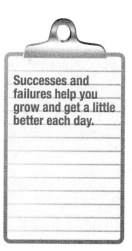

Successes and failures help you grow and get a little better each day.

Learn from Mistakes

Successful athletes learn not to stress over a missed putt, a strike out, a missed field goal, missed penalty kick, or a dropped pass. Instead they learn from these mistakes and move on thinking positively.

Being able to learn from mistakes makes you become a resilient student-athlete. You have the ability to "bounce back" and not dwell on an error, and focus on what you need to do to modify your actions so that you don't make the same mistake again.

F.E.A.R.

**False
Expectations
Appearing
Real**

Minimize Fear of Failure

Fear of failure is bigger than fearing mistakes. Athletes are often unsuccessful when they play not to lose rather than play to win. The bottom line is they have a strong fear of failure, which leads to feeling tight and freezing in competitions. This causes unwanted mental pressure in executing a routine play or a fundamental skill, and this is when athletes "choke." This fear can be eliminated by looking at the big picture. One out does not define your career, but it will help you learn from your mistakes.

"Derrek doesn't care about making an out. An out is just an out. He doesn't tense up because he has no fear of failure. An out is just an out—and that's it. It's just another at bat."

–Leon Lee, Hitting Instructor and Pacific Rim Coordinator for the Chicago Cubs, Describing His Son

Competition is not about being perfect, but about being your best each day. When perfectionists do not meet their own expectations, they become frustrated with themselves and do not learn from a mistake. An obsessive desire to be perfect leads to frustration, injuries and eventual burn out.

"The player who makes it to the next level is the one who strikes out three times in a row, but doesn't let it get to him. He forgets the strikeouts and comes back with a hit. It's the confidence."

–Kyle Saukko, Former JUCO National Champion, MLB Pittsburgh Pirates Minor League Player

Avoid Pressure to Win

Today, youth sports are taken very seriously because of our competitive culture and the common belief that competition and skill development at a young age are necessary to help student-athletes play collegiate sports. This pressure to perform comes not only from the athlete, but from parents and coaches as well.

Remember that sports should be fun. The fun of competition is playing the game or running the race —not the end of the game or race. Numbers get you into trouble, and scores and stats distract from the game.

Lower your Anxiety

Sports often lead to pressure situations and from these situations athletes can often face anxiety. Athletes reduce anxious feelings by focusing on their cue word or phrase, or locating a physical spot in the environment to get them to relax. Some athletes even write all their feelings that contribute to their stress and anxiety in a daily journal so that they understand what feelings and/or actions trigger nervousness. Anxiety is just another form of stress. The more confident you are in you abilities, the less anxiety you will have.

Overcome Adversity

Adversity is defined as a state of continued difficulty. It can be a misfortune, disaster, or a hardship, like a death in the family, a serious injury, failing a class, or hitting an athletic slump. You could also have a difficult coach or an annoying teammate.

When times are tough, who gets better and who gives up? Many view adversity as an obstacle, like a wall, but try to view adversity as a hurdle to overcome instead. That presents the opportunity for you to grow and evolve to get better. Try to stay positive, and forget about a loss or a poor performance so that you can succeed.

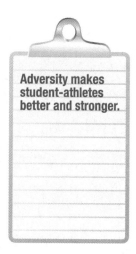
Adversity makes student-athletes better and stronger.

"**Everyone will face adversity.** How you will respond will determine your success. We underestimate ourselves and overestimate others. Positive words make you strong and negative words make you weak."

–Roger Crawford, Motivational Speaker and Author

Support

Hopefully, you have adults and friends in your life who act as a support system for you. Their role is to provide understanding and empathy while encouraging you to work hard and learn from your mistakes. They need to help you focus on the task and not the outcome. Successful student-athletes have people who support and believe in them.

"**Honestly, thinking back to playing football** in front of the large college crowds, the pressure around school, the media aspect, and the atmosphere in general, it is the mental side that makes the difference. Since everyone at the college level can play, it comes down to who can play in pressure situations. I think those who play the best, handle the pressure with controlled breathing techniques. I prepare the night before. I had a routine the night before where I visualize myself on the field and see myself do everything right. I visualize being successful. I visualize all the little things so I can adjust in pressure situations. So in the game, I feel like I had already been there. This really helped me. I didn't appreciate learning about peak performance in high school because I felt I was learning about things that didn't affect me. And, when I was in junior college, the atmosphere was mellow and there was no real pressure. I didn't appreciate it until I got to this level. When you are young, you don't absorb what people are saying or what they are going through until you experience it and can understand it. When I took it very serious, it really helped me and I will never forget learning it in high school. I am confident in my ability."

–Scotty Enos, University of Hawaii Kicker
Semi-Pro Football Player

PEAK PERFORMANCE: From Being Confident and Focused to Being a Leader

In addition to being mentally tough, athletes must be coachable teammates who exhibit good sportsmanship. Obviously, college coaches and scouts recruit talented and coachable athletes, but they build their programs by recruiting good communicators and leaders for their teams. This is why they view student athletes beyond the playing field—they watch them interact on the sidelines, the pool deck, and the gym; they watch how they interact with their parents and teammates; they watch how players react to officials and their high school coaches; and they watch how they respond to adversity. Most college coaches contact high school coaches for character references and call club teams for sport specific athletic ability. John Wooden, Legendary UCLA Basketball Coach, is remembered for saying, that a perfect day is when a person helps another who can't help him self and gets nothing in return. Are you working toward living perfect days?

KEYS TO COMMUNICATION & LEADERSHIP

College prep student-athletes need to develop some or even all of the following qualities to be a well-balanced student-athlete:
  - Coachable/Teachable
  - Good Teammate
  - Sportsmanship
  - Communication Skills
  - Leadership Skills
  - Community Service/Volunteer

Coachable/Teachable

Are you coachable on the field and in the classroom? NFL Dallas Cowboys formative coach, Tom Landry, stated accurately that coaches make you do what you don't want to, so that you can get what you want. Take advantage of the opportunities from your coaches and teachers throughout your high school prep years.

An ancient Chinese proverb says, "Fish for a man and feed him for a day; teach a man to fish and feed him for a lifetime." What a student-athlete can take from this is that if you are willing to learn from the adults and players around you, you will discover skills and qualities that will enable you to be successful, not only in your sport, but in life. Are you open to both criticism and support? Are you listening to your coach, or are you thinking about what excuse you are going to use to justify poor performance?

Good Teammate

We learned a valuable lesson from Scott Winter and Lain Hensley at *Odyssey Performance Enhancement Network:* at all times you are either contributing to or taking away from an experience. There is no such thing as non-behavior. If you are contributing, you are exhibiting positive behaviors, and if you are exhibiting negative behaviors, you are taking away from an experience. You are always contributing to or taking away from a class, team, performance, or any situation in any time or place. Being idle is taking up space, thus taking away from an experience. Distracting another in a classroom or at a practice is taking away from a situation.

Texting during class or practice is "Taking Away" behavior. Talking when your teacher or coach is talking is "Taking Away" behavior. Daydreaming or thinking about something other than what you should be focusing on is "Taking Away" behavior. Not actively participating in class or during practice is "Taking Away" behavior. Making fun of classmates or teammates is "Taking Away" behavior.

Contributing behaviors are encouraging others, paying attention, focusing, leading by example, and participating positively, among other things. Make a chart for take away and contributing behaviors—spell it out specifically. Your behavior and attitude influence those all around you, and will contribute to or take away from your team or class.

You will get out of any team or class situation what you put into it. Maximum effort and participation will get you maximum satisfaction and achievement.

Sportsmanship

If you are gracious in losing and winning, respectful of your opponents and the officials, manage your emotions well, and support your teammates and coaches even when you disagree with them, you are exhibiting good sportsmanship. An example would be when you manage your emotions by not showing anger and frustration by throwing a bat, or your helmet.

An all-star team that was favored to win did not continue on because the players were very critical of one another, constantly yelling negative comments and blaming each other leading to a situation where the team competed against itself as well as its opponents. Your opponent should only be the other team, not your teammates. Teams can't win fighting both themselves and their competition.

Communication

Good communication prevents misunderstandings. How many times have you experienced a situation where your parent, coach, or teacher is mad at you because you didn't understand the directions?

"The quality of your life depends upon the quality of your communication."
–Lain Hensley, Odyssey Performance Enhancement Network

Good communicators practice active listening and speaking with clarity. Communication is a two-way street: there are speakers and listeners, so you must practice both listening and speaking.

Listening requires paying attention, an open mind, being present, eye contact, open body posturing, and appropriate responses. Many times, we hear, but we are not really listening. Pay attention and stay involved in the conversation.

Speaking is the other half of good communication, and requires delivering your thoughts in a clear and articulate way.

While speaking and listening, if you try to dialogue instead of discuss a topic, you will find yourself communicating more positively with classmates, teammates, teachers, coaches, and parents. Discuss is when we tear down different ideas to find the best idea and dialogue is where we build upon different ideas to find the best idea. Be sure to dialogue when your goal is to be an active listener and work together to come together.

Leadership—Leading Yourself and Others

Leading Self: Leadership is directing your self first, and then others. To lead yourself, you need to organize, plan, and prepare as if its involved with your life. You need to be a role model, to stretch your comfort zone, to be absolutely coachable, and to contribute to your team. (See Chapter 7 to learn how to set goals and manage your time.)

Don't be a robot. You have heard the saying that leadership, character, and integrity are what you do when no one is looking, so be that athlete that takes the initiative to do what needs to be done, especially at practice when no one is looking. Don't wait to be told what to do when you can determine it on your own. Coaches notice.

Alex Diemer wasn't the tallest player, but she was a sought after volleyball recruit for Boise State University because she played hard, had a work ethic, and most importantly, she was a leader who inspired her teammates to play hard.

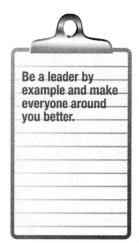

Be a leader by example and make everyone around you better.

Leading Others: Once you feel good about leading yourself, you might want to consider "servant leadership." Roger Crawford, a highly respected motivational speaker challenges student-athletes to lead a life of significance –that is, to make a difference for others.

A strong team leader is someone who is also a problem-solver. When they see disharmony in their team, they work with the individuals to solve problems, or if there is a conflict with a coaching decision, a leader can be the team's spokesperson. A leader needs to be an active listener who offers possible solutions so that the team can excel.

Student-athletes have to be mentally tough to compete in sports today. Coaches are looking for athletes with positive attitudes, who also possess leadership skills. If you feel that you don't currently have communication or leadership skills, you can develop them throughout high school. You need to have the mindset that you can learn more and grow, as long as you push your comfort zone and challenge yourself, getting a little better each day.

A winning coach at any level will tell you that championship teams have players that are leaders on and off the court or field and serve as a two-way communicator between the coach and the players. A winning team will have a teammate who will lead by example and is relentless at motivating his/her teammates to play hard and to win. An outstanding teammate is the one who makes everyone around them better. Leadership is a requirement to win.

Leadership Opportunities in High School

"The foundation of academic success lies in the success of activities and athletics programs. You will find opportunities to pursue a passion, try something new, and build friendships."
–Ron Severson, Roseville Joint Union High School District
Assistant Superintendent

Take a leadership class in high school, sign up for the student government class, or join a student government activity or club. While you will make posters, organize events, and manage activities, you will make friends and learn invaluable lessons, like service leadership, conflict management skills, communication skills, and how to advocate for yourself.

Read about how a leadership class helped these high school students...

"Being a leader gave me the foundation I've needed in my careers as a college admissions counselor and an employment recruiter."
–Alison Guzenski

"During my interview for the RA (resident assistant) position at UC Davis, half of my answers were examples from my time in student government. I talked about initiative, humility, integrity, and conflict management."
–Joe McIntosh

"Student government alumni are equipped for college and for handling career because of the skills they learned as student-leaders. They will be productive students in college, and more willing to approach professors or to organize an event in their dorm or for their athletic team. Students will be ready to face anything that comes their way because their student government experiences have prepared them for the real world."
–Tamara Givens, Student Government Adviser

Leadership training and experience will help prepare you for college –for academics, athletics, dorm life, Greek life, and any college pursuits you find yourself seeking.

Community Service

Some high schools require that all students complete community service, and they will often give you a list of ideas for where to volunteer. If your high school does not require community service you should still commit to volunteering your time to a worthy cause. Not only is it good for you, but most college applications and scholarships require that you share what you have done in the way of community service. Some students volunteer at pet shelters, work in a hospital, serve Thanksgiving dinners at homeless shelters, or coach youth sports programs. Check with your college and career center or your counselor for more ideas on how you could get community service hours.

Final thoughts...
Peak performance is an optimal state to be in while playing sports and competing. You have to practice the techniques to develop these mental skills. Building confidence, learning how to focus, visualizing your athletic success, and overcoming nerves and adversity are all part of performing your best in pressure situations. Once you come to the realization of just what you are capable of and what you can do, your world will be full of endless possibilities. You need to believe in yourself, and you will earn confidence by working hard, learning from mistakes, and competing in the present. Play Hard. Play Smart. Play Forward. Play with a volcanic heart of passion.

Chapter 6
Top 10 Plays

1. Have a positive attitude

2. Realize what you can and cannot control when competing

3. Believe in yourself

4. Write affirmations so you will talk to yourself in a positive way

5. Use visualization and imagery to help you focus

6. Find balance between relaxation and intensity—get "in the flow"

7. Focus on your task, not the outcome

8. Learn from your mistakes

9. Be a positive influence on your team

10. Lead yourself first, then lead others

Chapter Game Plan

MAKE YOUR GOALS HAPPEN

- Smart Goals Defined
- S: Specific
- M: Measurable
- A: Action-Oriented
- R: Realistic (Relevant, Reasonable, Rewarding)
- T: Timely (Time Based, Time Deadline)

HOW TO SET YOUR GOALS— FIRST: REFLECT

- Controllables

SECOND: SET GOALS

- Steps to Set Goals

HOW TO ACHIEVE GOALS

- FIRST: Manage Your Time Wisely
- SECOND: Reflect to Get Better
- THIRD: Use Your Time Wisely in the Summer

KEEP IT SIMPLE

Dream big but have a purpose in your heart.

MAKE YOUR GOALS HAPPEN

How are you going to go through high school? Lain Hensley of Odyssey Performance Enhancement Network claims we must "Make it Happen". What he means is that student-athletes are not spectators. They are proactive and set priorities and goals and challenge themselves for peak performance. Make a plan, open doors, promote yourself, and revise or reinvent yourself continually. Don't be a spectator on the sidelines. Participate. Play hard. Play smart. Develop the "I CAN" attitude. Make the sacrifices and stay committed.

Student-athletes must meet high school, NCAA, and individual college requirements.

Students and student-athletes alike must set and accomplish goals. To do this, you need to have a plan in three areas: academics, athletics, and peak performance. In terms of academics, high school counselors can help students set four-year academic plans, and now most middle schools also assist students in setting up six-year academic plans. In terms of athletics, if you want to play college sports, YOU must make sure that you meet the NCAA academic eligibility requirements because this is not a focus for counselors. With this being said, some schools have counselors who have an interest, and the knowledge, to help you make sure you meet NCAA requirements. Note that student athletes not only have to meet NCAA requirements, but each university also has its own academic requirements for admission too (read Chapter 9 for details). Do not rely on your school counselors, as they have numerous responsibilities. This is **your** responsibility.

Yogi Berra, an admired and successful New York Yankee player and manager understood the importance of setting goals for success. Winners have goals and a plan!

Winners...
- expect good things to happen
- set high goals
- are always learning, growing
- strive for excellence
- turn success into a habit by practice
- are driven by desires not fears
- anticipate and welcome change
- do not quit
- are positive

"You've got to be very careful if you don't know where you are going, because you might not get there."

-Yogi Berra, Former New York Yankee

Dreams are when you daydream and wish that you could do or have something in the future. You really don't work toward that dream, you just think about it, and they are often unrealistic. In order for you to make the dream realistic and achieve it, you must turn it into a goal and make it something you work toward, not just something you think about. You must take steps to reach your goals and these individual steps make up your plan. Meaningful goals align with your convictions and dreams. The best goals require that you stretch yourself in order to achieve them.

Devise goals to keep you focused, and to provide you with the steps to be successful. A goal is not a real goal that will get you somewhere unless it has important, specific elements. The acronym **SMART** gives you these elements you need to know to write your academic, athletic, and peak performance goals.

Winners realize that goals are more than dreams.

Mikey Beck, a former high school and current college baseball player overcame his wall by asking his teammates to run and catch with him every day in the off-season. He was committed to do this day after day, week after week, season after season. He didn't have the natural talent that some of his teammates had, but he had the passion, desire, work ethic, and commitment that gave him the motivation to sacrifice time to work on his game. No one thought Mikey would pitch an inning in high school, but he became a pitcher in the rotation for his high school team. Mikey was a high school senior with a 4.6 GPA. During his senior year, he sent out 150 letters with transcripts and profiles to college coaches to increase his exposure.

Some say he was living in a dream world, far from reality. Maybe he was, but he was developing an incredible work ethic and becoming a person of character and fortitude that will undeniably lead to a successful adult life no matter the profession he chooses. Mikey was offered almost full tuition to Menlo College, which was a NAIA school, based on his family's financial need and his excellent grades, but he was not going to make the baseball team. So he enrolled at American River College and played fall ball, got cut and then transferred to Yuba City Community College in the spring. He did a redshirt year as a sophomore. He is still keeping the dream alive by playing wherever he can until he has no opportunities. He will probably continue after community college and find a DIII school in the middle of the country where he can earn a degree and still play baseball.

Smart Goals Defined

A **SMART** goal (or a real goal) has five elements. The goal will be…

S - specific

M - measurable

A - action oriented

R - realistic

T - timely

Your goal should be stated in one sentence and should meet these five elements. Goals explain exactly what is expected. Answer the following questions to guide you in setting **SMART** goals.

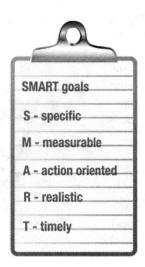

SMART goals

S - specific

M - measurable

A - action oriented

R - realistic

T - timely

S: Specific

‣ A specific goal has a much greater chance of being accomplished than a general goal
‣ Describe your goal in precise terms so there is no confusion as to what needs to be accomplished
‣ Answer the journalist's questions: Who, What, When, Where, Why and How?
‣ What will your goal look like when you reach it?

M: Measurable

‣ When you measure your progress, you tend to stay on track
‣ Make sure you include the measures you will use to judge your progress toward achieving the goal
‣ How much? How many?
‣ Can you monitor and track your progress?
‣ How will this goal be measured?
‣ How will you know when it's accomplished?

A: Action-Oriented

‣ This needs to be something that you can "do"
‣ This is stated with a verb
‣ This needs to focus on working on your behavior
‣ What is it you want to change?
‣ What is it that you want to achieve?

R: Realistic (Relevant, Reasonable, Rewarding)

‣ Your goal must be realistic, yet challenging
‣ Your goal should relate to attaining something that is necessary and of value and that supports your educational and athletic vision
‣ Don't set it so high that in the back of your mind you know failure will eventually happen
‣ Do you truly believe that you can accomplish this goal?
‣ Is the goal consistent with your other goals?
‣ Do you have the resources, knowledge, and time to achieve this goal?

T: Timely (Time Based, Time Deadline)

‣ Determine a date, time frame, or schedule for your goal.
‣ There is a starting and ending point.
‣ There is a clear target date.
‣ When should you reach your goal?

The reason some student-athletes have difficulty accomplishing goals is that they have not designed goals with the 5 elements. Below are examples of general goals and **SMART** goals.

Example of a vague, general goal:
 ‣ To get a better grade in English.
 ‣ To be a better player on my team.

Example of a **SMART** goal:
 ‣ To score at least 80% on my literary analysis essays in English 9 by the midterm.
 ‣ To move from being ranked #6 to #4 on my tennis team's ladder by the start of league matches.

SMART *Goals Summary*

It is important to set specific, measurable goals with an action verb that are challenging yet attainable with hard work, and within a specific time period. Successful people write down daily, weekly, and monthly goals. They also continually evaluate how they are progressing toward these goals.

Now that you can define goals vs. dreams and know how to set **SMART** goals, you need to answer some really important questions about what you really want and what you are willing to do to achieve this. Student-athletes wanting to perform at their peak realize that it takes sacrifice, meaning you have to give up things such as hanging out with your friends, watching TV, staying up late, texting, and playing computer games. Instead, your time will be focused on being successful in school and going to bed early so you are fresh to work-out, practice, or attend games. This does not mean that you will not need to find time to relax and to rejuvenate yourself as you will need time off, not only to avoid burnout, but to enjoy playing sports. Remember, sports are supposed to be fun! This is why you play. (Remind your parents of this!) Student-athletes must find a **balance** between enjoying their free time and dedicating themselves to hard work in order to achieve both challenging and meaningful academic and athletic goals.

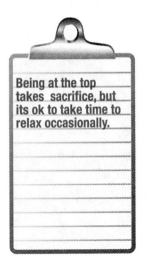

Being at the top takes sacrifice, but its ok to take time to relax occasionally.

"It took a lot of hard work and persistence over the years to achieve a scholarship. I had to balance out schoolwork and continue to train at a high level, and then perform at the tournament level. I stay motivated because I constantly strive to continue getting the results I know I am capable of. Knowing that I will be playing in college is also very motivating because I want to be as best prepared as I can be going into it next year. Time management was key and I was able to do that. I am very proud to be receiving the scholarship and feel I deserve it because of the work I have put in over the years."

–Max Vogt,
Tennis Scholarship to Bryant University, Smithfield, RI

HOW TO SET YOUR GOALS—FIRST: REFLECT

Start to set your goals by completing the Goals Questionnaire to help you develop a clear picture of your goals. Write your answers on the template or download a copy from our website.

GOALS QUESTIONNAIRE

Academic Goals:

1. What GPA do you want to achieve this year?
2. What grades do you want to earn in your core and elective classes?
3. Do you consider yourself a "college prep" student?
4. What do you need to do to earn excellent grades in your classes?
5. Might you need after school help or a tutor for any classes?
6. Are you developing good study skills and habits?
7. Are you spending time reading?
8. What are you going to do to improve?

Athletic Goals:

9. Do you plan on competing at the highest level in your area for your age group?
10. How much time do you expect to spend on designated practice time and on your own?
11. Do you work on your fitness, which includes strength, conditioning, agility, speed and nutrition?
12. Are your parents supportive of your athletic goals?
13. Do you want to be a college-recruited athlete?
14. What are you going to do to improve?

Peak Performance Goals (Mental Toughness, Communication, Leadership)

15. Do you recover from losses and learn from adversity?
16. Do you visualize and imagine positive outcomes both in school and in sports/ performances?
17. Do you know how to relax?
18. Do you allow a wait time before responding to conflict?
19. What are you willing to sacrifice to achieve your goals?

20. Are you working on your listening and speaking skills?
21. Do you speak to yourself in a positive manner?
22. Are you leading yourself by respecting others, making the right choices, and being accountable for your actions?
23. Do you want to lead others by leading by example or by developing interpersonal skills?

Reflect on your responses to see what is important to you. Are you willing to work toward these goals? Will you be committed? Be honest with yourself. It's much easier if you have someone to support you in accomplishing your goals—like your parents, a relative, a coach, or a counselor.

Controllables

Now that you have thought about your goals, you need to know that you can only do what you can control. You remember from Chapter 6 we call these controllables.

Student-athletes must recognize and focus on what they can control in school and sports. They also need to recognize what they cannot control. To help you think about this concept, complete the following activity.

Think about all the things that could affect you when you are performing in school and in sports by using both charts below. In the box on the left, finish filling in some of the things that many athletes make excuses for, or things that they have no control over. In the box on the right, fill in what you are actually able to control.

CONTROLLABLES

What can you control?

What is out of your control?

School Uncontrollables	School Controllables
‣ instructor's teaching style	‣ my attitude
‣ other student distractions	‣
‣	‣
‣	‣

Sports Uncontrollables	Sports Controllables
‣ umpire, ref, judges	‣ my attitude
‣ weather, wind	‣
‣	‣
‣	‣

What a student-athlete can learn from this activity is that there are some specific things you cannot control, but you can control your response or reaction to what happens. For instance, if your team is losing or you make a mistake, spend 30 seconds thinking about what happened, learn from it, and move on. This is why you hear the saying, "Great athletes have terrible memories." Focus on how to positively influence your own performance or your team's. This is being resilient.

RESILIENCY

The ability to bounce back from adversity, to recover quickly from setbacks

On the other hand, you have probably learned from this exercise that there are in fact, many things that you can control that will affect your performance in school and in sports. You can encourage and motivate yourself and others around you to do their best. Take control of what you can and change the outcome. You have the power.

HOW TO SET YOUR GOALS—SECOND: SET GOALS

Now let's talk about setting academic and athletic goals. Take care of business and work on controlling your attitude and effort to achieve good grades.

You need to know that your Grade Point Average (GPA) and SAT/ACT scores are two of the most important measurements, outside of athletic ability, that colleges and coaches will consider when they recruit student-athletes. The higher your GPA, the lower your SAT/ACT scores have to be according to the NCAA Academic eligibility sliding scale. (See Chapter 9 for details.)

Some high schools are moving to a progressive, comprehensive, college planning service, Naviance. This web-based program is used for academic advising, high school course selection, counseling, college planning, and letters of recommendation. This site is designed to help students and parents with colleges, careers, and academic planning, and also, matches students with colleges and scholarship opportunities.

Steps to Set Goals

Step 1

Complete the recommended forms and plans to help you work toward good grades. Your school counselor or college and career center will have these forms or they are available on the dcipress.com website:
  ‣ 4-year high school academic plan—get this from your high school counselor since they are specific to each high school
  ‣ NCAA worksheet for prescribed course of study
  ‣ GPA calculation (paper and online at individual university sites)
  ‣ Academic goals template
  ‣ Athletic goals template
  ‣ Time management planner
  ‣ Reflection to review goals—evaluate & check progress

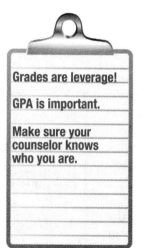

Grades are leverage!

GPA is important.

Make sure your counselor knows who you are.

Step 2

Meet with your counselor when you are in junior high school and/or high school to complete your four-year academic plan, using a college prep course selection list.

Talk to your counselor about wanting to attend college and playing college sports. Even if you are not sure if you will actually end up playing college sports, keep your options open throughout high school. Tell your counselor you want help in making sure you are taking college prep classes so you can open all your doors for college options. You never know what is going to happen in the future, and you may change your mind several times while in high school. For example, you may think you are going to go to a community college and may end up going to a private college or state college right out of high school. By earning the best grades you can get, you will be able to make choices on where you can go. Remember, grades are the leverage for opportunities after high school.

Step 3

In addition to using your four-year high school plan, also use the NCAA worksheet to make sure you meet NCAA academic eligibility requirements.

We cannot emphasize enough that you must make sure that you refer to the most recent update of the NCAA academic course requirements since they continually change. Chapter 9 lists the current required course work. Go to ncaa.org to view the most current requirements and even to order, or print, the worksheet.

Step 4

Calculate your GPA. You will need to figure both your academic GPA and your cumulative GPA. Your high school grade printouts and your transcripts will calculate your current GPA. You can also plug in your grades on college websites for GPA calculations. If you want to calculate your GPA on your own, here is how to do it.

Academic GPA does not include elective or PE classes. Cumulative GPA includes all classes you have taken during high school.

CALCULATE YOUR GPA

CLASS	LETTER GRADE	POINTS
English		
Totals:		

Grade Values:

A	4
B	3
C	2
D	1
F	0

$$\frac{\text{TGP = Total Grade Points}}{\text{NC = Number of Classes}} = \text{GPA}$$

Add your grade points earned. That is the total number of grade points. (TGP)

In addition to your academic GPA and cumulative GPA, you will calculate weighted grades if you take Advanced Placement (AP), Honors, or International Baccalaureate (IB) courses. Go to each college website that you are interested in attending and enter your courses and grades and the website will automatically calculate your GPA based on their policy with weighted grades. Note that some colleges, such as Brigham Young University, do not weight AP, Honors, or IB grades.

Step 5

Set your goals using our Goal Setting Template for long-term and short-term goals.

Now it is time to actually write your academic, athletic, and peak performance goals. Since you know that goals must have elements of **SMART** and they must be something you can control, you are ready to commit to yearly and short-term goals.

If your major goal is to play at the college level, in actuality, your goals must be broken down to yearly academic and athletic goals for all four years of high school. Many high school counselors require students to create four-year academic plans. Student-athletes must, in addition, set four-year athletic plans. This way student-athletes clearly visualize and focus on what they need to do each year and evaluate their progress at the end of the year.

Climb the ladder by setting short term goals step-by-step to a long-term goal.

In order to meet your yearly academic and athletic goals, you must also set short-term goals, which are steps toward reaching your yearly goal. By approaching your goals in smaller steps, they are easier to accomplish than trying to make them happen all at once. It can be frustrating to set goals if you are not setting short term goals in addition to your major goal. They are like steps on a ladder.

Once you set your short-term goals, you need to consider what obstacles may get in the way of achieving your goals. If you list potential obstacles in the beginning and also list ways to overcome these setbacks, you will be ahead of the game. Additionally, think of someone who can help and support you, someone who will encourage you and hold you accountable. By sharing your goals with people around you, they will help you reach your goals.

Just DO it! Write down your goals.

As always, you can write goals in this book, make copies, and/or download templates from dcipress.com for your academic and athletic goals each time you set new ones.

ACADEMIC GOALS TEMPLATE

9th grade yearly goal: _____

Set specific, measurable goals with an action verb that is challenging, yet attainable with hard work, and within a specific time period.

Support Person: _____

The following short-term goals are steps to achieving your yearly goal.

SHORT TERM GOAL #1: _____

Actions—what to do to accomplish goal:

1. _____
2. _____
3. _____

Potential obstacles/possible solutions:

_____

_____

SHORT TERM GOAL #2: _____

Actions—what to do to accomplish goal:

1. _____
2. _____
3. _____

Potential obstacles/possible solutions:

_____

_____

SHORT TERM GOAL #3: _____

Actions—what to do to accomplish goal:

1. _____
2. _____
3. _____

Potential obstacles/possible solutions:

_____

_____

Use this chart to plan your ACADEMIC goals. You'll find another chart later in the chapter for your ATHLETIC goals.

Don't forget SMART

S - specific

M - measurable

A - action oriented

R - realistic

T - timely

SAMPLE ACADEMIC GOALS TEMPLATE

Academic Goal for 9th grade: To earn an A or B in freshman English

Support Person: My mom.

SHORT TERM GOAL #1: To score at least 80% on my literary analysis essays in English by the end of the semester.

Actions—what to do to accomplish goal:

1. To do all the writing practice my teacher assigns during class and at home
2. To go to the school tutoring center for help
3. Use teacher feedback to revise writing

Potential obstacles/possible solutions:

- Not enough time to get help from school because of after school sports practice and games—seek help before school and at lunch
- My teacher does not give very much feedback—seek help from older students, family members, other teachers

---

SHORT TERM GOAL #2: To improve my reading comprehension

Actions—what to do to accomplish goal:

1. Practice doing what good readers do such as PARTRR, annotating, highlighting and interacting with the text
2. Carefully read (for a purpose) all the assigned reading—remember there is a difference between reading for pleasure and leisure than reading to learn
3. Find a book that really interests me and read it for pleasure

Potential obstacles/possible solutions:

- I don't like to read—ask friends and your teacher for titles that might interest you
- I don't have time to read my homework—Get up early and read before school or on the bus or in the bleachers while waiting for games

---

SHORT TERM GOAL #3: To earn A's and B's on my quizzes and tests

Actions—what to do to accomplish goal:

1. Take Cornell Notes every day in English class
2. Create flashcards and study guides from my notes and books in class
3. Clarify and ask questions of the teacher about the expectations for the tests
4. Spend time every week night completing homework and studying or reviewing

Potential obstacles/possible solutions:

- I don't have flashcards and I was absent—cut up paper in squares and call a classmate for makeup work or email your teacher to schedule a time to meet.

ATHLETIC GOALS TEMPLATE

9th grade yearly goal: _____

Set specific, measurable goals with an action verb that is challenging, yet attainable with hard work, and within a specific time period.

Support Person: _____

The following short-term goals are steps to achieving your yearly goal.

SHORT TERM GOAL #1: _____

Actions—what to do to accomplish goal:

1._____

2._____

3._____

Potential obstacles/possible solutions:

_____

_____

SHORT TERM GOAL #2: _____

Actions—what to do to accomplish goal:

1._____

2._____

3._____

Potential obstacles/possible solutions:

_____

_____

SHORT TERM GOAL #3: _____

Actions—what to do to accomplish goal:

1._____

2._____

3._____

Potential obstacles/possible solutions:

_____

_____

Use this template to write down your (not your mother's!) ATHLETIC goals.

SAMPLE ATHLETIC GOALS TEMPLATE

Athletic Goal for 9th grade: To make the freshman baseball team at tryouts.

Support Person: My grandfather.

SHORT TERM GOAL #1: To improve my hitting and my batting average to .250–.300

Actions—what to do to accomplish goal:
1. Practice hitting 3 times a week in the fall (off-season) on the field or at the batting cages
2. Take 2 hitting lessons before tryouts
3. Practice swing fundamentals by hitting whiffle balls off a tee and having my support person video tape me

Potential obstacles/possible solutions:
- It could rain
- I could go to indoor batting cages
- I don't have enough $ for lessons—work with a high school coach or potential teammates

SHORT TERM GOAL #2: To improve my fielding fundamentals

Actions—what to do to accomplish goal:
1. Practice taking ground balls 3 times a week from my support person, parents, or friends
2. Focus on the proper technique and fundamentals while fielding ground balls
3. Develop proper footwork while fielding
4. Video tape and analyze fundamentals

Potential obstacles/possible solutions:
- I don't know a knowledgeable person to help me with fundamentals— ask parents or past coaches for help
- I don't have anyone to practice fielding with—seek out other travel teams/clubs or friends to practice with

SHORT TERM GOAL #3: To improve my throwing accuracy and fundamentals

Actions—what to do to accomplish goal:
1. Practice throwing 3 times a week with my support person, parents, or friends
2. Check out a book from the library, bookstore or online to research about throwing technique and practice specific throwing drills
3. Play catch 5 times a week since baseball is a game of catch

Potential obstacles/possible solutions:
- I don't have anyone to throw with—practice with a toss-back net or on a fence

HOW TO ACHIEVE GOALS

FIRST: Manage Your Time Wisely

Now you need to find the time to achieve your goals. You will have to learn how to manage or use your time wisely—put first things first.

Put first things first; organize and prioritize your activities.

We already talked about using a planner to organize yourself (Chapter 2). Now it is time to think about how you use your time so that you can determine how you will achieve your goals. Once you have set your goals, you have to carry them out. You have to make them happen. How do you manage all this? How much time do you have in 24 hours to get everything done? One idea is that every Sunday evening, take out your planner, along with your goals, and set weekly plans for academic, athletic, and peak performance. Then you need to set daily goals, setting time aside for studying, completing homework, practice, games, and most importantly, sleep. This is called time management. Once a week you should reflect on whether or not you reached your goals. Reset your goals for the upcoming week, making sure you complete any goals you did not reach the week before.

Many student-athletes have to make difficult decisions as to how to use their time, and often find themselves in tough situations. They feel like they are pulled in so many different directions at the same time, between trying to balance sports, homework, studying, extracurricular activities, family, and friends. This is an issue of time management.

Sean Covey, in *The 7 Habits of Highly Effective Teens*, divides the activities we have to do into four quadrants. The categories on the next page can help you decide what you need to do in order to manage your time.

TIME QUADRANTS

	Urgent	Not Urgent
Important	**Q1: The Procrastinator** Exam tomorrow Friend gets hurt Late for work Project due today Car breaks down	**Q2: The Prioritizer** Planning, goal setting Essay due in a week Exercise Relationships Relaxation
Not important	**Q3: The Yes-Man** Unimportant phone calls, *texts Interruptions Other people's small problems Peer pressure	**Q4: The Slacker** Too much TV Endless phone calls, *texting Excessive computer games Mall marathons Time wasters

Adopted from Sean Covey's *The 7 Habits of Highly Effective Teens*
*authors added new time-consumers of teens

For balance and sanity in your busy life, you need to find opportunities to relax and to give your brain and body a break. Take a break from time to time and play a game on X-Box. Try to spend time with your family and friends. Watch your friends when they compete in other sports or perform in a play. You will come back to your work refreshed and energized and thinking more clearly. Use your time wisely and you can do it all, and do it well.

Again, as we said in the second chapter, we highly recommend that you purchase and use a school planner or purchase one at an office supplies store. In your weekly planner, you need to write in all the activities that you need to accomplish for the week. At the end of every week, ideally on Sunday night, reflect on how well you used your time, if you achieved your goals, or not, and what you need to do for the new week. See the following sample.

"Discipline and time management skills are vital to school and work, and they can be developed through club sports. I can vouch for this because between going from school to a school sport to a club sport, I had to quickly establish a routine in order to get everything done. Overall, club sports can be very taxing on you and your family, and add unneeded stress. However, if you are a serious athlete and have a strong desire to compete and increase your level of play then this could be the key for you."

–Kristin Kurpershoek, multiple sport athlete

WEEKLY PLANNER/CALENDAR & GOALS

SMART Goals & Priorities for the week:
1. Create flashcards and study guides from my notes and books in class
2. Develop proper footwork while fielding
3. Listen more carefully to my coach

	Mon.	Tues.	Wed.	Thurs.	Fri.	Sat.	Sun.
School Projects & Tests	Re-search paper	Chap. 1 test	Buy English book	Health project due	Vocab. test	Work on essay	Review math, Study Spanish
Homework: Math English Spanish Health History							
After school activities	Practice 4:00	Game (away)	Practice 3:30	Game (home)		work	Batting cages
Personal & Social					Watch movie	tutor	Church

Weekly Goals Accomplished?

Academic?   Yes/No
Athletic?   Yes/No
Peak Performance? Yes/No

If you did not achieve your weekly goals, why not?

_____
_____

What can you do to accomplish them?

_____
_____

SECOND: Reflect to Get Better

The only way to actually get better every day is to reflect on your goals and accomplishments. At the end of each high school year, reflect on your goals so that you can re-evaluate and write new goals for the upcoming school year. Be honest with yourself about why you didn't reach your goals. Don't use scapegoats either.

Here is a sample.

END OF YEAR REFLECTION ON GOALS

What are you satisfied with in terms of your grades for the year and your GPA?

_____

_____

What would you do differently to earn higher grades?

_____

_____

What are your academic strengths (math, writing, note-taking, organization)?

_____

_____

What do you need to work on academically?

_____

_____

What are your athletic strengths (strength & conditioning, specific sport skills, nutrition)?

_____

_____

What do you need to work on athletically?

_____

_____

THIRD: Use your time wisely in the summer

You may focus your summer on both academics and athletics, or only one. Depending upon your developmental needs and the athletic competitions/ showcases you want to attend, you will determine how you will spend your summer.

WEEKLY GOALS, PLANNER/CALENDAR AND REFLECTION FOR THE SUMMER

SMART Goals & Priorities for the week:
1. Take an SAT test prep class.
2. Lift weights 3 times a week.
3. Eat more healthy foods.

	Mon.	Tues.	Wed.	Thurs.	Fri.	Sat.	Sun.
Academic	Send my profile to 25 DI and DII college coaches	Visit a potential college	Read a book for pleasure	Practice math for SAT		Work on college entrance essay	Study SAT vocab.
Athletic	Weights	Write thank you notes to coaches visited	Weights Run 3 miles	Practice	Weights	Practice	Run 3 miles
Peak Performance	Write imagery script	Practice visualization		Practice listening		Coach little kids	
Personal & Social		Go to movies			Visit Grandmother		Church

Weekly Goals Accomplished?

Academic?   Yes/No
Athletic?   Yes/No
Peak Performance? Yes/No

If you did not achieve your weekly goals, why not?

_____

_____

What can you do to accomplish them?

_____

_____

Goals are ladder steps toward reaching your dream.

Setting goals and reflecting on your progress is vital to improving. Be sure to work on assessing yourself both academically and athletically when setting goals. Be honest with yourself about why you did or did not achieve your goals. Don't blame others; don't scapegoat. Remember it is important to be flexible with your goals and to revise your goals as you change throughout high school.

Last words...
KEEP IT SIMPLE

Get organized and get it done.

- Make school and sports your priority. Work hard, practice, go to class with focus and do the work, take responsibility for yourself and your actions, ask for help from parents, counselors, teachers, coaches, ministers, use the kitchen table model, and make your goals public.
- Meet the college prep requirements so you open doors, and give yourself endless possibilities.

Setting goals is one thing; making them happen is another. You must be active and committed to making sacrifices to get to the next level in sports. Goals help you get a little better each day. And, it's ok to re-evaluate and change your goals, just make sure you're striving for something

"We are imperfect people working in an imperfect world so our goals are never going to be perfect either."
–Ron Severson, Roseville Joint Union High School District
Assistant Superintendent

Chapter 7
Top 10 Plays

1. Goals are dreams with a purpose, place in mind, and end dates

2. Set high standards for yourself

3. Reflect on what you really want –to set goals

4. Set **SMART** goals

5. Set short term and long term goals

6. Achieve goals by writing them down, managing your time, and reflecting on your progress

7. Find a support person to help you achieve your goals

8. Revise your goals to reflect your growth

9. Take one day at a time and work to get a little better each day

10. Make your goals happen

HALF-TIME

Inspirational Speech by Coach Guin Boggs

Guin Boggs' motivational messages have inspired thousands of young people up and down the West Coast. His presentations offer a priceless collection of humor, advice, encouragement, thought-provoking truths, and unforgettable stories that point young people to success in sports, school, and life.

Coach Boggs played basketball at California State University, San Jose and has coached at the high school, community college, and four years at the college level. He has been named "Teacher of the Year," "Most Inspirational Teacher," and "Coach of the Year" at the high school and college level.

"Join me for the next few minutes for the ride of your life. I am going to ask you to listen in three ways—with your ears, with your eyes, and mostly, with your heart.

I am going to start by asking you a question. Who do you think are the happiest people in America: the richest, most intelligent, best looking, most famous, or those with the most possessions? Actually, the happiest people in America are the most grateful—those that live life with an attitude of gratitude. A thankful heart will not only buy you a front row seat but it will invite you to be a participant in the greatest game of all—the game of life.

If it is to be, it is up to me! Attitude is everything. It is your on-off button for success. And the good news is that it's something you can choose. You can't buy it. You are not born with it. It is simply a choice. By choosing a winning attitude, you are choosing to live rather than just exist. Remember that your attitude is up to you—it will put you on life's victory road or keep you busy losing.

None of us were asked to be born. Life is a gift. Each morning you wake up with a gift package, which is your life. What you do with the package determines your joy, your purpose, and meaning. When you untie the ribbon and open the box you can see how awesome life is. This day you have 24 hours, and 1440 minutes to build, give, serve, grow, find things to be passionate about—TO BE, TO LIVE! Awesome! And the good news—you get the opportunity to open the package every morning of your life. With the approximate 25,000 mornings we are given, we are awakened to new thoughts, new hopes, new dreams and new opportunities we had not thought about before. With a vibrant, grateful attitude, we have to be careful not to waste any sunrises. With the right 'In Look' and 'Out Look' even on a cloudy day with the eyes of our heart we can still see the sun rising. And before it turns the top of the trees orange, it starts to warm our hearts.

Your attitude can detonate the powder keg of potential that you have been given. More importantly, it will be a driving force to help you be all that you were created to be. I share with you the words of Helen Keller, **'Life is a great adventure or it is nothing at all.'**

What is your game plan? I hope it is filled with inspiration, motivation, preparation, perspiration, and celebration. Life is a gift. Don't waste the gift. Live life with significance so you can succeed. You can be a spectator or a participant—get involved and hang on for the ride of your life! Winning in sports is great, but winning in life is the biggest victory of all. Make it a great day! Make it a great life!

It's not where you've been, but where you're going;
It's not what you've done, but what you're doing;
It's not who you were, but who you are becoming."

Coach Boggs

8

Considering
COLLEGE ATHLETIC OPPORTUNITIES

What really matters is what you do with what you have.

THERE IS A PLACE FOR YOU TO PLAY

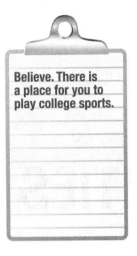

There are all kinds of opportunities to play sports in college. There are so many different types of athletic programs that there is a place for you to play and get a great education. You and your parents need to learn about all the many and varied choices beyond the NCAA DI sports and the top 25 teams covered on TV. Only a small percent are a fit for DI sports, but many are a perfect fit for DII and DIII sports programs.

There are different associations and divisions within these associations in order to meet the unique needs of individual student-athletes. Some student-athletes want to attend a small school where academics are more of a priority than athletics are. Others are looking for the big schools with the best athletic program in the nation. Research your options so you find the place that is the best fit for you, both athletically and academically, remembering to consider the size, reputation or status of the school, and opportunities for being recruited to the pros.

Ryan Motsenbocker chose to play intramural basketball at San Diego State University instead of playing NCAA DI basketball at Sacramento State because he wanted to live near the beach and play competitive intramural basketball with former high school players. Though talented and intensely competitive, he did not want to make sacrifices to meet the demands of a NCAA DI student-athlete. College intramurals were able to satisfy his competitive basketball needs and allow for a social life, whereas DI basketball would have been a job without much time outside of sports.

Different Athletic Associations

The following information is an overview of the different college athletic associations. Note the sometimes subtle differences, as well as the divisions within some of the athletic associations.

From the *NCAA Guide to Student-Athletes*: What is the NCAA?

The NCAA, or National Collegiate Athletic Association, was established in 1906 and serves as the athletics governing body for more than 1,300 colleges, universities, conferences and organizations. The national office is in Indianapolis, but the member colleges and universities develop the rules and guidelines for athletics eligibility and athletics competition for each of the three NCAA divisions. The NCAA is committed to the student—athlete and to governing competition in a fair, safe, inclusive and sportsmanlike manner.

NCAA—National Collegiate Athletic Association

- Determines guidelines and eligibility
- More than 1,280 colleges, universities, conferences, and organizations participate in it
- Offers competition at 3 levels:
  - » DI (3 Subdivisions: Football Bowl Subdivision, Football Championship Subdivision, and DI with no football)
  - » DII
  - » DIII

NAIA—National Association of Intercollegiate Athletics

- About 400 schools
- Specific sports at the college compete in NCAA
- Small schools (about 1,000 students)
- Mostly rural
- Limited sports programs
- Limited financial aid
- Admission requirements—must meet 2 of 3 requirements:
  - » Score 18 on enhanced ACT or 860 on SAT (excluding the writing section)
  - » 2.0 Overall GPA
  - » Rank in the upper half of your graduating class

USCAA—United States Collegiate Athletic Association (formerly NSCAA)

- About 100 schools
- Very small (under 1,000 students)
- Specific sport opportunities in baseball, basketball, cross country, soccer, and track
- Some colleges may compete in additional sports

NCCAA—National Christian College Athletic Association

- Christian-based perspective promoting outreach and ministry
- About 100 schools
- Specific sport opportunities in baseball, basketball, cross country, soccer, track and field and wrestling
- Some colleges may compete in additional sports

NJCAA—National Junior College Athletic Association

- Commonly referred to as community or city colleges
- Two year colleges to earn Associate of Arts (AA) Degree
- About 5,000 colleges nationwide
- An opportunity to improve academically and athletically or to be seen by coaches, recruiters and scouts with the goal of attending a four year college of choice after one or two years

- Some guarantee admission to a specific four-year college when specified grades and/or specified course requirements are met
- Some have strong reputations for having their athletes recruited by universities
- No SAT/ACT requirement for entrance
- "JUCO" is short for junior college and is a term you will hear TV announcers use to refer to players who played at a two year school initially, earned an associate's degree, and then transferred to a four-year college with two seasons of eligibility remaining. These players do not have to sit out a year like other transfer students. "JUCO" players can fill roster spots left open by transfers or players leaving DI schools early.

As you can see, beyond NCAA DI college sports, opportunities range from NCAA DII and DIII to other athletic associations including NAIA, USCAA, NCCAA, and NJCAA to club sports and intramural sports at respective schools. The smaller athletic associations focus more on the student in student-athlete and don't have the big athletic budgets. They also don't have the same pressures to win from the media and the boosters. They do, however, offer financial aid and academic scholarships to student-athletes.

Differences in NCAA Divisions

The differences between NCAA DI, DII, and DIII fall into categories: number of required sports, scheduling, and financial aid.

Divison I

DI schools must offer a specific number of men's and women's sports, in each season (fall, winter, and spring,) including at least two team sports for each gender. Also DI teams have to play a minimum number of contests against other DI teams, which varies by sport.

DI schools must also give a specific amount of financial aid. There are two categories of athletic scholarships: headcount sports and equivalency sports. Headcount sports, which include basketball and football, have a maximum number of student-athletes that can be on scholarships in any given year. For example, men's DI basketball can give only 13 and women's DI basketball can only give 15 full scholarships. On the other hand, equivalency sports, like volleyball, soccer and baseball, have a set amount of scholarship money that can be divided up between players. Coaches may divvy up the specific number of scholarships however they wish among all their players. For example, DI men's volleyball can divide 4.5 scholarships among two or more players and DI woman's volleyball can divide 12 scholarships between two or more players on the team, allowing multiple players to receive partial scholarships rather than each player being awarded a full scholarship.

DI Football Bowl Subdivision teams have 85 athletes on full scholarships, while DI (A and AA) Football Championship Subdivision teams are only allowed 63 scholarship equivalencies. Also, DI programs follow spectator attendance rules and offer a certain number of sports.

Division II

DII schools must sponsor at least ten sports: five sports for men and five sports for women, or four sports for men and six for women. There are no attendance requirements.

Division III

DIII schools must sponsor at least five sports for both genders and two team sports, and does not have an attendance rule.

Note that NCAA DIII and NJCAA DIII sports programs are not allowed to offer athletic scholarships.

Comparing the Divisions

Normally, DI schools have the best student-athletes, excellent facilities, full-time strength coaches, and the best competition. The drawbacks, however, are big class sizes, athletes have to travel across country to compete, and there is often pressure to perform in front of large crowds. DII schools have smaller class sizes, and athletes travel less and feel less pressure to perform. With that, however, comes less money for the athletic program and facilities. DIII schools travel regionally, and have small facilities and less fan support. NAIA schools have less recruiting regulations and there is less pressure to perform. Two-year colleges have lower entrance requirements and athletes can often play right away. Students can improve their GPAs in order to transfer to a 4-year university. Community colleges normally do not provide money and offer little in terms of facilities and fan base, but tuition costs are very low compared to 4-year schools.

Lastly, there are club and intramural sport opportunities in all colleges. Some schools offer club sports that are more competitive and fulfill students' needs for enthusiastic competition without the intense practice and game preparation schedules. Colleges offer intramural or recreational sports and a variety of instructional PE courses. However, there is no money available at this level of sports.

FIND THE RIGHT FIT

There are numerous schools across the nation that will be a fit for you. When researching and deciding on a college, you must consider what level of competition and type of athletic program and association works for you. There is a great college out there where you can study and compete—depending upon your academic and athletic qualities and your goals. Just be realistic.

In addition to considering the different competitive athletic levels, you will want to consider your academic goals. Perhaps you want to study engineering or nursing. Some student-athletes have found it impossible to achieve these academic goals and compete at certain schools because their major's classes are only offered in the afternoon during athletic practice or require too much outside time and keep students too busy to play intercollegiate sports.

Educate yourself on these different programs and guidelines for recruiting and eligibility. NCAA DI & II schools have different recruiting and eligibility rules than NCAA DIII and other athletic associations. Make sure you understand the difference between NCAA DI, DII, and DIII and the difference between athletic associations beyond the NCAA.

Other Options

Beyond competing in sports in the above college environments, there are other intermediate options for student-athletes with specific needs.

Early High School Graduation

▸ Graduate after 1st semester senior year
▸ Attend NCAA DI college earlier than normal
▸ Acclimate to college life while working out with the team

Prep School Bridge Programs and Feeder Programs

▸ An additional senior year of high school
▸ Allows you to improve high school grades and/or SAT/ACT scores, or to complete more rigorous course work (advanced math, English, foreign language, AP courses, academic literacy courses, etc.)
▸ Allows you to improve athletically
▸ Some prep schools are feeder schools for specific colleges
▸ Allows you to get bigger, stronger, more mature, and experience a few classes in the spring without using up NCAA eligibility before competing for the team
▸ These programs are a good alternate to the junior college route

Geoff Blumenfeld attended Navy's feeder high school as a 5th year high school student to gain eligibility to the Naval Academy. With patience, he eventually became a successful starting kicker for the Navy's football team. With his strong academic and athletic experience, he is now a very happy helicopter pilot for the Navy.

Additional Year Before High School

Similar to the "prep" year between high school and college, is a situation where parents opt to have their student-athlete postpone entering high school by either repeating 8th grade or getting homeschooled an additional year before entering 9th grade. This allows the student to mature physically and emotionally before entering high school. Sometimes a student is not ready for 9th grade expectations, and is either academically, socially, or athletically immature. This is a decision that individual families will need to make depending on what they believe is best for their student-athlete.

ELIGIBILITY RULES ONCE ENROLLED IN COLLEGE

NCAA 5-Year Eligibility Duration

Once a student-athlete enrolls full-time in college, he or she only has a five-year window to compete in college athletics. Therefore, student-athletes may choose to "redshirt" or "grayshirt" (explained below) if they are injured or want more time after high school to develop academic and/or athletic skills before joining a college team. In essence, this is like deferring for a semester or year. In rare cases, a special 6th year medical hardship waiver may be given to a student-athlete with a reoccurring injury documented by the college trainer. Check ncaa.org yearly to make sure you are meeting eligibility requirements with your GPA and the number of units you are taking.

TRUE Freshman

- This is when a first-year student competes in athletic contests during his/her freshman year of college
- Many freshmen "redshirt" rather than compete their first year in college to get bigger, stronger, and faster

"Redshirting"

- Technically not an official term used by the NCAA
- Has nothing to do with grades
- You attend college and practices, but do not compete in games during the academic year
- Allows athlete to mature physically during the first year of college
- You can redshirt at any point in your athletic career—allows additional season of competition during the 5-year period of eligibility
- You must take a full academic load to be eligible the next year
- An injured or ill athlete can be granted a "medical redshirt" when they are injured after participating in a limited amount of competition during a particular academic year. This may lead to qualification for a Medical Hardship Waiver. The participation rule is set and is different for different sports.

"Grayshirting"

- Not an official NCAA term
- Offers opportunity to mature physically and acclimate to college academics
- Does not use up a year of eligibility
- Cannot receive scholarship yet
- Able to work out and practice with the team
- Does not start the five year window eligibility period
- Prospect signs letter of intent but doesn't report to team
- Delay college entry until mid-year
- Not full-time student; only part-time student status

Student-athletes need to consider all of their options for recruiting, including what level they want to play at and whether or not to redshirt. In some sports, like football, athletes redshirt more often than other sports. You need to do what is best for you.

Miserable and Want to Transfer?

What if you are in college and have been very unhappy your first year? What if you are struggling or bored academically? What if you don't get along with the coach or your athletic experience is not what you thought it was going to be? What now? What are your options? While many freshmen experience homesickness after moving away from home, if you have given yourself some time to get used to a new routine and make new friends and your school still isn't the right fit, you may consider transferring. Some freshmen will be homesick if they moved far from home. Give yourself at least until spring before you make any drastic changes.

Student-athletes should not stay at a college if they are miserable. You have options to go to a community college or transfer to another college that would be a better fit both academically and athletically.

Research all your options and the NCAA transfer rules in terms of athletic eligibility, transferable course credits, and academic and athletic scholarships. It is important to communicate with coaches and your parents, and then make a decision based upon what is best for you.

Last Words...

If you really want to play sports at the college level, there is a place for you to play, whether it be a big DI school or a small, local community college. Make sure that the school you pick is the right academic, athletic, and social fit for you.

Chapter 8
Top 10 Plays

1. There is a place for you to play beyond NCAA DI sports

2. Be realistic about your athletic and sport-specific talents

3. Be honest about your academic goals

4. There are other athletic associations besides the NCAA where student-athletes can find desirable sports competition

5. NCAA DI & DII sports programs must follow specific recruiting rules, regulations, and calendars

6. NCAA DIII & NAIA sports programs play by different rules than DI & DII

7. The eligibility clock starts when you enroll in college

8. Redshirt is a year in college where you practice but don't play and Grayshirting is a delayed college start to first improve athletics or academics

9. Community college is a great fit for those needing extra time for academics, athletics, social, or financial reasons

10. Consider all your options to find the RIGHT FIT for you!

9

BECOMING A QUALIFIER

NCAA Academic and Athletic Eligibility

Never settle for less than what you can be.

QUALIFIER STATUS

The NCAA is a national organization that determines rules of competition and guidelines for student-athletes in terms of academic and athletic entrance requirements and eligibility. What this means is that student-athletes must meet not only the college admissions requirements, but also the NCAA requirements (unless the student plans on competing in another athletic association such as NAIA).

The NCAA publishes a very helpful, yet complex, guide for high school student-athletes wanting to play sports in college. Order or download this free *NCAA Guide for the College-Bound Student Athlete* at ncaa.org. Use this guide to insure you make yourself a qualifier and meet eligibility requirements. It covers the following topics:

‣ Academic Eligibility
‣ Amateurism Eligibility
‣ Financial Aid
‣ Recruiting Rules

This section of the book explains and gives information on how to navigate through the required college preparation and application process in terms of academic eligibility for athletes. Note that since NCAA regulations are always changing, check the website (ncaa.org) and the *NCAA Guide* for continuous updates.

NCAA ELIGIBILITY CENTER

In the beginning of your junior year, register and pay the fee online with the NCAA Eligibility Center. This organization determines if you are academically eligible to participate in DI or DII collegiate athletics as a college freshman. Be patient while registering online, as you could experience initial loading delays. Also, be sure to receive an email receipt.

Academic Eligibility

The NCAA has set specific academic eligibility requirements for incoming freshmen and transfer students for DI and DII athletes. However, all student-athletes must first meet individual college admission requirements to be accepted. Be sure to carefully check specific academic admission requirements for every college you wish to attend. The most important preparation for the student-athlete is to work at and maintain the best possible study habits and grades. Focus on one semester at a time and on earning good grades in order to gain that leverage. If you fall behind academically, consider taking a summer school course or two.

"Remember, good athletics is about winning at competition in games. Good academics combined with athletics are about winning in life. So, keep education as your top priority."

- Myles Brand, NCAA President 2006-07

Student-athletes have 2 important goals for academic eligibility

1. Earn Good Grades

‣ Begin your high school career taking the most demanding academic path that you are capable of, which will give you the opportunity to meet the most rigorous admissions standards at the most desirable colleges. Recognize that certain colleges have specific requirements that your high school and the NCAA do not. No matter what classes you take, earning good grades must be your focus throughout high school since being academically eligible is a requirement to compete in sports. College coaches and scouts will generally visit high school offices to check on grades before ever coming out to the athletic facility to observe.

2. Meet NCAA Requirements

‣ Make yourself what the NCAA denotes as a "qualifier" throughout high school so you will have opportunities for college options. A "qualifier" is a student who meets NCAA DI and/or DII eligibility requirements.

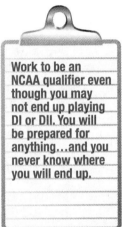

Work to be an NCAA qualifier even though you may not end up playing DI or DII. You will be prepared for anything...and you never know where you will end up.

For specific NCAA DI and DII programs go to ncaa.org and read the *NCAA Guide for the College-Bound Student-Athlete*. The NCAA makes yearly updates on this guide. The next part of the chapter is a brief overview of the requirements in the guide.

Academic Eligibility Requirements for Division I

Students who intend to compete in college athletics and/or earn an athletic scholarship must meet requirements as written in the *NCAA Guide*. Below is a summary, but consult the *Guide* for more details.

1. Graduate from high school
2. Complete core courses
3. Earn a minimum GPA in your core courses
4. Earn a combined SAT or ACT score that matches your core-course GPA and test score on the sliding scale (see scale in the *NCAA Guide*)

You are a **qualifier** if you meet the DI requirements.
You *CAN*:
- Practice or compete for your college or university during your first year
- Receive an athletic scholarship during your first year
- Play four seasons in your sport if you maintain eligibility from year to year

You are a **non-qualifier** if you do not meet the DI requirements. You *CANNOT*:
- Practice or compete for your college or university during your first year
- Receive an athletic scholarship during your first year, although you may receive "need based" financial aid
- Play four seasons; you can only play three in your sport if you maintain eligibility from year to year
  - » You can earn back a 4th season if you complete at least 80% of your degree before beginning your 5th year of college

Farrah Bradford moved to Georgia for a volleyball scholarship only to find out after a few weeks there that she was not academically eligible. She did not take the necessary foreign language class to meet NCAA academic eligibility. She had to return home and attend a community college where she took foreign language in order to make herself eligible for the NCAA.

Academic Eligibility Requirements for Division II

Students who intend to compete in DII college athletics and/or earn an athletic scholarship must meet requirements as written in the *NCAA Guide*. Below is a summary, but consult the *Guide* for more details.

1. Graduate from high school
2. Complete core courses
3. Earn the required GPA in your core courses
4. Earn the required combined SAT or ACT sum score. There is no sliding scale

You are a **qualifier** if you meet the DII requirements
You *CAN*:
- Practice or compete for your college or university during your first year
- Receive an athletic scholarship during your first year
- Play four seasons in your sport if you maintain eligibility from year to year

You are a **partial qualifier** if you **do not** meet all the DII academic requirements, but you have graduated from high school and have met some of the eligibility requirements. Again, consult the *NCAA Guide*.

You *CAN:*

- Practice with your team at its home facility during your first year
- Receive an athletic scholarship during your first year
- Play 4 seasons in your sport if you maintain eligibility from year to year

You *CANNOT:*

- Compete during your first year

You are a **non-qualifier** if you do not graduate from high school or if you graduated and are missing the both the core-course GPA average or the minimum number of core courses and the required ACT/SAT scores.

You *CANNOT:*

- Practice or compete for your college or university during your first year
- Receive an athletic scholarship during your first year, although you may receive "need based" financial aid

You *CAN:*

- Play four seasons in your sport if you maintain eligibility from year to year

Academic Eligibility Requirements for Division III

DIII colleges do not use the NCAA Eligibility Center. You need to contact your DIII college for eligibility requirements, practice and competitions, and financial aid/scholarships.

You MUST make sure that you meet all requirements specifically set by each college you apply to. Also, just because you meet the NCAA requirements, does not guarantee college admission —**you must apply for admission.**

Core Courses

Core courses are defined in the *NCAA Guide* as:

- Academic courses in English, math, natural or physical science, foreign language, non-doctrinal religion or philosophy
- Four-year college prep (no remedial, special education or compensatory courses)

Check the NCAA Eligibility Center website to make sure your high school courses are on the NCAA List of Approved Core Courses.

If you take a course that is not on the NCAA approved core list, it will not count toward your academic eligibility. Courses on your transcript must match exactly what is on the NCAA core list.

College courses taken during high school may be used to satisfy core-curriculum requirements if the courses are accepted by the colleges you apply to and meet all other requirements for core courses. For NCAA DI only, such courses must be placed on the student's high school transcript. Courses taken at a college will NOT appear on the NCAA list of approved core courses. The high school's NCAA list of approved core courses will include only those courses taught/offered by the high school.

Core-course Grade Point Average (GPA) calculation

To determine your academic eligibility, the NCAA Eligibility Center will calculate your GPA for your core courses on a 4.0 scale. The NCAA allows you to use your best grade achieved in core courses. Grades from any additional core courses will only be used if they improve your GPA. This NCAA core GPA is different than a high school overall GPA because it is calculated using only NCAA approved core courses, and high school GPA is calculated using all courses in grades 9-12.

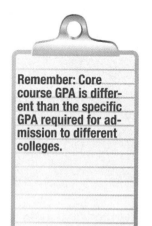

Remember: Core course GPA is different than the specific GPA required for admission to different colleges.

The following values are assigned to letter grades:
A = 4 points
B = 3 points
C = 2 points
D = 1 point

The lowest grade that will count for a core course depends on your high school's policy concerning lowest passing grades. Normally, the grade D is the lowest passing grade. "Plus" or "minus" grades are not used to calculate your NCAA core-course GPA.

Weighted grades for honors or advanced-placement courses are factored into the core GPA for initial NCAA academic eligibility. If your high school only weights grades to determine class rank (and not calculate GPAs), then weighted grades cannot be used for NCAA eligibility. Note that for individual college applications, certain colleges weigh grades differently.

Go to ncaa.org website to download a form to calculate your core course GPA for NCAA academic eligibility.

SAT/ACT Test Score Requirements

The SAT and ACT are the two test options for college admissions. Check carefully to see which test your institution requires. Many schools will take either test, but some require one over the other for admission purposes.

The SAT has two types of tests. The SAT I is a reasoning test divided into 4 parts: mathematics, critical reading, multiple-choice writing, and a short essay. There are also the SAT II tests, which are subject tests on any of the following topics: biology, literature, US or world history, math (levels 1 and 2), biology, chemistry, physics, and a number of foreign or world languages (including Chinese, French, German, Modern Hebrew, Italian, Japanese, Korean, Latin, and Spanish).

The ACT measures student's knowledge and skills in English, math, reading, and science reasoning. The writing test on the ACT is optional.

The essay section on both the SAT and ACT will not be used to determine qualifier status.

All students must meet the minimum SAT/ACT score requirements in relationship to their GPA. Students may take the test as many times as they want, and for the SAT, may use the best sub-scores from different tests to compile their best possible overall score. The ACT grade is calculated using your best scores from a single test sitting.

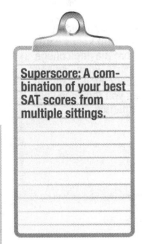

Superscore: A combination of your best SAT scores from multiple sittings.

For example:

Test (Date Taken)	Math	Critical Reading	Total Score
SAT (3/09)	570	660	1230
SAT (5/09)	620	630	1250
Superscore	620	660	1280

Both the SAT and ACT are offered several times throughout the traditional school year. See the SAT/ACT websites, your counselor, or your high school's career center for national testing dates. When you register, be sure to bubble in the code 9999, as well as the codes of any schools you are interested in, to make sure your score is reported directly to the NCAA Eligibility Center and those additional schools. Test scores will not be accepted if they are only reported on the high school transcript.

Most colleges require you to take the SAT/ACT by December of your senior year so that your scores can be reported in time for college admissions deadlines. The *NCAA Guide* states: "You must achieve the required score on an SAT or ACT test before your full-time college enrollment, whether you are a citizen of the US or a foreign country."

Go to the NCAA website (ncaa.org) for the NCAA Quick Reference Sheet which has the freshman academic eligibility standards and DI sliding scale for correlating the minimum requirements for core course GPA and SAT/ACT test scores.

Summary of Academic Eligibility and Recruiting Opportunities

A student makes himself a desirable or prospective recruit when he is a "qualifier." It is highly recommended that you work to meet all DI academic requirements in case you are able to participate in DI sports.

Grades shouldn't be what keeps you from playing college sports. Focus on your academics as much as you focus on your athletics.

It doesn't matter if you want to go to a university, state, private or community college—maintain your "qualifier" status so you have options. If you plan on transferring, four-year colleges prefer junior college transfer students to already be confirmed "qualifiers" so that eligibility is already verified when transferring. Set your goals high to maximize your potential.

Again, be sure you are a "qualifier" your entire high school career. Some high school students, unfortunately, believe the myth that freshman grades do not count for eligibility, which is not true. Grades in your core courses, from 9th through 12th grade, count for NCAA eligibility. This is why 9th grade is, in fact, a very important academic year.

In addition to being a "qualifier," student-athletes must make sure they also meet specific college entrance requirements. Most colleges require more academic core courses than DI and DII. For example, two years of a foreign language is a requirement for many colleges, but not for the NCAA academic eligibility requirements.

Ideas to Remember:
> Earn the best possible grades, especially in core classes
> Maintain a qualifier worksheet throughout all of your high school years
> Take advanced classes when possible
> Make your senior year challenging rather than kick back (to continue to prepare yourself for college academics)

"My coach always told me that college coaches go to the high school office first to check our grades and GPA, and if they weren't good enough they wouldn't even come out and watch us."

–Miles Burris, Former San Diego State University
Linebacker and Current NFL Football Player

Amateurism Eligibility

In order to be eligible to play college sports, you must be certified as an amateur student-athlete, meaning you can't be a professional athlete and then play college sports. See the *NCAA Guide* at ncaa.org for an overview of the amateurism bylaws and details. Any of the following actions could jeopardize your amateur eligibility status:

- Entering into a contract with a professional team
- Accepting salary for participating in athletics
- Accepting prize money
- Playing with professionals
- Trying out, practicing, or competing with a professional team
- Receiving benefits from an agent or prospective agent
- Entering into an oral or written agreement with an agent
- Delaying full-time collegiate enrollment and participating in an organized competition

When you register with the Eligibility Center you will be asked questions to determine your amateurism eligibility for initial participation at an NCAA DI or DII School. DIII colleges conduct their own certification. Once you are in college, a compliance officer monitors your academic and amateurism eligibility throughout your college career.

Financial Aid (Athletic Scholarships)

The NCAA financial aid refers to scholarship money. NCAA regulates the number of scholarships by sport for DI and DII schools for both men's and women's athletics. This does not mean, however, that each school offers the full amount of scholarships available for each sport. For example, some programs are penalized if they do not meet the Academic Progress Rate (APR) numbers. See Chapter 16 for more financial aid information.

Recruiting Rules

The NCAA establishes recruiting rules and guidelines for contact periods and coach evaluations. Please see Chapter 11 for recruiting regulations.

Last Words...

Student-athletes must meet the NCAA requirements to be eligible to compete and to get a scholarship at NCAA DI or DII colleges. Students must take core classes, and earn minimum GPAs and SAT/ACT scores in order to ensure eligibility. In addition, they must register with the Eligibility Center, and complete the amateurism questionnaire and request final amateurism certification.

Chapter 9
Top 10 Plays

1. Make yourself a qualifier by taking required core courses, maintaining a specific GPA, and reaching a specific SAT/ACT score

2. Earn good grades in high school so you are eligible for both high school and college sports

3. There are different academic eligibility requirements for DI, DII, and DIII sports programs

4. There are specific amateur athletic eligibility regulations

5. GPA is based on performance in classes taken in grades 9-12

6. Register with the Eligibility Center by your junior year

7. Use the sliding scale to find how high your test scores need to be

8. Use the Eligibility Center as a guide to make sure you are on track to be a qualifier

9. Grades and athletic skills go hand-in-hand. You need both to get a scholarship

10. Take the SAT/ACT multiple times to maximize your possible score

NCAA ELIGIBILITY HIGHLIGHTS

Adopted from the NCAA website. NCAA eligibility rules change. Check ncaa.org for updates and full disclosure.

CORE COURSES

- ✓ **Division I** requires 16 core courses
- ✓ Beginning August 1, 2016, 10 core courses (7 must be in English, math, or science) must be completed by your 7th semester (beginning of your senior year) and are locked in meaning they can't be retaken to improve your grade after your 7th semester begins. You can receive athletics aid and practice with the team, but you can't compete if you don't meet the 10 course requirement
- ✓ **Division II** requires 16 core courses on or after August 1, 2013

DIVISION I - 16 CORE COURSES

- ‣ 4 years of English
- ‣ 3 years of math (Algebra I or higher)
- ‣ 2 years of natural/physical science (1 year of lab if offered by high school)
- ‣ 1 year of additional English, math, or natural/physical science
- ‣ 2 years of social science
- ‣ 4 years of additional courses (from any area above, foreign language or comparative religion/philosophy)

DIVISION II - 16 CORE COURSES (2013 AND AFTER)

- ‣ 3 years of English
- ‣ 2 years of math (Algebra I or higher)
- ‣ 2 years of natural/physical science (1 year of lab if offered by high school)
- ‣ 3 years of additional English, math or natural/physical science
- ‣ 2 years of social science
- ‣ 4 years of additional courses (from any area above, foreign language or comparative religion/philosophy)

TEST SCORES

- ✓ **Division I** uses a sliding scale to match test scores and core grade-point averages. See the sliding scale at ncaa.org and note the scale will change in 2016
- ✓ **Division II** requires a minimum SAT score of 820 or an ACT sum score of 68 (no sliding scale)
- ✓ NCAA uses only the SAT critical reading and math sections (not writing section) for score purposes
- ✓ NCAA uses the ACT sum of four sections: English, math, reading and science
- ✓ Use the NCAA Eligibility Center code 9999 when registering for the SAT/ACT

GRADE-POINT AVERAGE

- ✓ Your GPA is calculated using only courses on your school's list of NCAA courses. See the list at eligibilitycenter.org or ncaa.org
- ✓ **Division I** core grade-point-average requirements are listed on the sliding scale at ncaa.org
- ✓ DI sliding scale matching GPA & test scores will change for students enrolling after August 1, 2016
- ✓ DI sliding scale will be added for academic redshirts for August 1, 2016
- ✓ DI students enrolling after August 1, 2016 must have a minimum 2.3 GPA in the 16 core courses to compete but can receive athletics aid (scholarship) and practice with a 2.0 GPA
- ✓ Must also graduate from high school
- ✓ **Division II** core grade-point-average requirement is a minimum of 2.0 with no sliding scale

QUALIFIER STATUS

The new NCAA DI Initial-Eligibility Academic Requirements result in 3 scenarios for student-athletes enrolling full time at an NCAA Division I college or university on or after **August 1, 2016**:

1. A full-qualifier may compete, receive athletics aid (scholarship), and practice the first year

2. An academic redshirt may receive athletics aid (scholarship) the first year, practice in first regular academic term, semester or quarter

3. A non-qualifier may **not** receive athletics aid (scholarship), practice, or compete the first year

10

Researching
COLLEGES & THE ROLE OF SPORTS

The spirit, the will to win, and the will to excel are things that endure.

You must find the academic and athletic fit specifically for you!

FIND THE RIGHT FIT

Do your research to find the athletic, as well as academic, opportunity that is the best fit for you. We can't say it enough—it is all about the right fit. Be honest in your evaluation of yourself and seriously consider colleges that realistically want you! Many student-athletes unfortunately narrow their focus and do not realize that there are many colleges that could be right for them. Create lots of options and keep them open until it is time to commit. Unless you are a blue-chip athlete, chances are you won't be recruited by your dream school.

A good start is to read the respected best-selling college guide, *Fiske Guide to Colleges,* and use the search feature at collegboard.org. Go beyond the well-known schools to find all the opportunities available. Loren Pope's book, *Colleges that Change Lives,* is about 40 lesser-known schools outside the traditional Ivy League universities that are similar to the Ivy League experience. If students can't gain admission into highly competitive Ivy League schools, these other colleges might become viable and desirable options.

Again, do your research and seek out all your options. There are more than you think. Rarely is there only one perfect school, but rather there are many good choices for most students.

I had to find a place that was a right fit for me where I got along with the coach."

–AJ Herlitz, Football Player at Southern Oregon University

What are your college goals?

Most importantly, students must ask themselves:
- What are my college goals and what do I want from my college experience?
- What role will sports play?
- What are my academic and career goals?
- How important is the college environment, including its physical, cultural and social aspects?
- Can I gain admissions to this school and how much will it cost me?
- What is realistic for me financially?

Research is key when answering these questions. Be sure to note that college is not high school. Many first year college athletes return home for breaks and explain to their friends, family, teachers, and high school coaches how different college sports are from high school and club sports. In high school sports, coaches try to build relationships with players and show concern for them. College coaches, however, are in the business of winning and recruiting the best players to get the wins. Keep this fact in mind when determining what the role sports will play in your college career.

Caitlyn Murphy and Alex Diemer were incredibly unhappy at their chosen colleges. One did not get the playing time she was promised and found that the team was not as it seemed during the official visit. The other did not like her coach. One of the girls left college with a sour taste for DI athletics and enrolled in a junior college where she did not play sports. The other transferred to another college to play volleyball. If they had known college sports are so different from high school sports, they probably would have made different choices.

What role will sports play for you?

As a student-athlete you must make difficult, yet important, decisions about the role of sports in your college education and your role in sports during your college career. You must determine if your abilities and potential are a fit academically and athletically for a specific NCAA division, college, or athletic association.

Kyle Schlehofer gained admission to his dream school, the University of Oregon, but was not offered any scholarship money, nor was he a recruited walk-on. He considered but decided not to play community college ball because his goal was to go to medical school and he felt he needed to go to a four-year university to reach his long term goal of medical school. A month after high school graduation, Kyle was offered a partial athletic scholarship of 25%, or a 50% academic scholarship to St. Mary's College in California—his second choice college. He took the offer, and made the decision so that he would have the opportunity to play ball while getting an undergraduate education. After two seasons, Kyle gave up baseball to focus on his academics, although he would not have traded the experience of playing on a college team.

Student-athletes must also consider their chances of participating in their sport at a specific college. For example, someone might qualify academically at a Division I college, but not have the athletic ability to play at that level of competition. The opposite might be true of an athlete who could be offered a DI scholarship, but not be able to qualify academically. You might have the skills to compete at the DI level, but are you willing to make the commitment to compete at the highest level—with pressures to perform and win? We have interviewed many former DI student-athletes who quit because the game wasn't fun any more and instead became like a business. You have to know what is important to you—whether you just want to play, or if you want to play at the highest level possible.

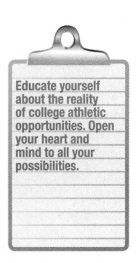

Educate yourself about the reality of college athletic opportunities. Open your heart and mind to all your possibilities.

You need to realize that there are no guarantees. Student-athletes must be honest about their role in sports during their college career. Because of the competitive nature of sports, being given a spot in a program does not guarantee that you will actually have the opportunity to play. Each year new players are recruited who may bump you from your position. You need to be aware that you can end up being anything from a starter, to a substitute, to a scout player, or to being cut from a program. There are no guarantees.

"This program may not be the perfect fit because I am a receiver but block more than catch in our run style offense. But, I really like the school and am happy."

–Brandon Michalkiewicz, Football Player at
California Polytechnic State University

Community college is a realistic option for some student-athletes. It is highly recommended that each student-athlete be a "qualifier" even if he or she wants to go to a community college before attending a 4-year school. It is easier to transfer from a community college if you entered it as a "qualifier." And, you can transfer after only one year as long as you maintain a certain GPA and take the right classes.

Community college student-athletes who are non-qualifiers, must earn an Associate of Arts (AA) degree in order to be eligible for transferring to a 4-year university. Also, be aware that some colleges do not accept transfer students. Do your research before considering a community or junior college as an option.

Katie Oddo knew what role she wanted sports to play in her college career. "I played competitive club soccer since I was ten years old and always knew I would play college soccer. I wanted to play in the ACC (Atlantic Coast Conference). I wanted to do something different than all the girls in my club—going to Los Angeles to play. I wanted a new start. My club coach helped me with official visits to Marshall University in West Virginia and the University of Miami. I could have been a starter at Marshall but I didn't feel it would be enough of a challenge to fulfill my competitive drive. I wanted to have to work really hard for playing time. And the visit made the difference. When I walked on the Miami campus, I loved the feel of the school. It had a comfortable home feeling. All of the players were so nice. And, since my grandma lived in Miami, I had family there. It wasn't a big deal that I didn't get very much playing time. I hardly played my freshman year, played some my sophomore year, played even less my junior year, and then started every game my senior year. It felt good that I had to work so hard for it. My advice to student-athletes is to have fun. We sometimes get wrapped up in playing time. Enjoy the ride and you will become the person you are because of your experiences—it translates to life."

☑ WHAT ROLE WILL SPORTS PLAY IN COLLEGE?

Use the following questions to help you think about your college fit, both athletically and academically.

- ☐ Are you only using sports to help you get into the college of your dreams?
- ☐ Are you using sports as your focus and plan on picking a school for its sports team?
- ☐ Are sports more important than the specific college?
- ☐ Is it important that you are a starter or is it ok if you are a role or a practice player—such as a scout team player, or a benchwarmer?
- ☐ If you get injured or don't play once you are already in college, will you be happy at that institution?
- ☐ How important is the coach? What about the assistant coaches? Realize that the coach might not be there the next year due to hiring and firing. While the coaching staff is very important, the coach should not be the basis of your decision since they are not permanent to the athletic program.
- ☐ What about the reputation of the athletic team?
- ☐ What is the culture of the team and the make-up of the individuals on the team, especially the student-athletes that are part of your recruiting class?
- ☐ What if you are only a practice player and don't get to travel with the team?

☑ Are you a fit athletically?

- ☐ Is your commitment and passion at the same level as your potential college teammates?
- ☐ Are your physical and athletic abilities at the same level as your potential college teammates?
- ☐ Do you enjoy playing with the pressure to win and perform?

☑ Are you a fit academically?

- ☐ Are you earning good, or excellent grades in your high school classes?
- ☐ Have you taken honors, AP, or IB courses and done well in them?
- ☐ Are you currently attending a rigorous high school?
- ☐ Beyond high school, can you maintain good grades and compete in any college?
- ☐ Is the academic rigor not enough or too much?
- ☐ What are the graduation rates? (Remember, you can't play sports your entire life and only a small percent of athletes go on to the pros...so your educational choices are very important to your future.)
- ☐ Have you developed the necessary study skills and habits to be successful in college?

In a perfect world, a college will give you both the athletic and educational opportunities that you want. Be sure you select a college with a balance between athletics, academics, and a social life. If something happens that takes you out of sports, would you still want to attend the college you select? Consider some of the possible scenarios that could happen to anyone.

Although Nick Young really wanted to play college baseball, he declined an athletic scholarship to an out of state school and walked on at UC San Diego, a highly academic and desirable in-state university. If he got injured and couldn't play, he wanted to be at a university in his state. After one year, he left because the program was not a big deal on campus and he wasn't getting playing time. Nick ended up across the country in Delaware where he enjoyed a college baseball career and earned a great education in business.

What if:

▸ What if the pressure to perform is too great? Or not nearly enough?

▸ What if injuries prevent you from playing? Would you still want to be at this particular college?

▸ What if the time commitment for college sports is too much?

▸ What if you have to sacrifice too much, including a social life, the opportunity to study abroad, future career internships, etc.?

▸ What if you become frustrated from either not playing well or not getting enough playing time?

▸ What if competing at the college level is not fun anymore?

▸ What if you don't feel like you belong with your teammates?

▸ What if the coach you like leaves and you don't like the new coach?

"When you are young, you have dreams that seem easily attainable because you are a rising star. I swam for the competitive swim club and did cross fit dry land conditioning for four years of my life. The sophomore years are cool years because you get lots of letters. Then you can get discouraged because you become realistic about your size and start realizing you are not a top star. I was not a superstar sprinter and had to be an endurance swimmer to make a difference. You have to ask what do you want from the sport and where can you go. You don't realize all your opportunities until you look at DII and DIII in addition to the DI schools. You have to fit in the academic spectrum too. You can make yourself a better prospect if you have an academic background to push yourself forward. I had to be proactive because I didn't get a lot of phone calls. Calling was too time consuming, but I sent emails to so many coaches. I read college rosters to compare my times and emailed coaches my profile. It's just like completing college applications because you have to send emails to safe, dream, and targeted schools. I sent emails to Ivy League schools because I wanted to get out of California and see what's out there. You have to be headstrong. And, it's really a personal choice where you want to be."

–Jordan Caines, Cornell University Swimmer

Research Colleges to Help You Decide

Now that you've thought about the role of sports for you in college, you will want to consider what college is right for you based on researching and later narrowing down your choices. Remember you are researching colleges with a purpose—academically and athletically.

There are a variety of educational options for you:

▸ **Community college:** offers a two year-degree, Associate of Arts (AA) or certification in specific occupational fields. You could compete in a sport for two years, which would count toward your 4 years of NCAA eligibility.

▸ **State University:** offers a 4-year degree, either a Bachelor of Arts (BA) or Bachelor of Science (BS). Most offer graduate Master's degrees. Some offer doctorate (PhD) degrees. You can compete in sports for 4 years.

▸ **Private Colleges and Universities**: offer AA, BA, BS, and Master's degrees. Many also offer PhD programs. You can compete in sports for 4 years.

▸ **Ivy League:** these are elite private East Coast colleges with demanding admissions requirements. Being an elite athlete could help you gain admissions.

Career Considerations

There are additional considerations when you are researching colleges. First, some of you have an idea of what type of career you are aspiring toward. Some of you also know already what field you want to major it. If you know this, your first step will be to find colleges that offer the major you are looking for. If you do not know what career path you want to take, you can take a career inventory that will provide you with careers that reflect your aptitude, personality, and passions. Go to collegboard.org and take the test. Print out your results and put them in your college file, box, or crate. In terms of careers, you will also want to think about the following:

Collegboard.org offers services to help with decisions about majors and career paths. It also compares colleges, side-by-side. This is an incredible site and service!

▸ The job environment (inside or outside, travel or not)

▸ What you would be doing in that job

▸ Working with people or independently

▸ Working hours and conditions

▸ Stress level

▸ Typical salary (beginning and maximum)

▸ Education and training

▸ Special skills and abilities

▸ The demand for your major

If you are a highly academic student who plans on pursuing a graduate degree in a highly competitive school (medicine, law, pharmacology, dental, veterinary or PhD) you may want to go directly to a 4-year college rather than attending a community college first.

After high school, Scotty Enos attended his local community college to get better grades and to get bigger and stronger to make himself a valuable football kicker. He gained valuable athletic and academic experience and even learned about living on his own. After a successful two-year community college football career, he was offered an athletic scholarship to the University of Hawaii where he set multiple kicking records. He left Hawaii two courses short of graduation to play semi-professional football in Kentucky and then in Iowa, but later returned to Hawaii to complete summer school and obtain his 4-year college degree. He will continue working hard toward his goal of getting drafted by an NFL team and making a career out of football.

College Environment

Whether you do or don't know what career you want to pursue, the next step in narrowing down your college choice would be to look at the environment of the schools you are considering. Consider the physical, cultural, and social aspects of the campus and surrounding community.

- Visit your college/career center at your high school, introduce yourself to the counselor, and gather materials

- Request course catalogs—look at graduation requirements, course offerings in majors you are considering, etc.

- Attend college presentations (usually made by college representatives) on your campus—ask specific questions about your interests

- Attend college career fairs normally sponsored by your high school counseling department

- Tip for college fairs: bring pre-printed address labels to paste on college information cards so you don't have to write it on all the forms—include your name, address, email, phone, high school, and year of graduation

- Explore websites for career, major and college exploration tools, including My Road (collegboard.org); this site allows you to assess your personality, profile, academic fields, and review future occupations

- Take online "virtual tours" of colleges—consider average temperatures, rainfall, weather, etc.

- To get an idea of where colleges are located across the nation, look at a US map

- Visit colleges and take tours

- Watch the team you hope to join play or compete

- Make unofficial and official visits
- Ask questions about academics, athletics, cultural, and social life
- You will also want to consider your real options based on your abilities, athletic and academic performance, and potential.
- Consider attending summer school courses as a high school student to experience what college is like on that campus

Your options depend on where you fit athletically and academically.

WHAT KIND OF SCHOOL DO YOU WANT TO ATTEND?

When choosing colleges, there are athletic, academic, environmental and cultural considerations. To determine your preferences, fill in the number scale below. 0 is no preference, 1 is not important, 2 is somewhat important, 3 is important, 4 is very important. When you're done, go back and see what your most important preferences are, and use that to shape your potential college list.

⓪①②③④   Athletic program (DI, DII, DIII, NAIA)

⓪①②③④   Scholarship or financial aid packages

⓪①②③④   Team dynamics

⓪①②③④   Head coach and staff

⓪①②③④   Athletic playing time/performing arts opportunity (starter, walk-on, scout team, understudy, etc.)

⓪①②③④   Student-body support for athletics

⓪①②③④   Club sports and intramural opportunities

⓪①②③④   College's commitment to players' academic success

⓪①②③④   Academic support programs for student-athletes

⓪①②③④   Academic support for students with learning disabilities

⓪①②③④   Percentage of scholarship players who graduate

⓪①②③④   Admission competitiveness—how difficult to get in and stay

⓪①②③④   Major/Minor degree programs & declaration deadline

⓪①②③④   Academic environment (competitive or cooperative)

⓪①②③④   Class size and access to professors

You will find that some of these considerations are important to you as you select a college while others aren't as important.

⓪①②③④ Internship programs available

⓪①②③④ Networking or job opportunity support after graduation

⓪①②③④ Graduate Programs

⓪①②③④ Proximity to home

⓪①②③④ Accessibility (how long would it take you to travel there? Is there a nearby, convenient airport? Cost of flights from home?)

⓪①②③④ Environment (beach, city, mountains, urban, rural, etc.)

⓪①②③④ Climate (cold winters, mild, hot summers, windy, etc.)

⓪①②③④ Surrounding community

⓪①②③④ On & off campus living conditions (dorms, fraternities)

⓪①②③④ Size of campus and classes

⓪①②③④ Difficulty in getting classes and ability to graduate in 4 years

⓪①②③④ Culture of campus and of students (intellectual, social, religious, political, fashion, life-style, etc.)

⓪①②③④ Social life on campus (fraternities, student government, clubs, activities, extracurricular activities, athletics, performing arts, parties, intramurals, etc.)

⓪①②③④ College rules (no drinking, smoking, drugs, on or off campus)

⓪①②③④ Living arrangements (separate male/female dorms)

⓪①②③④ Religious affiliation

⓪①②③④ Cost (tuition, room & board, rent)

⓪①②③④ Transfer policies for student athletes to other colleges

OTHER CONSIDERATIONS

Many student-athletes factor in admission requirements and college costs before applying to a school.

Admission Requirements

Research the admission requirements for the colleges you are considering. Find out the minimum requirements for the SAT/ACT and your GPA. For NCAA academic eligibility (different than individual college admission requirements), the higher your GPA, the lower your SAT/ACT scores can be. Also, for NCAA eligibility, if your SAT/ACT scores are very high, you can get in with a lower GPA. Remember that college admission requirements are different from the NCAA core course GPA eligibility requirements. You need to meet both requirements.

Also, you need to know exactly which tests colleges require. Some colleges will take either the SAT and the ACT, while some may only want one or the other. Some require specific subject tests, while others may not require any. It is very important that you know exactly what each college you are applying to requires. Carefully check the exam requirements of the colleges you intend to apply to, as well as any other specific admission requirements.

> Regardless of what the NCAA requires, it is best to have the highest GPA & SAT/ACT scores possible.

Betsy Barr was an incredible soccer athlete—probably the best female athlete that graduated from her high school. She could have played anywhere in the country, but she did not fit everywhere academically. She chose to attend the University of Portland because she loved the environment, the coach, the girls on the team, and the program's goal of reaching the NCAA championship. In her senior year, she led the team to a national championship, and now enjoys coaching club soccer and teaching high school.

In addition, you need to take specific high school subjects for different college admissions requirements. For example, in California, you need three years of a foreign language (middle school does not count) for the University of California system, while California State Universities require two years.

Costs of College

Another consideration could be how much college will cost you and your family. For example, you might be able to get a full-ride scholarship at a small private college while a DII college could only pay for your books. Although the small school might not be your first choice, you could pick it because you will be a starter for that team and have four years of college paid for. This is something you would need to consider and talk about with your parents. Collegboard.org offers free resources to help you figure out college costs and expenses, and determine how much you need to save for college. It also delineates different savings plans. The website explains

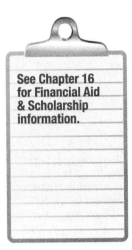

how to find college scholarships and financial aid and how to secure a loan. There are also tools for calculating and comparing loans and aid. Individual college websites should have a breakdown of the cost of attending that school as well.

See Chapter 16 for Financial Aid & Scholarship information.

Note that tuition for private schools is much higher than public schools in your state. Costs will vary depending upon the financial aid and/or academic or athletic scholarships you receive. Even though private schools are more expensive, many offer significant academic scholarships.

Use the chart below to estimate your college cost. Some categories like books, supplies, food, entertainment, and phone will vary depending on the student. If you buy your books online from a used bookstore (we suggest amazon.com or half.com), it will cut the cost of books considerably. You can also rent textbooks online but you will need to file a waiver. Your computer supplies will vary depending on the type of computer you purchase (Mac vs. PC), and food purchases will vary depending on how often you eat out (which depends on how much you like the cafeteria food). Housing and food costs will also change if you move off-campus after your freshman year. Typically off-campus housing and cooking for yourself is less expensive than the cost of living and eating on-campus. Also, if the student is covered on his or her parents' health insurance plan, you may not need to accept the college's insurance plan, which can reduce costs as well.

Compare costs for different colleges after filling out these charts. There will be extra charts on dcipress.com.

ESTIMATE YOUR COLLEGE COST FOR COLLEGE

Estimate what it will cost you to attend college for a year. Go to each college website that you are interested in for its list of costs and information to estimate your scholarship and financial aid.

Costs & Expenses	$ Yearly Amount		
	#1	#2	#3
Tuition			
Fees (parking, health insurance, etc.)			
Housing (on or off campus)			
Books			
Supplies (computer, notebooks, etc.)			
Transportation (airfare, busses, gas, etc.)			
Clothing			
Food			
Entertainment			
Phone			
Utilities (gas, electric, cable, internet, etc.)			
Other			
Total yearly cost:			
Estimated scholarships & grants:			
Total actual cost:			

Create a list of colleges

Think about where you would like to attend based on how you filled in the charts in this chapter. Ultimately, you will end up with a list that is prioritized with schools at the top that are highly desirable, to schools you would like to attend, down to those that you know you could attend, but are not going to be your top choice. It is important to have schools where you know you meet entrance requirements and that satisfy your athletic desires.

Find the fit. Perhaps you are a perfect fit for a 4-year college experience. Or, maybe your local community college offers the best fit for you right out of high school. Perhaps your grades and/or athletic ability and strength/size are a match for a community college before transferring to a 4-year college.

Keep in mind, however, that competing at a community college is not a given. Community colleges are increasingly recruiting bigger, faster, stronger athletes. You may need to check around with local community colleges to see where you fit on their depth chart. The competition to make the team is higher than ever. On the other hand, more college student-athletes are being recruited from community colleges—just read rosters to see the number of transfer students.

"**Not everyone can afford college**. I had to go to a JC unless I had a scholarship. I had a great college career starting at Butte Community College, then transferring to Chico State for three years of great baseball."
–Jamie Sprague, California State University, Chico Baseball Player

Campus Visits

In addition to researching the right college fit, you should visit the campuses and surrounding communities to get a feel for what you do and don't like. Try to visit campuses during college prospect camps, showcases or combines, to differentiate between the college communities. However, if you are competing during the summer, visit when you can, even if school is not in session. Making campus visits early will help you narrow down choices before submitting costly applications.

It's important for athletes to keep their options open when considering colleges in case they change their minds later on in the application process. Adam Wagner began wrestling in 5th grade, and was a successful competitor throughout middle school and high school. He attended many tournaments on his own and with his high school team, and placed in the top 12 in California during both his junior and senior years. He applied to several colleges throughout the country that had wrestling programs with the intention of competing at the collegiate level. However, in the spring of his senior year, he visited and fell in love with the University of Arizona, a school that didn't offer wrestling as a sport. He decided to attend the university, opting for a more social and academic college experience rather than continuing to wrestle competitively.

Last Words...

In the end, the most important task is to find a good fit! When researching colleges, carefully consider your college goals and role of sports for you. Remember, that there are many good options for you. Choose the college with a coach that wants you! And be honest in the evaluation of your athletic (and academic) ability so you find a place where you can play and succeed in the classroom.

Matt Laughrea played soccer since he was five years old, but gave it up at the end of his sophomore year to play football his junior year with his brother who was the varsity quarterback. Matt worked hard over the spring and summer and won a starting position as a wide receiver his junior year. He had a great year and loved playing football with his brother.

Matt remained on his high school volleyball team where he had been a varsity player since his freshman year, and he also continued playing club volleyball. During his junior year, a number of colleges were interested in him for volleyball, but he thought he might be able to get a scholarship for football. Unfortunately, he had little time to market himself in football since he was heavily committed to school and club volleyball. His summer was filled with volleyball tournaments across the state and Junior Nationals in July. He was not able to attend any football camps or combines.

During the summer before his senior year, Matt made visits to a number of DI volleyball colleges and one DII college, UC San Diego. He had numerous DII and DIII colleges interested in him, but he was recruited by UC San Diego at the Junior Nationals. In the fall of his senior year he made an official visit, and ultimately signed a letter of intent. Even though DII colleges have little scholarship money to offer, Matt chose UC San Diego because he really liked the volleyball team and he wants ultimately to go to medical school. UC San Diego has a terrific reputation as a feeder school for medical schools. He made his choice based on his ability to play at a DII school and for the college's outstanding reputation for academics.

Chapter 10
Top 10 Plays

1. Find the right fit athletically, academically, and socially

2. Really think about the role you want sports to play in your college experience

3. Consider what you will do if you get injured

4. Research your post-high school options

5. Determine the kind of college environment you are looking for

6. Consider the school size and distance from home that best fits you

7. Research admission requirements

8. Consider the costs of attending

9. Make college visits to find the right school

10. Remember it's about playing college sports AND getting a good college education

11

Understanding
RECRUITING

What you lack in size, you can make up in heart.

RECRUITING OVERVIEW

Recruiting is a two-way proposition: student-athletes hope to get recruited and coaches are looking for athletes to enhance their programs. There are all kinds of recruits, including highly sought after athletes who are on the top of college coaches' lists, as well as potential college athletes that no one knows about. Recruiting starts very early for some and last minute for others. The goal in recruiting is to create a match for the college, the athletic program, and the student-athlete. For the highly desirable recruits, it is important to ask the right questions about scholarship money and the program, and for others, it is a matter of getting your name in the recruiting scene.

"Recruiting is the most significant, yet difficult part of my job because of the time and resources it requires—all away from my floor coaching duties. I have a better chance of recruiting athletes if I start when they are in 9th grade."
–Guin Boggs,
William Jessup University Women's Head Basketball Coach

Since national college recruiters make it their business to find blue-chip athletes (the best athletes in regions across the nation), the highly sought out exceptional athletes are already on college coaches' radars. College coaches are identifying potential recruits in 7th and 8th grade and offering scholarships before these athletes even enter high school. Most DI programs have identified athletes by the end of their sophomore year of high school.

Obviously, colleges compete for the best student-athletes because they want to have the best athletic program and win games. DI college sports have become big businesses, where winning brings in lucrative TV contracts and money, and recruiting the best athletes is key to building winning programs.

Recruiting is highly competitive and a numbers game. College coaches are continually looking for athletes for their programs and spend numerous hours each day searching for talented athletes with good grades. To build a recruiting database, college coaches attend AAU, travel, club tournaments, Junior Olympics, "nationals" as well as some high school competitions. They communicate with high school, AAU, and club coaches, and even with other college coaches. They also use the Internet to research stats and information on high school athletes. Sometimes the head coach is not necessarily the recruiting coach. Many head coaches delegate recruiting to assistant coaches.

Since recruiters go to showcases and tournament events more than they attend high school sporting events, many athletes play with a club team and attend showcases in addition to playing on their high school team. It is more cost and time effective for coaches to see a lot talent in one place such as a showcase tournament. Football is the exception where recruiters visit high schools with outstanding players in the off-season to meet the student-athletes and check on their grades. College football coaches also attend the football playoff and state championship games.

DII, DIII, and NAIA schools also recruit to compete for the best student-athletes, but not to the extent that DI schools do. They do not have the resources, budget, or personnel to recruit as aggressively as DI schools. If you are interested in playing a DII or DIII sport, you especially need to be proactive to help college coaches find you.

You need to know that college coaches all network with one another and with high school coaches. Many of them have played sports or worked together on other coaching staffs. They might not be able to use you on their team, but they could put in a call to a friend at another college and recommend you. DI coaches will often make calls to DII and DIII coaches to inform them of the athletes they did not offer scholarships to.

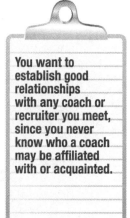

You want to establish good relationships with any coach or recruiter you meet, since you never know who a coach may be affiliated with or acquainted.

Recruiting Terms and Regulations

There are strict rules in today's highly competitive recruiting environment, and it is critical that you understand the terms and rules for your specific sport so that you maintain your eligibility.

There are two websites that appear very similar: ncaa.org and ncaa.com. The ncaa.org site is the official website for the National Collegiate Athletic Association, while the ncaa.com site is a commercial website that offers information regarding DI, DII, and DIII, men's and women's sports.

Use the ncaa.org site as your resource for recruiting rules and regulations, and note that they are different for individual sports. Be sure to note that changes are being made to promote academic success of student-athletes so academic requirements will be more rigorous.

The ncaa.org site provides information about the differences among DI (including the football bowl subdivisions), DII, and DIII and covers academics, rule compliance, health and safety, championships, resources, and finances. There is a simplified summary of recruiting rules for each sport, and information about religious missions, banned drugs, transfer rules, and even the probability of a high school student going pro.

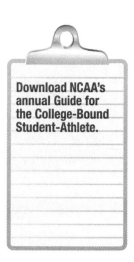

Download NCAA's annual Guide for the College-Bound Student-Athlete.

Start your research by going to ncaa.org and downloading a free copy of the NCAA Eligibility Center's annual *Guide for the College-Bound Student-Athlete*. This guide is a "must-read" for all student-athletes and their parents because the most current edition reflects the constant and important rule changes. This chapter will assist you in interpreting the rules and regulations of recruiting.

The following recruiting terms and regulations are defined and modified from the *NCAA Guide for the College-Bound Student-Athlete*. While the guide lists these in alphabetical order, we have put the terms in chronological order based on how you will encounter them.

Prospective Student-Athlete

‣ You are a prospective student-athlete once you begin 9th grade or before you enter 9th grade if you receive benefits from a college
‣ If you play basketball you are considered a prospective student-athlete once you begin 7th grade

Contact

‣ Any face-to-face contact off the college campus between the coach and you or your parents

Contact Period

‣ During this time a college coach may have face-to-face contact with you and/or your parents on or off the college campus
‣ College coach may visit your high school and watch you play
‣ You can make college visits
‣ The coach may email, write, or phone you

Evaluation

‣ College coaches evaluate your academic and athletic ability
‣ Coaches look at your transcripts to check out your grades

Evaluation Period

‣ During this time, college coaches can watch you play or visit your high school
‣ College coaches can not have any face-to-face contact with you or your parents off the college campus
‣ You and your parents can visit a college campus
‣ College coaches may email, write or call you or your parents

Recruiting Calendars

‣ Go to ncaa.org for specific NCAA DI recruiting regulations for each sport and also DII & DIII recruiting calendars

Recruiter or Recruiting Coordinator

‣ The recruiter is the head coach or an assistant coach on the college coaching staff (these coaches must be certified annually by passing a written test)
‣ Each sport limits the number of coaches able to go on the recruiting road

NCAA Eligibility Center

‣ Athletes are required to register with the Eligibility Center to verify that they are academically eligible to play DI or DII sports
‣ Athletes must register prior to receiving athletic scholarships and practicing and competing for a college
‣ Register online with the Eligibility Center at the beginning of your junior year of high school
‣ At the beginning of your junior year, send a transcript of six semesters of grades to the Eligibility Center
‣ Send your SAT or ACT scores directly to the Eligibility Center (by using code "9999") whenever you take the exams

Quiet Period

‣ During this time, college coaches may not leave their campus to do in-person recruiting with you or your parents
‣ College coaches may not watch you play or visit your high school
‣ You and your parents may visit a college campus and college coaches can have recruiting contact with you if you happen to bump into them on the college campus
‣ College coaches may write or phone you or your parents

Dead Period or Non-Contact Period

‣ During this time, no face-to-face contact between the coach and you or your parents, on- or off-campus can be had
‣ College coaches can write and call you or your parents

Unofficial Visit

‣ Any college visit you make that you and your parents pay for
‣ College can pay for three passes to home athletic contests
‣ You may make unlimited unofficial visits at any time
‣ It's best not to make an unofficial visit during the dead period since you cannot talk to a coach during the dead period

Official Visit

‣ Any college-paid visit you make
‣ The college will pay some or all of the following costs:
  » Your transportation to and from the college
  » Room and three meals per day
  » Reasonable entertainment expenses (including three complimentary passes to home athletic contests)
‣ BEFORE the college can invite you, you must provide the college with the following:
  » A copy of your high school transcript (DI only)
  » Your SAT, ACT, or PLAN score
  » Proof of registration with the Eligibility Center

Verbal Commitment

- A student-athlete's commitment to a college before he or she signs or is able to sign a National Letter of Intent
- Students can announce a verbal commitments at any time
- A verbal commitment is NOT binding for the college or the player

National Letter of Intent

- All DI schools (except the military service and Ivy League schools) and most DII schools are part of the NLI signing program
- No DIII, NAIA, prep school, or two-year schools participate
- The NLI is a voluntary written agreement sponsored by the Eligibility Center that is binding for one full academic year to the corresponding college
  - » The coach will want to get a verbal commitment before mailing you the National Letter of Intent
- There is both an "early" and "late" signing period for NCAA DI
- Signing, in addition to a financial aid agreement, is binding to both the school and the player
- Signing means the athlete agrees to attend the college for one academic year
- Signing means the college must provide athletic financial aid for one academic year (if the student is eligible for financial aid under NCAA rules)
- Signing means you are committing to the institution, not the current coach—if the coach leaves, you are still committed to the university (coaches regularly accept new coaching jobs)
  - » It is not binding to a coach or team, meaning signing the letter does not guarantee an athlete a place on the team or playing time, rather the athlete is guaranteed the athletic scholarship for a minimum of one full academic year
- Read any restrictions affecting eligibility (national-letter.org)
- Once a student-athlete signs, other schools cannot recruit the athlete

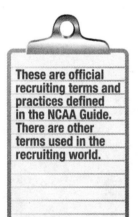

These are official recruiting terms and practices defined in the NCAA Guide. There are other terms used in the recruiting world.

In addition to the terms defined in the *NCAA Guide*, there are other terms and recruiting practices listed below.

Blue-Chip Athlete

- A highly recruited student-athlete
- College coaches make contact with these athletes by their sophomore year (some contact players when they are 13 years old)
- Actively recruited by many college teams because they are the best at their positions, and will have an immediate impact on their college team because of their current athletic skills, rather than their potential athletic skills
- Coaches attend games/tournaments to watch blue-chip athletes

- Coaches visit high schools to talk to and even watch blue-chip athletes during off-season or informal workouts
- Coaches email and have conversations over the phone with these athletes frequently
- These athletes have typically earned "All-League," "All-County," "All-Section," or "All-State" recognition
- Coaches or recruiters may make home visits to these athletes
- These athletes receive invitations for paid, official visits during their senior year
- This term comes from the 'blue chips' in poker, which are of the highest value

Recruited Walk-On

- Coaches seek out these players but have no athletic money to offer them
- These athletes receive no athletic scholarship money but often receive academic merit scholarships
- On the team in pre-season— but not automatically on the roster for travel and do not necessarily make the team during the season
- Possible benefits include gaining admission to the college, priority registration, living in the dorms with athletes, tutoring services, and advising

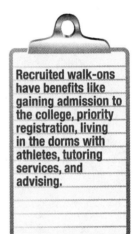

Recruited walk-ons have benefits like gaining admission to the college, priority registration, living in the dorms with athletes, tutoring services, and advising.

Walk-On

- Student-athlete is already admitted to the college
- Has not been recruited by the college coach, but asks before the season to tryout and possibly work out with team over summer
- Do not show up the first day of practice without notifying the coach and expect to try-out and make the team

"Bumping"

- Some college recruiters and coaches inadvertently "bump" into sophomore high school athletes while visiting high school campuses, mentioning how interested they are in them. While this happens on high school campuses, this is really a contact and technically not legal during the non-contact or dead period

Equivalency Sport

- Specific sports such as volleyball, soccer and baseball have a set number of scholarships that can be divided up between players. Coaches may divvy up the specific number of scholarships however they wish among all their players

Headcount Sport

- Other sports such as basketball and football have a maximum number of student-athletes that can be on scholarships at any time
- These are full scholarships

Beyond the terms and regulations of recruiting, you need to understand how recruiting works so that you can create opportunities to play college sports. The process is not usually linear. Often the sequence of events within the recruiting process can be very different from athlete to athlete. As with anything in life, timing, luck and networking will play a huge part in this process. Athletes who initiate and maintain contact and a relationship with coaches and recruiters will have an improved chance of being recruited.

"This college recruiting process is a tough one. I remember from football that everyone wants to talk to you but very few deliver on anything they say. I think it is truly most teenagers' first real taste of adult life. People will tell you anything to keep you interested up to the point where they don't need you anymore. I say, 'Keep positive', and make a decision based on the sports, academics, and social life."
—Ron Loder, parent

Recruiting Opportunities

College coaches and scouts recruit the best they can with the resources they have. Big name DI schools have a much bigger budget to recruit student-athletes than smaller DII and DIII schools do. These smaller schools are viable options for student-athletes and offer many opportunities that teens and parents may be unaware of. Remember, less than 1% of high school student-athletes receive a full DI scholarship and since the competition is stiff and spaces in DI programs are limited, students must open all doors for opportunities to play college sports including DII, DIII, NAIA, and even two-year community college programs. Unless you are a blue-chip athlete, narrowing your focus on DI programs only is unwise.

"There are thousands of smaller colleges where normal people can play. You need to be good and have a grasp of reality. You can play if you pick and shop for the right place."
–College Scout, Coach, and Author, Terry Battenberg

Recruiting is a Numbers Game

Recently, Niven Jones, parent of a high school baseball player went through the recruiting process and learned that a college baseball opportunity is a numbers game. As a California resident, the numbers were stacked against his son. The parent compiled numbers from high school baseball player estimates, the College Board, and the Department of Education, finding that the ratio of California baseball players looking to be recruited compared to the number of available roster spots in California colleges was huge compared to other states. He defined the number of positions available each year using a hypothetical 35 player college roster with 25% of the spots being filled by incoming freshmen or transferring juniors.

He estimated the number of players competing for one roster spot at a four-year college in various states as follows:

California	45 players
Texas	34 players
Oregon	27 players
North Carolina	16 players
Ohio	16 players
Pennsylvania	12 players

By not limiting his options to his home state of California, his son found an opportunity to earn a great education and play college baseball in Texas where he started on a top-notch DIII team, loved the coach and his teammates, and competed in the NCAA championship. His message was that if your child has difficulty finding a college to play their sport in, then expand your horizons for college choices beyond your own backyard.

Recruiting & Grades

Academics now play a big part in recruiting. Most college coaches make sure that the recruited student-athlete has the potential to succeed academically at their institution to ensure they will be academically eligible and able to contribute to the program. Recruiters do not want to bring a student to their college only to have them drop out because of failing grades. Colleges must meet Academic Progress Rate (APR) scores and when student-athletes drop out, it affects the APR and thus the amount of scholarship dollars available.

"Education is leverage when playing the recruiting game."
–Leon Lee, hitting instructor and Pacific Rim coordinator for the Chicago Cubs

Communication with Coaches

College coaches may not call student-athletes until July 1st before their senior year. However, they may call high school coaches, who, in turn, give instruction to student-athletes to call the college coach. This is legal. If you are given a college coach's phone number, make sure you call back in a reasonable time. You can call or email as often as you want, but don't be a pest. After July 1st a college coach may only call you once a week, and may begin to have face-to-face contact with you as well.

Mail

NCAA coaches can send unlimited mail to athletes, and athletes can send unlimited mail to coaches. However, coaches cannot respond to students' mail until July 1st after their sophomore year of high school.

Email

Like regular mail, college coaches can send and return unlimited emails. And, like with mail, coaches cannot respond to students' emails until July 1st after their sophomore year of high school.

Phone Calls

The NCAA limits the number of calls coaches can make to student-athletes, but athletes can make unlimited calls to coaches. Check ncaa.org regularly for variations of rules for specific sports since they change frequently.

Boise State University quarterback Jimmy Laughrea exchanged emails and chatted over the phone with four different DI college football coaches from the PAC 10 (now PAC 12), Big Sky, and Mountain West Conferences on a weekly basis during April and May of his junior year. Coaches would email him that they were in the office and ask for Jimmy to call them back. This allowed the coaches to talk to him without violating the rules.

Other Electronic Communication

The *NCAA Guide* explains the rules about social media sites (like Facebook and Twitter) and recruiting. Since technology is changing rapidly, be sure to check ncaa.org for the most current rules. Any texting, instant messaging, or leaving messages (on a user room, chat room, or message board within a social networking website) between a coach and a recruit is banned. DI men's basketball is the exception to these rules and DIII has different guidelines than DI and DII, so check carefully to make sure you are not in violation of the rules. All of these rules are in place to shield prospective student-athletes from undue pressure from college coaches and recruiters.

Recruiting Letters & Emails from Colleges

A typical college coach will:
- Have a secretary type a generic letter, make 10,000 copies, and send this same letter to thousands of high school student-athletes
- Weed out possible recruits by narrowing his list to those who responded
- Call the high school coach to ask if the athlete is a good citizen and has a good attitude
- Ask for a DVD or go watch the athlete play
- Narrow the pool down to 20 and actively go after those high school students
- Find a handful of those 20 student-athletes who are interested

Recruiting at Showcase Tournaments

Showcases are a place where athletes play in front of numerous college coaches and scouts, hosted by colleges and private organizations. These showcases allow college recruiters to see some of the best talent in the area. They also offer student-athletes the opportunity to be seen by recruiters, scouts, and college coaches, not only from their local area, but also from across the nation.

There are events for teams and for individuals. Some showcases are "open" and anyone who wants to attend can pay the money and participate. Other showcases are "invitation only" for the elite athletes, and you must be recommended, usually based on your athletic ability, in order to get an invite. Potential DI athletes attend elite showcases for broad exposure. There are literally hundreds of showcase tournaments, so you need to research which ones are best suited for you. Many tournaments may not meet your needs, especially if the tournament is really only a money-maker for a private company or college.

Attending numerous showcases can become a financial burden. You need to set a budget and see what works for you. Remember there are also opportunities to attend college clinics or summer camps if you are specifically interested in one college.

College recruiters and coaches do not have the time, money, or resources to attend all the sporting events at high schools, but they attend showcases to see the top athletes in an area all in one place, and can compare these athletes in one day, one weekend, or week-long camp.

Recruiting at Academic Showcase Tournaments

Academic showcase tournaments are tournaments for the successful academic student. College coaches attend these tournaments because student-athletes must have a minimum GPA to participate, thus insuring a certain academic level of the players. Many require that students send transcripts that prove the student has a 3.5 GPA or higher. Many of these coaches need to recruit strong students so they have the potential to be successful at a rigorous academic school. Coaches do not want to recruit students who will become academically ineligible because of poor grades.

Recruiting at College Prospect Day, Weekend Camps, and Clinics

These camps are hosted by the actual head coach and assistant coaches at a specific college. Generally, only the coaches from that site will be in attendance. Some of these camps are not specifically recruiting camps, but are fundraisers for the college athletic program. They also serve the local community by offering inexpensive opportunities to learn and develop fundamental sports skills. These camps are offered during the off-season, and since the camps don't offer overnight accommodations, student-athletes must find hotel accommodations if necessary. In addition, these camps can serve as a campus visit, as the parents and players may tour the campus, meet the coaches, and learn about the philosophy of the athletic program and school. Student-athletes will be able to educate themselves to see if the campus and athletic program is a fit for them.

Recruiting at College Prospect Summer Camps

College prospect camps must meet NCAA rules, which means they are open to everyone, first come, first served. (Sometimes, there is a follow-up prospect camp, which is invitation only, for the athletes that stand out.)

Camps may be day camps or 3-5 days in length and are offered during the summer. Usually, student-athletes stay in college dorms and eat in the cafeteria. Research specific camps online for your sport and go to specific college websites to find sports camps that are offered.

Be careful about attending huge camps at universities since there will be so many players that you may be easily overlooked. Usually, the only coaches and recruiters in attendance are the ones from that university alone. Sometimes, several coaches within the same athletic league will work together to host a camp on one of the campuses. This is valuable because you can be seen by a number of coaches within a region at one time.

Recruiting at your High School

College coaches visit high schools during the season and off-season to watch athletes in games and practices. Coaches visit high schools that have highly-recruited athletes on their teams. Sometimes, coaches go to the front office to check transcripts of athletes before they watch them perform.

Football is the sport where college coaches closely watch the school season, playoffs, and state tournaments since there is no club football. College coaches also show up in the off-season to meet with high school coaches to find any athletes who may have been overlooked earlier.

Home Visits

Some college coaches with a recruiting budget will take the time to visit blue-chip student-athletes and their parents at their homes. When a student-athlete has a couple of options for college, the coach will come with the goal of persuading the student to attend and play for his college. Also, college coaches will make home visits to hold on to the athletes they have recruited so they don't lose them to another college before signing day.

Campus Visits

Student-athletes are allowed five official visits and unlimited unofficial visits. High school athletes cannot officially practice or tryout for a DI program, but they can for DII schools. Potential athletes can hang out with college players and play recreation ball, but college players cannot officially report back to the coach about the players' ability if the coach directed the players to play with the recruits ahead of time.

Verbal Commitments

Colleges and universities will offer verbal commitments to student-athletes to beat out offers that other colleges may make to an athlete. Verbal commitments are not legally binding. Some student-athletes will verbally commit early, during their junior year, to avoid the mental stress of recruiting during their senior year.

Again, verbal commitments are not legally binding, however, some believe that a verbal commitment is ethically binding. Recently, there have been more instances where verbal commitments are not honored on either the part of the player or the coach. In some instances, once a verbal commitment is made to you, college coaches may not allow you to play a sport in your off-season since you are a valuable financial investment to them.

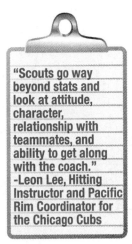

"Scouts go way beyond stats and look at attitude, character, relationship with teammates, and ability to get along with the coach."
-Leon Lee, Hitting Instructor and Pacific Rim Coordinator for the Chicago Cubs

Recruiting for Depth Chart

Recruiters, scouts, and coaches from colleges and scouting organizations evaluate student-athletes and create their depth charts for recruiting. The depth chart is the list of the athletes they are recruiting in the order they want the athletes. They must recruit more athletes than they really need because they are competing against other recruiters for the same student-athletes.

Keeping Options Open

If a number of college coaches have shown interest in you, show appreciation and enthusiasm. Tell coaches you don't want to rush into any decisions and that you need time to go on visits and to make an informed decision. Be leery if the coach says he needs to know your decision without giving you time to think.

You should maintain your options as long as possible by not rejecting a college offer, even if you think you don't want to attend there. In the end, a school that you did not think was a top choice might be the place you get a good offer from.

On the other hand, if a college makes an offer and you hold out, thinking you might get a better offer from a different school, the first school may rescind its original offer.

Since college coaches are part of a nation-wide coaching network, you should always be honest with coaches about your intentions and your desires about where you want to play. Lastly, whenever you are contacted by coaches, follow up and return all calls and questionnaires promptly, and always thank coaches or recruiters for their interest in you.

Recruiting after the Draft

Recruiting does go on after professional drafts for sports such as baseball and basketball. College coaches lose players and potential recruits because the athletes decide to go to the draft rather than finish their college career. When athletes leave college early to get drafted after their junior year, they leave more spots to fill. Also, college coaches can offer more money to recruits if they lose a player to the draft. Or, coaches will give the extra money to existing juniors or seniors because they are good, loyal players.

Jameel Ziadeh signed with Azusa Pacific University to play baseball, and was offered a partial financial aid package. It was understood that he would redshirt his freshman year and play his second year, however, the two junior athletes ahead of him in the depth chart decided to return their senior year. The coach could not offer him the money that he thought would be allocated for him until his junior year when the other two players graduated, and Jameel could not afford to continue to play at this college. He returned home to play at a community college. After a season, a college coach saw him play and offered Jameel a full-ride athletic package to Campbellsville, Kentucky, an NAIA school. He played his junior and senior years there, where they were one game away from going to the NAIA National Championships. During his senior year, his team won their conference tournament but lost in the regionals. He loved his baseball and school experiences in Kentucky, where he majored in sports management. He became an assistant baseball coach at Idaho Western Community College where they won the JUCO National Championship. He then became a graduate student and assistant baseball coach at Wayne State College in Nebraska.

NCAA Recruiting Guidelines

While coaches must adhere to NCAA recruiting guidelines, and most coaches have integrity, be aware that there are those coaches out there employing dishonorable recruiting tactics. Educate yourself about the NCAA Guidelines prior to starting the recruiting process.

Unethical Recruiting

Avoid unethical recruiting. Some coaches may make promises they really cannot deliver on. Beware of a coach who:

‣ Guarantees you will become a professional athlete
‣ Promises you a starting position
‣ Promises a position to one of your high school teammates
‣ Assures you a high paying off campus job
‣ Pledges "booster" support (financial, housing, sporting events, etc.)
‣ Assures you easy grades and teachers at their college
‣ Speaks negatively about other programs, colleges, or coaches
‣ Provides disreputable entertainment such as parties with alcohol, drugs, and/or sex
‣ Offers you any money or gifts, since this would make you NCAA ineligible

Over-Signing

Since it is a coach's responsibility to recruit talent, he/she has to offer more scholarships than are available. Because of this, it is in your best interest to get a recruiter's promise in writing. Sometimes student-athletes and their parents "hear" something different than what recruiters offer.

Over-signing happens when DI coaches sign more student-athletes than they actually have available scholarships. This happens because athletes may be ineligible academically, they may decide to attend elsewhere or they may get injured. Coaches worry that they may not have enough players for all positions, so they may sign extra prospects on National Signing Day. If all prospects show up, however, there would not be enough scholarships to give out for that year. Recently the NCAA has established new rules about the number of DI athletes coaches can over-sign. While these student-athletes will not play, they have the right to receive their scholarship for one full academic year. If this happens a college normally has no other option but to ask or "persuade" the student to grayshirt for a year. Some students may stay at that institution and wait a year; others may transfer to another school with the potential of playing for a different team.

Communication Between Coaches & Other Officials

Coaches do communicate regularly and often with admissions officers and financial aid personnel to help recruit athletes. For example, college admissions officers can assist a college coach by taking into consideration a student-athlete's potential contribution to the athletic program. Students who are not as academically desirable based on SAT/ACT and GPA as their peers might gain admission because their coach worked with the college admissions office. Athletic playing ability might become a consideration for accepting a student who is not competitive academically.

Admissions and Likely Letters

It is in the interest of universities to have their admissions office and financial aid office work with athletic coaches to help continue or build athletic success and traditions for the university. Coaches submit their recruiting needs and lists, along with the recruits' transcripts and profiles, to admissions. They work together to determine if the recruits academically fit the university. Admissions officers know that successful athletes can have characteristics that translate to success in the classroom.

Likely letters are letters sent to high school students notifying them if they will likely or not likely be accepted to a university. Colleges send likely letters to help them compete in the recruiting process for student-athletes since some private schools do not send out acceptance letters until April 1st, long after the signing date for National Letter of Intent. Likely letters can be mailed as early as October 1st, but many go out between January and February. Likely letters give more information to the student-athletes about their opportunities. This can help them decide if they want to pass up a scholarship deadline in February, for example, and wait for an acceptance letter to a non-athletic scholarship school.

Recruiting Offers and Scholarships, Grants, and Financial Aid

It is a plus for college programs when a high school student gets, for example, a Pell Grant. Since the federal government pays for the student's college, coaches don't have to use their limited athletic scholarship money on that student-athlete— meaning they can use the money to recruit another athlete. Coaches might also offer a job plus tuition— which amounts to a work study program— again saving athletic scholarship money for another athlete. (See Chapter 16 for information on scholarships and financial aid.)

Title IX

Football has such a big roster and offers so many scholarships that to comply with Title IX colleges need to offer women more scholarships. Recently, more and more colleges are eliminating men's sports because of financial cuts to athletic departments. This increases a female athlete's chance of getting a more substantial scholarship, while reducing men's scholarships in some of the smaller athletic programs, like volleyball and track.

Last Thoughts...
Recruiting is stressful, even for blue-chip athletes and the high-achieving academic students. Understand that recruiting is time consuming, confusing, often unfair, and exciting at the same time. Be prepared to manage the stress while trying to get recruited. By the time athletes are seniors in high school, they can't wait for the college recruiting and college decisions to be over. Signing day is the ultimate stress reliever.

Chapter 11
Top 10 Plays

1. Knowledge is power, so do your reading about recruiting

2. Download NCAA's annual *Guide for the College-Bound Student-Athlete* at ncaa.org

3. Consult the recruiting calendar for contact rules for each sport (found in the annual *Guide for the College-Bound Student-Athlete* at ncaa.org)

4. Know that the NCAA is reforming the academic requirements to be more rigorous

5. Know that recruiting occurs at key showcase tournaments and some prospect camps

6. Understanding the depth chart is vital if playing time is your most important consideration

7. Know that the National Letter of Intent (NLI) is binding for one year, but doesn't guarantee a starting position, playing time, or even a spot on the team

8. Being a recruited walk-on is an attractive option when your goal is to get admitted, not necessarily to play on the team

9. Be aware of any unethical recruiting practices

10. Recruiting opportunities are out there if you are realistic

12

Gaining Exposure &
MARKETING YOURSELF

Some succeed because they are destined, but most because they are determined.

MARKETING OVERVIEW

How do student-athletes get themselves recruited to play college sports? The recruiting process is basically the same for all athletes, but the timeline and the path to get there may be very different. Rare athletes may be recruited as early as seventh grade, a few when they are high school sophomores. Most are recruited during junior and senior year, while others may not be recruited until the summer after they graduate. Some may play at a community college and then get recruited to a four-year college.

Even though recruiting is a two-way proposition where both college recruiters and student-athletes can initiate the process, you need to help them recruit you! Since most athletes are not DI blue-chip college prospects, they must initiate the recruiting process and market themselves to gain exposure. It is ultimately the player and parent responsibility to communicate with college coaches.

You will want to initiate the recruiting process and create opportunities to be seen by recruiters and coaches. Since most coaches create their recruiting lists as early as freshman or sophomore year, you want to do everything possible to be seen by recruiters and coaches by your junior year. And even though coaches from big schools with big budgets seek student-athletes when they are sophomores and juniors in high school, it is not too late to get recruited if you are a high school senior.

Even if you are involved in a team sport, being recruited by colleges and getting accepted as a student-athlete are individual processes. Setting yourself apart as a desirable asset and getting noticed by coaches and schools are vital to the recruitment journey. When asked about self-marketing and the recruitment process, Stanford University sophomore pole vaulter Katie Zingheim said, "At the end of your junior year or beginning of your senior year, start sending out emails to anywhere you want to go. Find emails online, go through Facebook, and just contact the coaches of schools you want to go to to keep your options open."

High school coaches are not responsible for marketing you. Most lack contacts with college coaches across the country to be able to do so. You have to market yourself with your talent and your desire. Some high school coaches take an active role n helping their players get recruited. Most will help if asked and some feel it is not part of their job.

There are several ways of marketing yourself to get on college coaches' radars, including sending letters and DVDs, uploading videos to websites, playing with a travel club, and attending college prospect camps, clinics, sports summer camps, and showcases or combines. Work to get discovered. Go to college camps and compete on a club team to get the most exposure. Make unofficial college visits, keeping in mind that you will be making an important first impression.

Student-athletes spend time and money traveling and playing with competitive travel teams not only for player development, but for networking, exposure, and recruiting help. Good clubs market and connect their athletes to college coaches. They offer valuable services including building player profiles, uploading highlight and game film, hosting college information nights, introducing their players to college coaches, recommending colleges to their athletes based on the right fit, and other recruiting help.

There are also professional sport-specific and general recruiting agencies that offer communication, exposure, or recruiting services. These companies promise to market you to prospective colleges. They will help you create a profile, make and upload highlight and game DVDs, write cover letters, and send your information to numerous colleges. Some will even offer player development, networking, and exposure through mini camps, clinics, and tournaments.

Based on our interviews with athletes and their parents who have used these types of services, we heard mixed reviews. Some claimed the experience was impersonal, too expensive, and didn't help their teen get recruited. Others found the service valuable and helpful. Do your research before committing to a recruiting agency. Ask if any college coaches endorse this company. Ask for phone numbers of athletes' parents who have used the service in the past, and ask if there is a money-back guarantee. Evaluate what works best for you within your abilities and financial situation.

"I would use the NCSA baseball scouting service again if I had to do it all over. It's worth the money. I would advise other parents to use it, especially if you take advantage of all the services it offers."

–Kim Boone, parent of DIII recruit

Know that getting recruited can be very time-consuming, stressful, and exciting at the same time. Playing club or travel sports to get exposure, competitive experience, and recruited requires sacrifices for most parents, families, and athletes. Club practices, coaching fees, tournament entry fees, and travel and accommodations are expensive and time-consuming. But, on the bright side (the very bright side), it is priceless to be able to spend quality time with your family. For many parents and teens, this is a once-in-a-lifetime opportunity for one-on-one time together and an opportunity for parents to watch their teens play sports. The recruiting process parents go through with their child, even with the inevitable head butting, is so rewarding because it is invaluable to spend the focused time together.

There are multiple ways to gain exposure and get on coaches' radars. You can do it yourself, or there are plenty of college sports placement and recruiting services out there. The real question is which recruiting services and which tournaments and teams or clubs do you join in order to help you get recruited. It depends on what you are looking for and what you are able to do yourself. And, always remember that you are going to get yourself recruited because of your athletic ability, not because of the services you use. Recruiting services are growing in numbers and gaining clients because parents really don't know what to do when it comes to recruitment. Services offer what you can do yourself and take advantage of uninformed parents, who end up paying too much for information that is easily attainable. Do your research.

Coaches need to know who you are and see you play.

"Some prospective student-athletes pay to register with scouting services. This can be an effective way to get your name seen by a broad range of coaches. However, you do not need to do this— particularly if you have pinpointed some of the schools you'd like to attend. With a little effort, you can put together a packet to 'market' yourself to college coaches."

The UC Davis Student-Athlete Guidance Services website offers tips on how to contact a coach:

›   A typed letter of introduction which includes your full name, current address and social security number; this also should indicate when you will start college (for example, fall 2014)
›   An unofficial copy of your high school transcript
›   A list of classes you are currently taking (if they don't appear on your transcript)
›   PSAT scores, if you have not taken the SAT or ACT yet
›   SAT or ACT scores (or projected date of when you will take the test) information on your athletic accomplishments including best events and/or specific times
›   Other optional information that prospective student-athletes sometimes send to coaches:
›   DVD of an athletic performance (unedited)—this may be especially helpful for coaches to evaluate student-athletes in team sports
›   Highlight DVD
›   A resume or personal profile that includes academic and athletic awards
›   Personal and family information

—http://athletics.ucdavis.edu/academicservices/Old/SAGS/Where.htm

HOW TO MARKET YOURSELF

There isn't one set way to get your name out there as there are many paths and timelines to get recruited. The following are suggestions for marketing yourself. No matter what, be proactive and flexible. You will need to market yourself as a desired applicant, that is, a well-rounded academic and athletic student-athlete to gain the leverage you need to be recruited. Work to earn good grades, prepare to get high SAT/ACT scores and compete at the highest athletic level that you can.

Initiate the Recruiting Process

▸ Get your name out there. Remember that there are many opportunities, beyond DI, to get a great education and to participate in sports. DII, DIII, NAIA, and JUCO colleges do not have the budget and resources to find you, so you need to help them find you.

▸ Depending on your sport, you will start sending emails to coaches beginning the spring of your sophomore year through the fall of your senior year. Pay attention to other athletes in your sport. Are they already sending out emails and videos? Are they taking unofficial visits to colleges and meeting with coaches? Are they playing in key showcase tournaments? If so, you will probably want to do the same.

▸ Again, you can hire professional marketing services to help you get recruited. Be sure to do your research so that you know what you are paying for. Note that free offers usually are on a trial basis and will cost you money eventually. It is very difficult to know how effective these services will be for you since it's dependent on how many college coaches make use of the services.

» There are numerous college recruiting websites like recruitingrealities.com and informedathlete.com that explain the many myths and realities of college recruiting and simplify complexities of the NCAA rules and guidelines. Spend some time researching websites to better understand the NCAA and recruiting. The perfect starting place is ncaa.org.

» Be sure that you are not in violation of NCAA regulations if you pay for a recruiting service that is actually an agent. Adhere to the NCAA General Rule: **"An individual shall be ineligible for participation in an intercollegiate sport if he or she ever has agreed (orally or in writing) to be represented by an agent for the purpose of marketing his or her athletics ability or reputation in that sport."** (eligibilitycenter.org.) It is imperative that you or your parents contact the NCAA before hiring any sports "professional" as you pursue college scholarships.

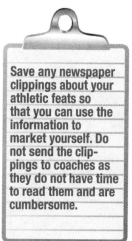

Save any newspaper clippings about your athletic feats so that you can use the information to market yourself. Do not send the clippings to coaches as they do not have time to read them and are cumbersome.

Brian Geist played baseball up until his junior year of high school, then decided to try out for the crew team. He joined a club crew team and transferred his work ethic to his new sport. He had the opportunity to compete in crew at east coast colleges during his senior year. He was selected to row in the Junior Olympics where he was seen by many college coaches in Greece. He would have never considered going to college on the East Coast until Yale University offered him an athletic scholarship. He graduated from Yale, and now coaches a women's club rowing program. He tells his girls that if they are athletic, hard working, and meet desirable size requirements (basically 5' 9" or taller), they have a good chance of getting a crew scholarship.

Build Your Student-Athlete Profile

- ▸ Make an attractive one page profile with your personal information, academic information, athletic achievements, and possibly a link to your YouTube video. Write it truthfully.

Use the following sample student-athlete profiles as models to create your own profile and market yourself to help college coaches identify you. These are sample student-athlete profiles. When creating your own:

- ▸ Use fonts that are easy to read. We suggest sans-serif fonts like Helvetica (sans-serif means there are no decorative marks on the ends of letters that are seen on Times New Roman). Only use black text.

- ▸ Stick to 3 categories: Athletic Information, Personal Information, and Academic Information.

- ▸ When designing your student-athlete profile, keep in mind that coaches will only quickly glance at your profile, so the most important information needs to be readily available.

- ▸ If you are including a picture, use free online editing software (if you don't have software on your computer already) to edit the picture. Increase the brightness and contrast to make your photo more crisp, and when you place it into your Word Document, put a black or dark gray outline around it.

- ▸ If you are including a paragraph of text for any reason, make sure it is left justified. This makes it easier to read because all of the text lines up on the left side.

- ▸ If you want to cut out your picture like the image below, you can use basic software like Paint. Open your image in Paint, zoom in, and use the eraser tool to erase the background. Or, you could print the picture out, cut it out with scissors, and scan the new photograph again.

Photo credit//Gary Jones, The Winning Shot

JOHN DOE

 **Quarterback #11**

PERSONAL INFORMATION

Age: 17 (February 26, 2002)

123 Elm Street
Anytown, USA 91234

Home Phone: 123-456-7891
Cell Phone: 123-456-7891
E-mail: student@email.com

Youtube URL: www.youtube/highlight.com

Parents:
Jane Doe: 123-456-7891
parentname@email.com
Joe Doe: 123-456-7891
parentname@email.com

ATHLETIC STATS

Position: Quarterback
Throws: Right
Height: 6' 2"
Weight: 190

22 Games
Passing Yardage: 2,675
Passing Touchdowns: 23
Completion Percentage: 61.2%
40-Yard Dash Time: 4. 65
Multi-Sport Athlete: Football and Baseball

ATHLETIC HONORS

» 2019 League Champion
» 2019 Section Champion
» 2019 State Bowl Runner-Up
» All-League First Team MVP
» Regional All-Star Game

COACH CONTACTS:

Varsity HS Coach: Jimmy Doe   123-555-2000
          The Best High School
          name@email.com

Throwing Coach: Mark Doe   123-555-2000
          Retired NFL Player
          name@email.com

ACADEMIC INFORMATION

The Best High School
Class of 2020
240 Awesome Ave.
Anytown, USA 91234
123-456-7891

9-12 GPA: 3.7
Class Rank: 208/552

Advanced Coursework:
» AP Government
» AP Microeconomics
» AP Macroeconomics

SAT: December 2019
Math: 650
Reading: 650
Writing: 650

SAT II: June 2019
Math 2: 650; Spanish: 650

Intended Major: Economics

» Honors Chemistry
» Honors Spanish 4
» Honors Pre-Calc

John Doe

Athletic Information

The Best High School Varsity Team
2020 Division II Section Runner-up

Position: Pitcher
Throws: Right
Bats: Right
Ht: 5' 9"
Wt.: 150
Age: 17 (July 26, 2002)

Varsity HS Coach: Mark Doe   123-555-6206
       The Best High School
       name@email.com

Pitching Coach: Rick Doe   123-555-4207
       Retired MLB Pitcher
Travel Team: Dave Doe   123-555-5386
       Baseball Academy

2020 Senior Fall Classic

Video:
youtube.com/baseballvid
Or DVD available on request

Photo Credit// Scott Hall
Spring 2020
Varsity Easter Tournament

Personal Information

John Doe

     123 Elm St.
     Anytown, USA 91234

     Home Phone: 123-555-8459
     Cell Phone: 123-555-8274
     E-mail: name@email.com

Parents:
   Joe Doe: 123-555-8558
       Teacher/Coach   The Best High School
       name@email.com

   Jane Doe: 123-555-9465
       Teacher/Coach   The Best High School
       name@email.com

Academic Information

The Best High School, Class of 2020
     240 Awesome Ave.
     Anytown, USA 91234
     123-555-2845

9-12 **GPA**   **3.7**
Class Rank   208/551

Junior Academic Merit Award

Advanced Coursework:
   AP Government
   AP Micro Economics
   AP Macro Economics
   Honors Chemistry
   Honors Spanish 4
   Honors Pre-Calculus

SAT   Dec. 4, 2019
       1670
       Math: 650, Reading: 510, Writing: 510
SAT II   Math 2: **610**; Spanish: **480** (6/2010)

Intended Major: Economics/Math

Create a Highlight Video

▸ Start videotaping yourself as early as your freshman year. Depending on the sport, some athletes will send videos out their sophomore or junior year, while other athletes will not send videos out until their senior year.

▸ If you can afford it, invest in a good digital video camera or borrow a friend's equipment. Your high school coach or school media director might loan you a camera to get footage of you in action.

▸ Edit the video with the appropriate angles and clips that college coaches are looking for. Ask parents or friends to videotape you while showing off fundamental skills and playing in game situations. For example, an outfielder would highlight his/her hitting mechanics and live hitting in a game. Then, he would capture the outfielder's first step to the ball after it comes off the bat. Finally, he would want to film the outfielder's catch, footwork, release and flight of the throw to all the bases.

▸ Many student athletes send a highlight video that doesn't help coaches. Coaches want to see certain actions and skills in the video to evaluate what they are specifically looking for. Ask college coaches, recruiters or scouts who may visit your school, club coaches, or some high school coaches for information about your specific sport. Ask them directly what they would like to see in a highlight video.

▸ When you are ready, you can either email college coaches with a video link or you can make a DVD (5-7 minutes) with personal highlights and, if needed, game film. Find out what coaches are looking for. We suggest you make both a DVD, and upload your video to YouTube or to a video website. Since most sites charge a fee, YouTube is one of the most frequently used sites.

▸ When you create your DVD and/or upload highlight videos to the web, make sure that they are of professional quality. Coaches receive a lot of videos that they describe as flat out hilarious back-yard videos because they are like those funniest home video clips that are poorly filmed and don't help the recruiter evaluate your skills. With these videos, coaches often do not see what they want to see.

▸ Create an introduction slide that includes a picture of yourself, your name, high school, city, state, graduation year, height and weight, and position.

▸ If you use music, make sure it is appropriate.

▸ Do not include parent/videographer commentary in the background. Also, do not include dead time.

- You could also create a conclusion, where you make a short statement about yourself, such as, "I work hard on and off the field. I have a passion to improve both academically and athletically. My goal is to play at the college level."

- Clearly label your DVD with your name, graduation year, position, possible jersey number, email and cell phone number

  » **Do not** send actual DVDs unless requested by the college coach

  » **Do** send your profile with your video link embedded to YouTube or websites for coaches to easily access.

SAMPLE LETTER TO GO WITH GAME/HIGHLIGHT FILM

If you are sending a DVD in the mail, type a letter to go along with it that presents you as confident and respectful. Keep it to one page.

Your Name   **Position:** _____
Your Address
Your Phone Number
Your Personal Email
Your High School/ Club Coach

College Coach or Contact Name
Title
College
Street address
City, State, Zip code

Date

Dear Coach **_Coach's Last Name_**,

I am writing to you because I am very interested in **college team name. (Now write why you are interested in this program).** I am currently a **your year in school and playing position** at **your high school.**

Include some of your highlights in your sport. Demonstrate evidence of improvement.

Not only am I working diligently on my athletics, but I have also been achieving success in the classroom. **Include information about how you are doing well academically in core classes, your current GPA and your class ranking. Include information about any testing results—ACT/SAT.**

I am sending a **DVD highlight or game film, profile, and/or competition schedule, etc.** to provide you with a more complete picture of who I am and what I can offer your program.

Sincerely,

Sign your name

Fill in all blue areas with your information, or the information for the college you are writing to. Be sure not to confuse different colleges you are writing to!

Use the Internet to Communicate

‣ Another option is to use an account on a social network website like Facebook where you can include highlight tapes and personal profiles. If you use one of these sites make sure that there is nothing inappropriate on them (including comments from friends) that might reflect negatively upon you.

‣ A few athletes build their own websites with a password (to keep personal information safe) from web hosting sites. This allows them to email the website link and password to college coaches. Be sure to maintain the website in a current and professional manner.

Make Contact

‣ Know the communication regulations and guidelines for phone, email, letter, and face-to-face contact. (Go to ncaa.org for specific sports' rules.)

‣ When coaches send you their athletic questionnaire or a letter of interest, make sure you respond. If you don't return questionnaires, the school may assume that you are not interested in its program.

‣ Go to the website of each school you are interested in and complete the student questionnaire. This will put you in the college's database.

‣ Communicate your playing interests to any schools of interest to you. Contact coaches via email and phone, but do not keep contacting a coach if he or she does not return your calls or emails. Be persistent, but don't be annoying.

‣ Write a short, concise two or three sentence email, using the college coach's name. Attach your profile with a playing schedule and video clip link to YouTube so coaches can view it if they wish.

‣ Be sure to employ email etiquette at all times, including proper grammar and spelling, and check your email regularly.

> Get a free email address to use in the recruitment process. Do not have a cheesy email address with inappropriate nicknames. Be professional.

Get Seen

- Recruiters want to see you play. Normally, just sending a DVD and/or hiring a scouting service to send out your information is not enough.

- Coaches recruit after seeing athletes in live games, not videos. Your video may get you noticed, but if you are fortunate, then someone will come to watch you compete, whether it is a head coach, an assistant, or a local recruiter for the college.

- If you haven't already, be sure you register with the NCAA Eligibility Center at the beginning of your junior year so that you work toward your "qualifier status." College coaches want to know what juniors are out there. Some college camps require you to do this before you attend their camps. Registering can be frustrating and take longer than you think. The website may not initially load so be patient and give it time. Make sure you receive an email receipt.

Attend College Camps

Attend college prospect summer camps. These are similar to weekend camps but they generally last 3-5 days. Student-athletes have the choice to commute or to stay in the dorms. This is a great opportunity to get noticed by the coaches of your favorite school. Athletes have gained acceptance to colleges, even as recruited walk-ons, by showing effort, desire, hard work, and character during an off-season or summer camp after impressing college coaches.

▸ To get seen, go on the Internet and search your sport and "college prospect camps." Or, go to the college website to find the various sports camps that are offered.

▸ During the off-season, attend weekend college prospect camps and clinics sponsored by the athletic programs of the colleges you want to attend. This will allow the college coaching staff to see you and will expose you to the different coaching philosophies, styles, and relationships.

▸ Send emails to coaches letting them know that you will be participating in the camp. These camps will help you gain a sense of how you perform in relationship to other athletes who attend. This is also an opportunity to see the athletic facilities, the campus, and the surrounding community.

▸ The value in attending multiple camps or clinics is that it gives you a sense of how you fit in with the program at that college.

▸ Generally, female athletes start attending these camps as high school freshman and male athletes during the sophomore or junior year. (Girls are often recruited earlier than boys as they mature sooner.)

Rachael Gross Thomas became a recruited walk-on and gained admission to UC Berkeley after being seen by the head coach at the school's soccer summer camp. She was not a highly recruited blue-chip athlete but demonstrated a coachable, intelligent, hard-working, positive attitude. Soccer gave her the opportunity not only to earn an undergraduate degree from a selective university, but it also allowed her to play four years of soccer with teammates who later became her life-long friends.

Attend Invitational Camps, Tournaments, or Combines

Attend key tournaments, showcases or combines as an individual. Some are first-come-first-serve; others are invitation only. Invitational events are often very inexpensive, however few get invited to participate. The key national invitational tournaments are more valuable than all other tournaments in terms of recruiting the best players. The benefit is you could be seen at one event by many college coaches. Many believe that this exposure is significant in being recruited. It is advised that you participate in showcases sponsored by a variety of organizations to increase your chances of being seen by a variety of coaches and recruiters. Be sure the showcase or tournament is one where coaches in attendance are those you want to see you play. There is a lot of misinformation about what coaches will be attending specific tournaments. It is highly recommended that you be selective and call college coaches to ask them which showcases are reliable and which ones they will be attending. Research how many years a showcase has existed and which coaches are guaranteed to attend. Once you decide which you will go to, be sure to email coaches to let them know you will be there and to invite them to watch you play.

- ▸ Get your name on college coaches' recruiting lists since many coaches attend showcases with lists in hand. Contact coaches ahead of time so you can get your name on one of their lists. Their lists include names from recruiting services, pre-identified blue-chip athletes, and the names from athletes themselves.

"**I introduced myself** to the coaches and asked questions about them personally. I wanted to show I was interested in them and their program. I hustled during drills and practice games, and took the initiative to do the little things without having to be asked by the coaches. If I made errors during the drills, I kept my head up and persevered. I kept emailing coaches to show my interest until I got offered partial scholarship money."
—Riley Drogenson
University of the Pacific Baseball Player

Attend team tournaments

Play with your competitive team to get exposure. Research the tournaments and showcases your team is entered in and evaluate if the cost makes it a good opportunity for you. In many cases, you do not have the choice. Your club or travel team coach will decide which showcases to attend based on helping their athletes get recruited. The good news is that many clubs offer excellent recruiting help. Competitive clubs will be sure that college coaches see athletes play and provide them with a student-profile compiled in a team binder for college coaches to view. Also, clubs put the profiles on their website for coaches to see. Clubs also help with recruiting by aiding athletes in choosing colleges that are a fit. Many club coaches build a network of college coaches to connect them to their athletes.

There are showcases and camps for all sports, hosted by all kinds of recruiting services and colleges. Do research and find out if the camp will be productive, so you will get valuable instruction to improve your game or be seen by college coaches. Key national level tournaments are the best for real recruiting opportunities. Many other ones are expensive and not worth the value.

Camps Organized by Professional Companies

Sports camps that are sponsored by outside companies on high school or college campuses provide another opportunity to be seen by coaches and recruiters. However, some of these are camps where recruiting is the focus and others are for-profit events. You can email college coaches and ask what camps are good opportunities for being seen and networking with coaches. Valuable camps offer good player to coach ratio, include player evaluations, connect high school players and transfer players to coaches, offer recruiting lectures, allow parents and players to interact with the coaches in question and answer sessions, and are reasonably priced.

How to Act at Recruiting Camps

Be on your best behavior at athletic events—we suggest you follow the tips below when you are at camps, tournaments, combines, showcases, games or meets:

› If appropriate, email coaches to let them know you will attend the event

› Be on time (at least 15 minutes early is ideal)

› If identification is not provided, wear some sort of identification like a jersey or number to identify you

› Avoid wearing jewelry

› Hustle all the time

› Be positive, encourage others

› Introduce yourself to coaches and ask them questions about their program to show your interest in them

› Know that coaches and scouts are always watching you, even when you don't think they are (so don't do anything unethical, like cutting in line or throwing trash on the ground)

"The road to college baseball may be very bumpy. Life is not a straight path; there are a lot of bumps in the road. It's important for potential student-athletes to communicate with college coaches. You really have to communicate so that you can be successful. The coach's main goal is to find players, and you might just be who they want, but you have to show them that you want it. There are three important questions to ask the coach. You need to practice asking the questions before you meet with a coach. Ask them the following questions:

1. What kind of player am I?

2. Do I fit in your program?

3. Are you recruiting players for my position?"

–Nathan Trosky
Baseball Showcase Camp Organizer

Make College Visits

▸ There are many ways to visit a college. The NCAA has specific rules about unofficial and official athletic visits. In addition to athletic visits, students and student-athletes can visit, tour, and make appointments with various college personnel on the campus. Have a clear plan before you visit any colleges. If you visit colleges during breaks, like Thanksgiving or other holiday breaks, know that the campuses will have a different atmosphere because students are home for the break. Check to make sure the admission office will be open during your visit. Some colleges host special visit days for high school juniors.

▸ Call ahead of time and ask the coach when it is a good time for you to stop by. Dropping by unannounced when the coach is busy will get you nothing. The reason for the visit is for you to make an impression and personal connection with the coach. Most importantly, you want to see if the college is a "fit" for you—athletically, academically, and socially.

▸ During your visit watch team practices and games. Watch how the players interact with one another and the coaching staff. Note how the coach treats the players. Get a sense of the atmosphere and the program. For more details on college visits, read Chapter 13 on unofficial and official college visits.

Andrew Wilson, with the help of his parents, was proactive in his recruiting journey. As a 7th grader, he joined one of the local competitive baseball teams and played travel (in addition to high school) baseball throughout his high school years. Andrew played in tournaments for exposure, took bimonthly hitting lessons, worked out in the gym, and studied to earn the best possible grades. He challenged himself in school by taking honors and AP courses as well as an online SAT course so he could make himself an academically desirable college applicant. In his junior year, during the fall, winter, and spring high school breaks, his parents took him to several camps hosted by various DI, DII, and DIII college programs. He met coaches and asked if he would be a fit in their programs. During the fall of his senior year, he realized he was an athletic fit for DIII programs needing outfielders. He emailed lots of coaches brief two sentences and attached his profile, including a highlight video clip link to YouTube. He was able to narrow his recruiting efforts based on coaches' responses and focused visits to DIII programs with strong academics. He realized there are several DIII schools across the nation with very strong business programs. He made appointments with admission counselors and coaches at those schools on the west coast. Andrew's visit to Willamette University in Oregon made the difference. He attended a weekend camp that allowed him to get to know the coach, hang out with the players, interview with an admissions counselor, and tour the campus. The coach liked Andrew's hustle and desire, and Andrew liked the coach's philosophy and coaching style. Andrew's search for a school took him to all kinds of campuses and programs, but by refining and being honest about his academic and athletic goals, he found Willamette. Andrew created the opportunity to play college baseball because he was proactive and initiated the recruiting process.

Network with Coaches, Alumni, and Teammates

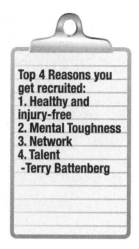

‣ In addition to the exposure the athletes gain by playing tournaments with clubs, many club coaches offer networking as a draw to their club. Club coaches are constantly developing relationships with college scouts and coaches to help their athletes get recruited. Some athletes choose to play on specific travel clubs because the coach knows lots of college coaches and can help their players find college opportunities. Those athletes on travel teams with a combination of good players and a schedule that includes tournaments to get exposure to college coaches, fair the best.

‣ Since college coaches belong to a loosely known "coaches' fraternity" you want to maintain great relationships with all coaches and recruiters, even if you are not really interested in a particular school. You never know when a coach may refer your name to a coach from a school that you really want to play for.

‣ Talk to other parents who may have insights into the recruiting process.

‣ Network with friends and teammates about their experiences to help you gather information.

‣ Contact high school alumni about their involvement in recruiting and college athletics.

"**I worked hard to qualify** for the Junior Olympics because I love pole vaulting and wanted to get my name out there. My family and I went across the country to show coaches I'm very involved in track, and serious about preparing for college athletics. I placed in the top 8 at a qualifying meet, top 5 in regionals, and then declared my intention to compete at the 16-17 Young Women Event. After earning a top 20 national ranking, I was noticed by college coaches. I was able to meet with them and learn about their programs. The experience boosted my recruiting opportunities and helped me to think about where I would be a good fit. I will send emails to follow-up, and complete lots of college questionnaires with my Junior Olympic marks. I am excited to see where track takes me."

–Annelise Spargo, high school pole-vaulter

Follow-up

‣ Send thank you notes to all coaches and college personnel you make contact with.

‣ Maintain email or phone communication with the head coach or assistant so they know you are sincere about your interest in their program. Keep your options open until you absolutely know which college you will attend.

Apply to Colleges

› Apply to many colleges and universities and try to gain acceptance so that you will have choices and can negotiate your options and scholarship/financial aid packages from different schools. Coaches frequently communicate with college admissions and financial aid personnel to get the best financial support package for you. Pursue your dream school, but always have a back-up college or two to attend. (See Chapter 15 for application details and Chapter 16 for scholarships and financial aid overview.)

▸ Check application deadlines. Schools are getting more impacted so they are more selective and expensive. Many applications can be submitted after October 1st.

⁝⁝

Chase Dickson was a realistic DIII baseball recruit. Even though playing baseball at the local community college was a realistic option, he made sure to become a qualifier, taking rigorous high school classes and preparing for the SAT/ACT. He played competitive travel baseball as well as high school baseball. In the fall of his senior year, he attended a showcase camp, two college prospect camps, and one national showcase tournament where over 300 college coaches watched. He attended the showcase camp to get exposure to several DI, DII, DIII, and NAIA coaches, and attended college prospect camps to visit the school and facilities, and also, to get evaluated and get advice on his pitching ability and potential fit. Before the showcase tournament, he initiated contact by emailing coaches two sentences informing them of the team he was competing on with field locations and game times. He also attached his student-athlete profile with a YouTube link to his pitching highlight video. He only selected schools he felt he had the ability to be an academic and athletic fit - based on his experiences and coach evaluations from previous camps. Several coaches watched him and many returned his emails. He followed up with visits to the schools and was welcomed by several DIII coaches. If he would not have initiated the recruiting process, he would not have had the opportunity to play college ball. However, while attending a new student admittance orientation, Chase realized that the school he was planning on attending was too small. He decided he would be a fit for a big campus with large class sizes, and PAC-12 sports program where he could be a sports fan. Chase's desire to play DIII baseball morphed into a desire for intramural sports, fraternity life, and a focus on his academics. He learned that athletes need to keep all their options open preparing for academics as well as athletics since they never know how their plans may change.

⁝⁝

Last Words...

Now you have a number of ideas, options, and tools to market yourself and get recruited. Many Division I schools with successful athletic programs have large budgets to recruit across the country, and know who the blue-chip athletes are and will find them. There are thousands of DII and DIII, NAIA and JUCO programs that cannot afford to recruit nationally which is why you need to be proactive in seeking exposure and marketing yourself. You will need to find a balance between getting exposed and the time and cost of attending numerous events. Remember, no one can guarantee you a place in college athletics.

Keep your options open.

Anything is possible.

Chapter 12
Top 10 Plays

1. Keep your options open—research a variety of colleges and sports programs

2. Make yourself a desirable student-athlete by earning good grades

3. Initiate the recruiting process

4. Build an attractive student-athlete profile

5. Create a highlight DVD or link on your profile

6. Make contact and email coaches with your profile

7. Get seen at camps and tournaments

8. Network with friends, coaches, teammates, high school alumni, and parents

9. Follow-up and communicate with coaches

10. Research recruiting services before committing

In your shoes...

Looking Back on the Recruiting Journey

"I think athletes should do the recruiting process on their own. My dad did not make a single call. This is the best way to go because it shows coaches your maturity. There are so many overbearing parents. Recruiting is starting earlier and earlier, but be sure to start making plans by your sophomore year. Look at schools informally your sophomore and junior years. Make a list of about 15 schools that you are interested in and be persistent. Decide how involved you want to be and do your best.

The fall of your junior year is key. You have to play your best soccer, attend showcases, and email coaches your tournament schedule. Regional showcases are so important. Olympic Development Program (ODP) is not essential but it was another recruiting opportunity for me. Being athletic and being able to run for days as well as getting game experience is key. Be realistic of what you are capable of on and off the field. Do not send game film unless a coach asks for it. After meeting coaches, send follow-up emails saying you enjoyed meeting them at the tournaments.

I applied to a range of schools and soccer programs. I applied to a few schools I knew I could get into and to those that were a stretch or reach to get into. Some college coaches have pull with the admissions offices. There is a network of coaches and some of them are friends and will pass on names of players they think would be a fit. Take all of your official visits. Ask what your role will be on the team and really be sure you are a fit for that program and coaching style. Athletics is not a career so pick a school to get the education you want also. I chose to attend Arizona State University because it was nice to be wanted by the coach. I was accepted into the honors college and received a 66% academic scholarship. The coach said he would take care of the rest of the costs.

My goal, after signing my National Letter of Intent, was to stay injury free and relax a little academically. In the spring of my senior year, I finally got to do what I wanted to socially. The summer before college should be spent getting stronger in the weight room. Take care of your back by using proper lifting technique. Most college coaches send their recruits summer workouts. In the end, you have to set your priorities and know what you have to get done. What I can control, I do. The busier I am, the better I do. You have to keep pushing yourself, but find balance or you will burn out. Be proactive and focus on both academics and athletics."

-Liz Harkin
Former Arizona State University Soccer &
U-20 National Team Play

Making
UNOFFICIAL & OFFICIAL COLLEGE VISITS

Chapter Game Plan

UNOFFICIAL VISITS

OFFICIAL PAID VISITS

- Visit Checklist
- Official Campus Visit Checklist
- Athletic, Academic, Environmental and Cultural Questions for College Visits
- Non-Athletic Related Overnight Visits for All Students

Ask all the right questions.

There are two types of NCAA regulated visits: unofficial visits and official paid visits. The NCAA has specific rules regarding both. There is a limit of five official visits a student-athlete may make, but there are no limits on unofficial visits. Official visits are paid for by the college.

UNOFFICIAL VISITS

Use the checklist in this chapter for your campus visit. Have a game plan or strategy when you visit to make the most out of your time there. Know ahead of time what to ask and what to look for.

Unofficial visits are paid for entirely by the student-athlete's family, and can be organized and planned by the family, or by the college coaching staff. Normally, it is the highly recruited athlete who will be awarded scholarship money who is offered a structured unofficial visit. Thus, the only real difference between an "official" and "unofficial" visit for a recruited scholarship athlete is who pays for the visit.

On the Wednesday after a Sunday Nike football combine, the Boise State quarterback coach emailed Jimmy Laughrea to say they were in the office and to give him a call. After Jimmy called, the head coach made a verbal offer over the phone for a full-ride athletic scholarship. The coach recommended that Jimmy visit the school before deciding. Jimmy's dad made airline reservations and accompanied him on the visit. The family paid for everything including the airfare, car rental, parking, hotel, and meals. Jimmy arrived and met the entire coaching staff, spoke with an academic advisor, took a tour, and went to lunch with the coaches (but paid for his own lunch). On the flight home, Jimmy decided to verbally commit to Boise.

On your own, visit, unofficially, as many schools as possible. Take tours. Observe athletic practices. Make an appointment with the coach and an admissions officer to ask athletic and academic questions. If you set this up beforehand, the coach will set aside a half hour rather than the five minutes you would get if you went unannounced. You will be demonstrating to the coach that you have interest in the school.

Be sure to check with the NCAA recruiting rules about what you can and cannot do during these visits, especially in regards to talking to coaches. If you are playing in tournaments, always try to make unofficial visits to nearby campuses. If you attend college prospect camps, turn those trips into unofficial visits too by touring the campus, checking out the facilities, and getting to know the feeling of the school environment.

Visits are very important in helping you distinguish the subtle differences of the various campuses and programs. They should help you determine what colleges you want to attend or compete for. You also want to consider if you would be happy relocating to that community after college. On the other hand, many student athletes go away for college athletics to experience a completely different environment, knowing that they plan to return home after college.

During an unofficial visit, be very careful not to violate NCAA rules. You must pay for all expenses on unofficial visits. Do not let anyone pay for your meals, transportation, sporting events, college t-shirts, etc. One exception is that the college can pay for three passes to a home athletic event. Sometimes, these visits can be very costly to student-athlete families, so chose them wisely.

Jill Wirt proactively sought out opportunities to play DII or NAIA college volleyball. On a trip to Southern California, her mom helped her set up appointments with coaches, financial aid officers, and student services to arrange for official campus tours. Jill was not a highly recruited scholarship athlete so she took the initiative to find opportunities to play college ball. She emailed numerous coaches about volleyball tournaments and Junior Olympics where she was playing. She sent the coaches her student-athlete profile, a highlight film and her club team schedule and her jersey number. Coaches then had an opportunity to watch her play at these events and to meet Jill.

OFFICIAL PAID VISITS

In terms of the NCAA official visit regulations, student-athletes can only take official visits when they are seniors in high school. (Note: many highly recruited blue-chip athletes have verbally committed before they are seniors in high school or before they make an official visit. Some even sign letters of intent, during the signing period, before they make an official visit.) Student-athletes are limited to the amount of official visits they can take. This is why you need to narrow down to five colleges (at most) for your official visits, since the NCAA DI and DII only allow five official visits total.

You may only make one official visit per college. Don't waste your or the college's time by visiting schools you are not truly interested in. If you are unsure about a school, take a visit, as it will help you make up your mind. Perhaps consider the distance from your home to the college and accept visits that are farther away. During your visits, take good notes, and make sure you always send a thank you note to all personnel you spoke with after the visits. See the *NCAA Guide* for rules and rule changes regarding official visits.

The school will work to impress the student-athlete during official visits.

NCAA Division III differs from DI and DII in that the DIII association has no rule about the maximum number of visits to college, (official or unofficial), although you can still only make one official visit per college. Student-athletes interested in DIII sports can go on 10 or even more official visits, although they can only officially visit each school once.

If you are offered an official visit and are interested in that school, take it. Ask many questions like how many other athletes are being recruited for your position, and about the depth chart. You may want to attend a particular college, yet the depth chart for your position is deep so your playing time opportunity may be limited. These are all factors you should consider when making your decision.

Coaches will make home visits when they are competing for a highly desirable blue-chip student-athlete.

Twin sisters Jessica and Alison Hamby competed together on AAU competitive and national water polo teams. They sacrificed many weekends when they would spend two hours traveling to competitive club practice and then three hours in the water playing. They lived much of their teen lives in the water, but were also very active in school activities and enjoyed competing on their high school water polo team. Their dad spent many hours emailing college coaches beginning in their sophomore year, while they traveled to AAU tournaments to be seen by college coaches. In the spring of their senior year, they narrowed their college choices ranging from small colleges on the East Coast to large universities on the West Coast. The girls visited campuses to help them determine which one would be the right fit. While they didn't get into their first choices they visited and fell in love with Marist, a small college in New York. Marist offered a financial aid and athletic package amounting to 50% of their education costs. They are extremely happy with the water polo program, their teammates, strength & conditioning coach, head water polo coach, and the academic and social life. They found the perfect fit because of their visit.

Visit Checklist

Since you will make an impression on the coaches based on what you wear, be sure to pack the right items. Stack Magazine suggests the following:
- Clothes
    - » Two pairs of socks (no holes)
    - » Two pairs of underwear
    - » A jacket (not a letterman's jacket)
    - » Nice jeans
    - » Three shirts/blouses: dress, long-sleeved, t-shirt—all color coordinated so you can layer depending on the weather
    - » Belt
    - » Shoes—not dress shoes, but not sneakers
    - » Pajamas (no sleeping nude)
    - » Khakis, tie, dress, dress shoes, boots (if you are visiting a prep school like Harvard)
- Extras
    - » Small pillow & blanket/sleeping bag

‣ Toiletries

   » If you are flying, make sure to have container sizes appropriate for air travel in a Ziploc bag

   » Shampoo/conditioner

   » Deodorant

   » Toothbrush/toothpaste

   » Lip balm

   » Towel

   » Shower shoes (flip-flops)

Official Campus Visit Checklist

Note to Parents: Your teen will spend most of the official visit with the team. Often parents have the opportunity to take the tour and to meet with college coaches, admissions and financial aid personnel. We do suggest that parents play a role in discussing financial aid, merit (academic) and athletic scholarship offers to obtain the best financial package. If a parent does accompany a teen on an official visit, please allow your teen to interact with the players and coaches without you.

‣ The host school will generally make all the visit arrangements, ranging from appointments, practices, tours, athletic events, meals, and overnight accommodations. Most official visits will be for a full 48 hours with little free time.

‣ Often you will be in a small group with other potential recruits.

In hindsight, Peyton Thompson wishes he had asked the right questions during his official visit. He realized once he was playing college football that he did not ask questions about athletic facilities, trainers, and fan support—which were some of the most important aspects of his athletic experience. Fortunately, he had a successful football career at California State University, San Jose and signed on with an NFL team, although he wishes he had known the right questions to ask during his visit.

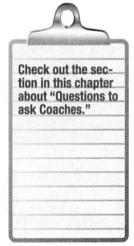

Check out the section in this chapter about "Questions to ask Coaches."

When you make any visits, take along a list of questions to ask when you are on campus. Coaches, tour guides, and admission officers will ask you if you have any questions, so always have a few pre-planned questions so you won't feel uncomfortable and speechless. Make it your responsibility to keep the conversation going.

☑ **CAMPUS VISIT CHECKLIST**

Note to Parents: This checklist can be used for an unofficial or official visit. For un-official visits, don't be helicopter parents (hovering every minute) during visits and tours. Allow your son/daughter to be responsible. Refrain from taking over and asking the visit questions. We do suggest that parents play a role in discussing financial aid, merit (academic) and athletic scholarship offers to obtain the best financial package.

Before the visit

☐ Call for an appointment with:
  » Head coach
  » Financial aid officer
  » Admissions officer
  » Compliance officer
☐ Make a reservation for a campus tour (some are booked up to 8 months in advance!)
☐ Download a map of the campus
☐ Take a notepad and questions with you
☐ Bring a camera and take pictures of sports facilities, dorms, etc. to help you remember the visit. Print pictures with notations and put in your crate.
☐ Attend the admissions office group information meeting if offered
☐ Be a great listener and note-taker
☐ Take a formal campus tour when classes are in session (this is normally between September and April)
☐ Meet with an admissions officer, and verify admission requirements
☐ Determine actual college costs
  » Ask about financial aid opportunities
  » Pick up financial aid forms
☐ Informally tour the campus with your parents
  » Talk to a student in the career center
  » Attend a class
  » Look at dorms you did not visit on the formal tour
  » Check out the college bookstore(s)—on and off campus
  » Eat in the cafeteria
  » Pick up and read a student newspaper
  » Read student bulletin boards on campus
  » Talk with students and alumni—
    ↳ ask why they chose the college
    ↳ ask what they dislike about the college
    ↳ ask what they do on weekends
☐ Observe an athletic practice
☐ Meet with the coach (if allowed)
☐ Talk to seniors and freshmen on the team; talk to those who play and those who don't
☐ Walk or drive around the surrounding community

After the visit

☐ Record all visits in your visit log
☐ Keep business cards of anyone you talk to
☐ Send thank you notes to those who spoke with you for considering you for their program
☐ Put all your notes in your college crate in the college folder

Below are some sample questions for you to review and get ideas. Visit our website at dcipress.com for an extra copy of this template.

POSSIBLE ATHLETIC, ACADEMIC, AND COLLEGE LIFE QUESTIONS TO ASK

College: _____   Date visited:_____

Athletic Questions to Ask Coaches

Circle athletic program: DI, DII, DIII, NAIA, JUCO

Notes: _____
_____
_____

‣ What role would I play on the team? (redshirt, practice player, starter, specific position)
‣ Where am I on your "depth chart"? How many players are competing for my position?
‣ Who else is being recruited for my position?
‣ Do I have to grey-shirt to eventually play?
‣ Will I be redshirted my first year?
‣ How much athletic playing time would I get? (Be careful if the coach is guaranteeing playing time. What if you get hurt? What if he discovers better recruits?)
‣ What is your coaching style and your philosophy for motivation and discipline? (Head coach and staff)
‣ What are the training and conditioning expectations in-season and off-season?
‣ What is a typical day for a student-athlete, in regards to classes, practice, studying and traveling? What are coaches' expectations?
‣ What is the current team GPA?
‣ Will I receive an athletic scholarship, and is it full or partial?
‣ Are there academic scholarship opportunities or financial aid packages that you (head coach) would assist me with?
‣ What is the traditional number of invited and uninvited (preferred or re-cruited) walk-ons?
‣ Can walk-ons earn scholarships/financial aid?
‣ What is your quota for walk-ons who receive special consideration for admissions?
‣ What are graduation rates for athletes in my sport?
‣ When does your coaching contract end?
‣ What is the networking potential that would help me to play professional sports?
‣ Will I be required to provide proof of medical insurance? Is medical insurance provided by the college?
‣ Who is responsible for my medical expenses if I'm seriously injured while competing?

Use questions on the day of your visit. Make a copy of it, or download it at dcipress.com before your visit.

Use these questions on the day of your visit. Make a copy of it, or download it at dcipress.com before your visit.

Academic Questions to Ask

Notes: _____

_____

_____

Ask these questions to an admission advisor

- What are the admission requirements and application deadlines?
- Are interviews required? Group or individual?
- Which standardized test scores are required?
- What qualities should prospective students have?
- How competitive is it to get into the college? Will being a recruited athlete help me get in?
- Is the college more competitive or collegial?
- What are the major/minor degree programs that are offered and when must a major be decided?
- How many students attend the college?
- What is the average class size?
- How available are professors during office hours?
- What is the percentage of courses taught by a professor vs. a graduate assistant?
- What percentage of scholarship athletes graduate?
- Are there academic services for student-athletes?
- What academic support programs are required for freshmen student-athletes? (ie. study halls, tutoring, study skills, etc.)
- Is there academic support for student-athletes with learning disabilities?
- Are there internship programs available?
- What is the cost of tuition, room & board or rent?
- When is the financial aid deadline?
- Do scholarship athletes pay for summer school?
- What are graduate program opportunities?
- What are the career placement opportunities and networking potential?
- Do career recruiters come on campus to hire graduates?

College Life Questions to Ask

Notes: _____
_____
_____

Use these questions on the day of your visit. Make a copy of it, or download it at dcipress.com before your visit.

- ‣ What is the college known for? Does it have a reputation and is it a valid concern?
- ‣ What is the physical and geographical environment? (beach, city, mountains, urban, rural, high altitude, etc.)
- ‣ What is the weather like? (cold winters, mild, humid summers, windy, etc.)
- ‣ What is the general atmosphere on campus?
- ‣ How safe is the campus and the surrounding neighborhoods?
- ‣ What is the culture of campus and of students (intellectual, social, religious, political, fashion, lifestyle, etc.)
- ‣ What is the social life on campus? (fraternities, sororities, student government, clubs, extracurricular activities, athletics, performing arts, parties, dances, concerts, fitness facilities, student recreation center, intramurals, etc.)
- ‣ Are there club sports and intramural opportunities in my sport and other sports that may interest me?
- ‣ What are the college rules? (drinking, smoking, drugs, curfews)
- ‣ What is the social life of the surrounding community? (nearby city, museums, parks, theatres, cultural events, concerts, etc. vs. rural environment with outdoor recreational activity)
- ‣ What percentage of students are residents vs. commuters?
- ‣ Do most students drive cars or ride bikes?
- ‣ How available is parking? Is there a cost to park?
- ‣ What are the on-campus living conditions like? (dorms, fraternities, apartments, etc.)
- ‣ How are the dorms set up? (suites, singles, doubles, triples, high-rise dorms, apartments, etc.)
- ‣ Are the dorms co-ed or single sex?
- ‣ How are roommates selected and how can they be changed if you are not compatible?
- ‣ Are the dorms noisy or quiet?
- ‣ What facilities are provided in the dorm? (Microwave, refrigerator, washer/dryers, etc.)
- ‣ What types of food services (cafeteria) and meal plans are available?
- ‣ What is the distance from freshmen dorms to the campus?
- ‣ Is there student housing guaranteed for four years? If not, how many years?
- ‣ What are the off-campus living situations like? (apartments, rooms for rent, houses)
- ‣ How expensive is it to live off campus?
- ‣ What are the rules for freshmen regarding living off campus?

After pole vaulting for over four years and placing third in state as a junior, Katie Zingheim was pursued by many colleges during her senior year to become a student athlete at their schools. After narrowing down her choices to UCLA, UC Berkeley, and Stanford, her official visits to the campuses were very influential in helping make her ultimate decision. The visits gave her a feel for the teammates and the overall atmosphere for the sport at each school, as well as the academic and social environment of the college overall, and after those tours she was able to make the right decision for herself. Katie will be a sophomore at Stanford University this fall and continues to pole vault.

Not only are you able to make athletic unofficial and official visits, there is a fairly new program where some private colleges offer overnight visits to all students. While this is not an athletic sponsored visit, student-athletes are encouraged to take advantage of this type of program if it is offered.

NON-ATHLETIC RELATED OVERNIGHT VISITS FOR ALL STUDENTS

Many colleges now allow students in their senior year of high school to make an overnight visit, between the months of September through April so students may learn what a day in the life of a student at that college is like. Visit specific college websites to find out how to make a reservation, and check to see how far in advance you need to arrange an overnight visit. You will be assigned to a student host. Most visits include:

‣ Meals on campus

‣ Visits to classes

‣ Meetings with professors and coaches

‣ Interviews with admissions and financial aid personnel

‣ A tour of the campus

‣ Evening activities on campus (concerts, sporting events, plays, etc.)

Last Words...

For most high school students, it is best to expand your options by making college visits. You may discover that certain schools do not appeal to you and that others are a great fit for you. When you visit campuses, make sure you take notes either on a notepad or on your phone to record notes, reactions and responses to what you like and don't like about the campus, team, and athletic program. Taking thorough notes and recording your immediate impressions can help you make the difficult decision of where you will study and compete when the time comes. Parents and students, note that high school student-athletes are not always supervised by adults during their entire official visit. If they are staying with upperclassmen, they may wind up at parties with drugs and alcohol. High school students may want to fit in and "be cool" and even experience peer pressure to participate. We have found that many parents are shocked at what transpires on college campuses during official visits. We suggest you have a discussion, prior to the visit, regarding appropriate and safe behavior.

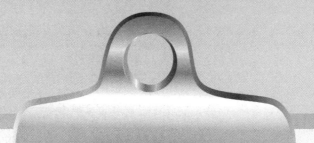

Chapter 13
Top 10 Plays

1. Make as many visits as possible to find a fit

2. Know that unofficial visits are paid for by the athlete and family

3. Be careful not to violate NCAA rules while visiting unofficially—
    call ahead and make appointments with the head coach, finan-
    cial aid officer, and an admission's counselor/officer

4. When at an athletic tournament, visit nearby colleges

5. Know that official visits are limited and paid for by the college

6. Know there is unsupervised time during official visits

7. Be prepared for peer pressure when making official visits

8. Take good mental notes or jot down first impressions of colleges
    to refer to when you return home

9. Ask the right questions –the stuff that matters to you

10. Parents, don't hover over your teens on unofficial visits; allow
    the student-athletes to communicate directly with college
    personnel

14

Taking
THE ACT &
SAT TESTS

Do your best when your best is needed.

Getting a college athletic scholarship depends not only on your athletic ability but other factors as well. Along with getting good grades, taking either the SAT or ACT and scoring well is one of the most important components of your college application.

This chapter will offer you an overview of the tests, registration, test-preparation plans, test-taking strategies, and will provide you with a wide variety of online resources.

AN OVERVIEW OF COLLEGE ADMISSIONS TESTS

As part of the application process, students must take standardized tests that colleges use to assess your academic readiness and potential, just as scouts evaluate you on your potential for college sports. Colleges require one of two tests: either the SAT or the ACT. To prepare for these exams, it is important that you take the preliminary practice tests, the PSAT or PLAN, as a sophomore to get feedback about your strengths and weaknesses on standardized tests.

Most 4-year colleges accept either test, so it is to your advantage to take both so you can choose the exam you perform better on. Even though you only have to submit one, taking both will allow you to discover which type of test matches your strengths.

There are a few differences worth noting about the ACT and the SAT. The SAT primarily evaluates critical thinking and problem solving, while the ACT is content based and measures what you have learned in school. The SAT tests more vocabulary than the ACT. The ACT includes science reasoning and trigonometry; the SAT does not. While the SAT has less difficult math, it has more math questions. The SAT has a guessing penalty; the ACT does not. The SAT requires writing and the ACT has an optional writing section (for those colleges requiring writing). The SAT is longer than the ACT.

A perfect score on the SAT is 2400 and a perfect sore on the ACT is 36. (Many "academic college showcase" tournaments require a minimum SAT score of 1700 to participate.)

ACT/SAT SCORE COMPARISON

If you took both tests, check your score comparison to find out which test score you should use on your college application.

| ACT Composite
English, math,
reading, science | SAT I
critical reading &
math without writing |
| --- | --- |
| 15 | 830 |
| 17 | 870 |
| 19 | 910 |
| 20 | 950 |
| 21 | 990 |
| 22 | 1030 |
| 23 | 1070 |
| 24 | 1110 |
| 25 | 1150 |
| 26 | 1190 |
| 27 | 1220 |
| 28 | 1260 |
| 29 | 1300 |
| 30 | 1340 |
| 31 | 1380 |
| 32 | 1420 |
| 33 | 1460 |
| 34 | 1510 |
| 35 | 1560 |
| 36 | 1600 |

–collegboard.org

Note that community colleges **do not require** SAT or ACT scores. However, some community college-bound students may want to take the SAT or ACT to use their scores for scholarship applications or if they transfer to a four year school after one year of community college. Students often change their minds, so taking the exams will keep more doors open as graduation nears. You might even get an offer at a four-year university late in your senior year and if you have taken the tests you will be eligible to attend.

The Details of the PSAT/PLAN and the SAT/ACT

In your sophomore year, you will prepare for the SAT/ACT by taking the PSAT and/or the PLAN.

PSAT (Preliminary SAT)

- Given only once a year, in October
- Measures critical reading, math problem-solving, and writing skills (in multiple-choice format)
- Is the qualifying test for the National Merit Scholarship Competition (NMSQT)
- Is used for the National Achievement and National Hispanic Recognition programs
- Students who score high will be contacted by many universities
- An asterisk by your Selection Index scores means you did NOT qualify for the NMSC competitions for awards
- Points lost for incorrect answers (except grid-in questions)
- Most students will not answer all questions correctly

PLAN (Preliminary ACT test)

- 4 sections: English (50 questions in 30 minutes), mathematics (40 questions in 40 minutes), reading (25 questions in 20 minutes), and science (30 questions in 25 minutes) for a total of 1 hour and 55 minutes
- Includes an interest survey, 65 minutes
- Free practice materials can be found at act.org

SAT

- Offered several times throughout the school year (check online or with your counselor for dates)
- 4 sections: writing (35 minute multiple-choice section & 25 minute essay section), mathematics (two 25 minute sections and one 20 minute section), critical reading (two 25 minute sections and one 20 minute section), for a total of 3 hours & 45 minutes
- The writing multiple-choice section emphasizes rules of grammar and usage. You must recognize errors, and improve sentences and paragraphs
- The essay in the writing section is expository. You will read a short excerpt or quotation and respond to a prompt that asks your opinion about an issue (see Chapter 4 for suggestions for expository essays)
- The math section features more advanced concepts taught in Algebra I and II, including functions, geometry, statistics, probability, and data analysis. Some answers are multiple choice, while other answers are student-produced
- Calculators may be used on the math section

- The three sections (writing, reading, and math) are worth up to 800 points each, add up to a score of 2400
- There is a penalty for wrong answers

ACT

- Offered several times throughout the school year (check online or with your counselor for dates)
- 4 sections: English (75 questions in 45 minutes), mathematics (60 questions in 60 minutes), reading (40 questions in 35 minutes), science (40 questions in 35 minutes) for a total of 2 hours and 55 minutes
- The English sections contain punctuation, strategy, grammar and usage, organization, sentence structure, and style
- The math section features pre-algebra, elementary and intermediate algebra, coordinate and plane geometry, and trigonometry
- The reading section covers excerpts from social studies, natural sciences, prose fiction, and humanities
- The science section includes data representation, research summaries, and conflicting viewpoints in biology, chemistry, physics and earth sciences
- Calculators may only be used on the math section
- The four sections, each out of 36 points, are averaged out, with the highest possible average being 36
- There is no penalty for incorrect answers
- Includes a career interests inventory
- There is an optional 30 minute essay, which some colleges require that costs an addition test fee. The prompt will present an issue and ask you to take a stance on it.

Need more information? Go to collegboard.org for information on the SAT, and act.org for information on the ACT.

AT A GLANCE: THE SAT AND THE ACT

	SAT	ACT
When is it administered?	Seven times per year	Six times per year
What is the test structure?	10-section exam: 3 Critical Reading, 3 Math, 3 Writing, and 1 random section. The random section will be either reading, writing, or math.	4-section exam: English, Math, Reading, and Science Reasoning. An experimental test is added to tests on certain dates only, and is clearly labeled as experimental.
What is the test content?	**Math**: up to 9th grade basic geometry and Algebra II **Science**: none **Reading**: sentence completions, short and long critical reading passages, reading comprehension **Writing**: an essay, and questions testing grammar, usage, and word choice	**Math**: up to trigonometry **Science**: charts, experiments **Reading**: four passages, one each of prose fiction, social science, humanities, and natural science **English**: grammar **Writing**: optional essay
Is there a penalty for wrong answers?	Yes	No
How is the test scored?	200-800 per section, added together for a combined score. A 2400 is the highest possible combined score.	1-36 for each subject, averaged for a composite score. A 36 is the highest possible composite score.
Are scores from all test sittings sent to schools?	Yes. If a student requests a score report be sent to specific colleges, the report will include the scores the student received on every SAT taken.	No. There is a "Score Choice" option. Students can choose which schools will receive their scores AND which scores the schools will see.
Are there other uses for the exams?	Scholarship purposes.	Scholarship purposes, and certain statewide testing programs.
Best time to register?	At least 6 weeks before the test date	At least 4 weeks before the test date

SAT/ACT AND NCAA ELIGIBILITY REQUIREMENTS

 ‣ Remember the NCAA has specific eligibility requirements for the SAT/ACT.
 ‣ DI has a sliding scale for your test scores and GPA.
 ‣ DII has a minimum 820 SAT score (excluding the writing section) and 68 ACT summative score (the sum of all four sections, not the composite score).
 ‣ NCAA uses reading and math scores on the SAT, not the writing section.
 ‣ NCAA uses the sum of the 4 sections on the ACT: English, math, reading and science. A perfect score is 144.
 ‣ NCAA requires that all scores be sent directly to the Eligibility Center by marking the code of "9999" when you register

SAT II Subject Tests

Like all of the campuses, some colleges have dropped the SAT II subject test requirement, although other colleges still need it. Check to see if the colleges you are interested in call for those additional exams. The NCAA does not require the writing tests.

If the college you are planning to attend recommends the SAT II subject tests, be sure you are prepared for it. Students can take up to three SAT Subject exams in one sitting, although most students don't take more than two tests in one day. Each test is one hour, and students cannot take both the SAT II subject tests and the regular SAT on the same day. It is important to work out your schedule so that you are able to take the SAT II test immediately after completing the corresponding high school course. Be sure to make your schedule early so that you have completed both the SAT I and SAT II exams by the end of your junior year.

The chart on the next page lists the different SAT subject tests and their corresponding class you should complete before taking the test. If you have not taken Honors or AP/IB courses, you may need to study and review a little bit more than others before taking the subject tests.

SAT SUBJECT TESTS

Go to collegboard.org for detailed explanations and practice questions for each test.

English
Literature

History
U.S. History
World History

Mathematics
Level 1 (2 years of algebra + 1 year of geometry)
Level 2 (requirements for Level 1 + pre-calculus or trigonometry)

Science
Biology, Ecological
Biology, Molecular (for pre-med & science majors)
Chemistry
Physics

Languages
French (listening portion optional)
German (listening portion optional)
Spanish (listening portion optional)
Others: Modern Hebrew, Italian, Latin, Chinese, Japanese, and Korean

Register to take the SAT

Visit your College & Career Center or go online to collegboard.org to find testing dates and registration information. Parents will need to provide credit card information for payment.

Create a free College Board account online. You need to obtain your high school code from your high school counselor, College & Career Center, or from your school's website.

Register to take the ACT

Register for the ACT online at act.org. You need to obtain your high school code from your counselor, College & Career Center, or your school's website.

Register to take the SAT II

If you are applying to a college that has impacted majors where they recommend that you take subject tests, you need to register for the SAT II test. Check with the college before registering for this optional test.

Reporting Scores

It is important when you register for the SAT and/or ACT that you identify the colleges you want the scores sent to. Take time beforehand to make a list of schools where you feel you will be a fit academically and athletically. You can send results to 4 colleges for free, but you will have to pay for each additional report that is sent out.

The **NCAA requires that student-athletes have their scores sent directly to the Eligibility Center. Use the code "9999"** when you register for the SAT or ACT, and know this report will count as one of your free reports.

Scheduling your test dates and test deadlines

A popular strategy with taking the SAT and/or the ACT is to start in December or January of your junior year to establish your baseline score. Then, after preparing to improve your score, take the tests again in the spring. When you take the SAT or ACT, you have the option to pay an additional fee to receive a list of your answers along with the questions you were asked. You can also pay to receive your scores on the written test, and can use this information to better prepare for the next test.

Juniors should take both the SAT and ACT by the spring of their junior year, and then re-test during the fall of their senior year if they want to improve their scores. Some athletes will need to schedule around their athletics, so taking tests in the fall of junior year might be preferable. Applicants will also need to finish testing in the fall for Early Admissions. Students will need to research individual schools to confirm the final date for testing.

TEST PREP

Just as you showcase your athletic talents, you also want to showcase your academic abilities. You will need to familiarize yourself with the structure and content of these tests, using any of a variety of ways to prepare. You can study by yourself, take online practice tests or mini-review courses, or attend in-depth review sessions from companies in the test prep business. There are also academic tutors who will work with you individually or in small groups, as well as academic advisors who offer many services including test preparation. However, fees for these classes and tutors can reach thousands of dollars.

Taking standardized tests is just like playing sports: how you practice will determine how you play, and how you practice SAT and/or ACT tests will determine they way you will perform on the actual exams.

Take the PSAT/PLAN

Start preparing by taking the PSAT in October of your sophomore year. Many high schools offer the test during the school year, but if your school does not, you can still sign up and take the test at a center. Some schools have a system that offers test-taking preparation development starting with EXPLORE in 8th or 9th, the PLAN in 10th, and the ACT in 11th and/or 12th. We really encourage you to take the PSAT and/or PLAN because they have no bearing on the decisions that colleges make, and offer the opportunity to prepare for the SAT or ACT. If you take the PSAT as a junior, your score could qualify you for a National Merit Scholarship. The PSAT and PLAN reveal what your strengths are and what you need to work on to get the scores you will need to gain admission into the college of your choice.

After you receive your scores, go to the College Board website and get started on your SAT test preparation. Click on the free tool, My College QuickStart, to get a detailed score report and a personalized SAT study plan. The site will help you understand your strengths and what you need to work on by offering specific practice questions that correspond with the questions you missed on the PSAT. It also suggests colleges and majors that might suit you based on your scores.

Practice SAT/ACT Tests

How much preparation should you do for the SAT/ACT? At the minimum, take a complete practice test that includes all the tested sections so that you become familiar with the directions and have worked under the time constraints. Then go through the answers to see how you did and why you missed particular questions. When you take these practice tests, use a timer or stop-watch to determine if you need to speed up or slow down on different sections.

TAKE PRACTICE TESTS!
Taking a few or even several practice tests is a great way to prepare for the SAT/ACT. Review the answers you missed and check your times on each section.

Before the test, make sure you:
- Familiarize yourself with the SAT/ACT so you know what to expect on test day
- Familiarize yourself with the different types of questions on the SAT/ACT, the directions for each type of question, and how the test is scored, so you know what to expect on test day
- Take test prep seriously and, if possible, take a test prep course
- Use the free materials available in your high school College & Career center to become familiar with the elements of the tests. Go online to find valuable resources. The following websites have free test-prep information:
  - » collegboard.org
  - » cavhs.org
  - » act.org
  - » number2.com
  - » gocollege.com

When students register to take the SAT online, they are able to obtain free practice materials, an official practice test, testing skills and insights, and an online score report. The College Board website also offers links to colleges and universities where you can locate information regarding admission profiles, so you can see what the average scores were for incoming freshmen at individual schools.

If you want a more structured program with a teacher facilitating your studying, there are many SAT/ACT workshops. Most student-athletes we interviewed agreed that taking a Kaplan or Princeton Review type of course improved their scores mainly because it required them to actually sit down and do the work of learning test structures and strategies. You will have to set aside additional academic time either for working on your own, in workshops, or with tutors to review material and practice taking tests.

How many times should you take the SAT/ACT? Colleges and universities do not care how many times you take the SAT, but will take your best score from each section of the test. For the ACT, colleges use different criteria regarding multiple ACT scores: some use your most recent scores, while others select your best scores from multiple test sittings. As a result, we encourage you to take the exams twice.

Beyond specific test prep, students need to be reminded of long-term academic skills:

- Challenge yourself throughout high school by taking rigorous courses, including at least 3 years of math
- Read and write as much as possible—both in and out of school
- Building your vocabulary is important – take advantage of the SAT word of the day by signing up for free at collegboard.org
- Different test prep companies sell flashcards for English and math practice. College Board sells conveniently boxed sets of vocabulary flashcards and math flashcards that are easy to use and very helpful.

TEST-TAKING STRATEGIES FOR SAT & ACT

These tests cover knowledge and skills that you have acquired since elementary school. You can prepare by reviewing topics that will be tested, as well as learn some test-taking strategies that will help you during the exams.

Become familiar with the test(s) you will be taking. Now that you understand the format of the exams, you also must become familiar with the rigid time limits and learn strategies for each section of the test. Determine which strategies below will help you.

Night before the test

Gather what you will bring to the test

- Picture ID (school ID card, driver's license, etc.)
- SAT admission ticket
- A watch—you cannot use your cell phone as a timer since they are not be allowed in testing centers. Make sure the watch doesn't beep!
- Two sharpened #2 pencils
- Calculator with new batteries
- A snack and water for breaks
- Directions to the test center
- Get a good night's sleep

Morning of the test

‣ Eat breakfast
‣ Wear a watch—make sure it does not have any alarms set
‣ Bring your already prepared items
‣ Get to the test center 30 minutes early. Consider weather, traffic, and any unforeseen problems like a flat tire

During the Test

‣ Keep your mind on your work, not your score
‣ Get in "the zone" and tune out distractions around you
‣ Use a #2 pencil (have an extra on hand)
‣ Budget your time—write down start and stop times for each section
‣ Write on your test booklet. Cross out wrong answers and write in question marks if you are guessing or unsure
‣ Do easier questions first; if you get stuck, move on, leave it blank, and return to questions later, if you have time
‣ If you change an answer, erase thoroughly, and fill in the correct circle completely
‣ If you leave an answer blank, make sure you carefully enter your next answer in the correct spot on the answer sheet
‣ For the SAT, do not make blind guesses. However, you should make educated guesses by eliminating some answers because there is a penalty for wrong answers.
‣ For the ACT, since wrong answers aren't penalized, make sure to answer every question
‣ Work only on the section you are supposed to be working on—do not return or move ahead to another section. You could have your test confiscated
‣ Use all of your time. Do not close up your test booklet. If you finish early, go back and check your answers
‣ Use your breaks to go to the bathroom, stretch your legs, walk, eat or drink to keep up your energy level, and relax
‣ Stay positive and focused

Topics & Strategies for Specific Test Sections

Become very familiar with the different sections of the tests. Practice with either online resources or with test-prep books until you know how the entire test is structured. Know the directions for each section, so you can skip them and use that time to answer questions.

SAT/ACT English Topics

✎ English (grammar)
  ‣ The following are the most common errors you will need to recognize and correct in the multiple choice answer section:
    » Fragments, run-ons
    » Noun/pronoun agreement
    » Subject/verb agreement
    » Verb tenses (past or present)
    » Adjectives vs. adverbs
    » Parallel construction
    » Diction (word choice)
    » Punctuation (commas, apostrophes, semi-colons, etc.)

✎ **Writing Section** (multiple-choice questions for the SAT only)
  ‣ 3 types of multiple-choice writing questions:
    » Improving sentences
    » Identifying sentence errors
    » Improving paragraphs

✎ **Reading Comprehension Strategies**
  ‣ Quickly preview the text
  ‣ Read the questions first (not the answers)
  ‣ As you read—look for answers
  ‣ Underline key words, phrases, and transitions in the text
  ‣ Every passage has a main idea or central theme
  ‣ Take advantage of your own outside knowledge about topics
  ‣ Review—quickly skim again for answers

✎ **Sentence Completion Strategies (SAT only)**
  ‣ Underline or circle key words
  ‣ Fill in blanks with your own words without looking at the answer choices
  ‣ Use process of elimination—cross out choices that do not make sense, then narrow down remaining options to the correct answer
  ‣ Make an educated guess if you are unsure of the answer
  ‣ Don't second guess yourself: Easy questions have easy answers; difficult questions have difficult ones

✎ Strategies for Timed-Essay Writing

‣ Budget your time. Pace yourself, saving 1-2 minutes to proof-read your essay at the end
‣ Answer the prompt—read the question carefully and be sure to respond to everything the question asks you to address
‣ Think critically about the issue presented in the essay assignment, then define and support your point of view, using reasoning and evidence based on your own experiences, readings, or observations (see Chapter 4 on expository writing)
‣ Organize your essay—jot down a brief outline or map. You should plan on writing 3-4 well-developed paragraphs for your essay, including an introduction, body and conclusion
‣ Have a clear thesis
‣ Use evidence
  » Think in advance about the books or short stories you have read, historical examples you could use, or current events that you have heard about. Create a list of potential evidence you could use for a variety of topics
  » Literary or historical, and current events
  » Personal experience or observations (friends & family)
  » Movies, TV
‣ Explain your evidence to show how it supports your point of view
  » Each paragraph and every sentence should make a specific point
  » You will be evaluated on how well you argue and support your opinion, not on what your opinion is
‣ Write legibly
‣ Follow formal writing conventions—avoid slang
‣ Don't use vocabulary that you are not sure of in an attempt to appear intelligent
‣ Write on the assigned topic, or else you will receive a zero
‣ Since this is a timed writing, the readers will
  » understand that the essay is a first draft
  » read quickly to gain an impression of the whole essay
  » look for and reward what is done well rather than what is done badly or omitted
  » not judge an essay by its length or the quality of handwriting
  » understand that grammar and/or spelling is not an overriding factor in determining an essay score unless errors interfere with understanding
‣ Here are some sample prompts from the past:
  » *What's more important: winning or losing?*
  » *Should you question authority?*
  » *What's more valuable: teamwork or individuality?*

Essay Scoring

Essays are scored by trained high school English teachers and college professors with experience in teaching writing. Each essay is scored independently by two readers according to a holistic scoring guide.

Just as athletes practice fundamental skills in preparation for a game, students taking admissions tests practice test-taking skills to prepare for the actual SAT/ACT tests. Spending some time reviewing sample prompts, writing timed sample essays and understanding the rubric will help you be successful on the essay. Be sure to practice writing under the time constraints so that on the day of the test you will feel relaxed and confident. Some people believe that longer essays earn higher scores, so don't be brief. Have a game plan by creating a list of possible examples that you could use, ranging from books or short stories you have read, to examples from history and current events.

For sample student-written essays and the scoring rubric, go to the College Board website.

SAT Math

You probably learned most of the math on the SAT by the time you completed middle school. It covers arithmetic, elementary algebra and geometry. The SAT math is a test of general reasoning abilities, and typically does not go beyond Algebra 2. A small portion of the test hits probability and counting, data analysis, functions and logical reasoning. You will need to spend time reviewing if you have not had a math class that covers these topics in over a year or more.

Topics on the SAT Math could include the following:

✐ **Number and Operations (Arithmetic)**
>> Fractions
>> Decimals
>> Percents
>> Ratios
>> Proportions
>> Averages
>> Integers
>> Rational numbers
>> Logical reasoning
>> Sequences and series
>> Sets

✐ **Algebra and Functions**
>> Exponents
>> Absolute Value
>> Rational Equations and Inequalities

- » Integer and Rational Exponents
- » Direct and Inverse Variation
- » Function Notation
- » Concepts of Domain and Range
- » Functions as Models
- » Linear Functions–Equations and Graphs
- » Symbols
- » Quadratic Equations and Functions

✐ **Geometry and Measurement**
- » Geometric Notation for Length, Segments, Lines, Rays, and Congruence
- » Slope and Coordinate Geometry
- » Properties of Tangent Lines
- » Coordinate Geometry
- » Qualitative Behavior of Graphs and Functions
- » Transformations and their Effect on Graphs of Functions

✐ **Data Analysis, Statistics, and Probability**
- » Data Interpretation, Scatter plots, and Matrices
- » Probability

Strategies for the SAT Math Test

Use a scientific or graphing calculator, but do simple math in your head to save time. You cannot bring handheld computers, palm pilots, or any calculator with QWERTY keyboards, that print paper, make noise or require an electrical outlet. You also cannot use your cell phone as a calculator. **Graphing calculators are permitted. Make sure you have good batteries so that your calculator doesn't die half-way through the test!**

- ‣ Manage your time
- ‣ Know that questions are arranged in order of difficulty
- ‣ Complete easy & medium questions before hard questions
- ‣ Don't spend too long on a problem you don't understand
- ‣ Plug simple numbers into equations
- ‣ Use approximation when answers vary widely
- ‣ If diagrams would help but are not given, draw them
- ‣ Look for like terms, especially in measurement.
- ‣ Look for key words like *is, of, more than, older than, less than, younger than, percent* for context clues
- ‣ Remember the formula **PEMDAS**—use the acronym "Please, Excuse, My, Dear, Aunt, Sally" for order of operations
- ‣ Draw pictures when they do not give you any, or if the picture is not drawn to scale
- ‣ With percent problems, use the formula is/of = %/100
- ‣ Eliminate fractions, decimals, and radicals whenever possible
- ‣ Estimate whenever possible
- ‣ Check the answers to see what units to convert to

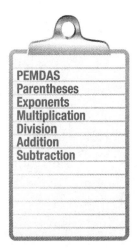

PEMDAS
Parentheses
Exponents
Multiplication
Division
Addition
Subtraction

When it comes to guessing:

‣ Use common sense
‣ Do not second guess yourself if you are in the easy part of a section
‣ Ignore or eliminate odd-ball answers!
‣ If there isn't an easy route to doing a problem, move on, and come back later
‣ Never pick a "non-answer" or a "super answer" unless you are certain

ACT Math

The math section of the ACT has 60 questions that are to be completed in the 60 minutes allotted. A calculator is permitted for use during testing. There are six content areas that are being evaluated during the exam: Pre-Algebra, Elementary Algebra, Intermediate Algebra, Coordinate Geometry, Plane Geometry, and Trigonometry. The following topics and sub-topics are listed on the ACT website at actstudent.org

✎ Pre-Algebra

‣ Operations with whole numbers, decimals, fractions, integers
‣ Square roots
‣ Exponents
‣ Scientific notation
‣ Factors
‣ Ratio
‣ Proportion
‣ Percent
‣ Absolute value
‣ Linear equations
‣ Data collection, representation, and interpretation
‣ Statistics

✎ Elementary Algebra

‣ Substitution
‣ Algebraic operations
‣ Solving quadratic equations through factoring

✎ Intermediate Algebra

‣ Quadratic formula
‣ Rational and radical expressions
‣ Absolute value equations and inequalities
‣ Quadratic inequalities
‣ Systems of equations
‣ Functions
‣ Matrices

Coordinate Geometry
- Relations between equations and graphs
  - » Points, lines, polynomials, circles, and other curves
- Graphing inequalities
- Slope
- Parallel and perpendicular lines
- Distance
- Midpoints
- Conics

Plane Geometry
- Properties and relations of plane figures
  - » Angles, parallel and perpendicular lines
- Properties of circles, triangles, rectangles, parallelograms, and trapezoids
- Transformations
- Proof and proof techniques
- Volume
- Geometry in three dimensions

Trigonometry
- Right triangles
- Trigonometric functions
- Graphing trigonometric functions
- Solving equations
- Modeling using trigonometric functions

ACT English

The English section of the ACT is similar to the SAT, but the ACT has 75 questions to be completed in the 45 minutes allotted. Five literary passages are presented for reading, followed by multiple-choice questions about that section. Questions are comprised of two categories: mechanics or rhetorical skills. Mechanics questions involve punctuation, grammar and usage, and sentence structure, while rhetorical skills include strategy, organization, and style. Unlike the SAT, spelling and vocabulary are not tested in the ACT. For specific details on the English section, go to act.org.

ACT Science

While the SAT does not include science, the ACT does include 40 questions to be completed in 35 minutes. This section tests reasoning, problem solving, interpretation, analysis, and evaluation of natural sciences. No calculators are allowed on this section. You will be provided with seven sets of scientific information in one of three formats (data interpretations, research summaries, or conflicting viewpoints) followed by multiple-choice questions addressing the same information. Information may be provided in the following formats: graphs, tables, charts, descriptions of experiments, conflicting hypotheses or viewpoints, and more. The ACT website says to review biology, physics, and chemistry, but students say that as long as you can read charts and graphs, you don't need to review many scientific concepts.

GOAL SETTING FOR THE SAT/ACT

Since most students take the SAT/ACT more than once, they are able to set more realistic and specific goals after receiving their test results. You should revise your goal chart after receiving scores.

Based on your practice tests results, what are your strengths?
1. _____
2. _____

Based on your practice test results, what are your weaknesses?
1. _____
2. _____

What specific sections do you need to work on the most?
1. _____   2. _____   3. _____

How much time do you plan to sacrifice to prepare yourself for the ACT/SAT?
Per semester: _____   Per week: _____

SAT Score Goals: _____   ACT Score Goals: _____

SENDING YOUR SCORES TO COLLEGES

Releasing scores: Most colleges, some scholarships, and the NCAA require that the College Board or ACT officially submit scores to them directly. This can be done when a student registers for the exam (four schools included in the exam fee) or after the test, for a fee of $11 per school. Note that there is an extra fee for rush orders.

Withholding scores: The College Board allows students the option to withhold some SAT scores, known as Score Choice. If a student tested in June with a lower score than in May, the student will have the option to send only the May SAT scores. If a student doesn't exercise Score Choice, the SAT report will include all scores in the student's file.

Last Words...
The SAT and ACT exams are extremely important when it comes to applying to and being accepted to many colleges. The effort to practice and prepare for them will make a significant difference in your score and widen your options for after high school. Reviewing material, writing practice essays, working out math problems, and getting used to the time constraints of the exam will improve your confidence while taking the SAT or ACT.

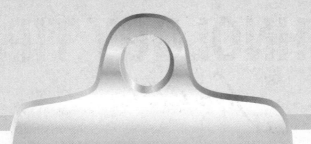

Chapter 14
Top 10 Plays

1. Take college admissions tests seriously—they are important pieces of your admissions package

2. Take the PSAT/PLAN in October of your sophomore year

3. Go to collegboard.org and click on My College QuickStart to get a detailed score report and a personalized SAT study plan

4. Register for the SAT and/or the ACT—be sure to meet deadlines and take tests starting your junior year

5. When registering, select the colleges you want your scores sent to—athletes must also have a report sent directly to NCAA Eligibility Center using the code 9999

6. Prepare for the tests—familiarize yourself with the tests by taking sample exams online, using an SAT/ACT prep book, attending prep classes, or hiring a tutor

7. Take SAT and/or ACT tests again to improve your scores during the fall of your senior year

8. Take the optional SAT IIs immediately after you complete the corresponding high school course

9. Go to bed early the night before the test and eat a good breakfast

10. Arrive early and bring a picture ID, pencils with good erasers, a calculator, watch, and water

👍 TECHNOLOGY TIPS
from Alison

How to Study for the SAT/ACT While Surfing the Web

> **Technology makes it really easy to cram some SAT/ACT studying in with your daily Facebook and email routine.** There are tons of websites out there with free test prep information, and they're much more interactive than boring ol' prep books. Here are some of my favorite studying websites:

👍 THE BEST PART

SAT Prep:
Easy-to-use videos (with NO ads!) explain how to do every single SAT practice problem in the College Board *Official SAT Study Guide.* You can also download the videos for free to your iPod or iPhone from iTunes

1. **khanacademy.org**
   » A well-respected educational site with videos on all different subjects. This website is one of the best because they want to provide free world-class education to everyone, so there aren't annoying ads and gimmicks to get your money.

SAT, ACT, SAT II Prep:
» Diagnostic Test so you'll know what to review
» FREE practice tests
» FREE online book on SAT strategies
» FREE interactive online books using SAT vocabulary words

2. **sparknotes.com**
   » *Spark Notes* isn't just for understanding Shakespeare. Their website is a great resource for SAT, ACT, and SAT II subject test prep (and they do AP test prep too!). The only drawback of this site are the obnoxious ads that are continuously running on the side of the screen.

SAT, ACT Prep:
» "Like" the official ACT Test page for deadline reminders
» "Like" Kaplan SAT & ACT Prep for *Question of the Day* to show up on your news feed
» Download the ACTStudent app or the SAT Score Quest™ from The Princeton Review

3. **f Facebook.com**
   » No, seriously. Go on a SAT/ACT test prep "liking" spree. Kaplan SAT & ACT Prep uploads a picture of the *Question of the Day,* so at least you can squeeze in a little studying while scrolling down your News Feed. And while your on Facebook, you might as well "like" the official ACT Test page, so you never forget sign-up deadlines.

What about apps?

Whether you're studying for the ACT or the SAT, or your weakness is vocab or critical reading, there's an app for that. Go to the App Store to find specific apps tailored to your needs. We suggest the Princeton Review SAT Score Quest and the official ACTStudent app.

THE BEST PART

SAT, ACT, SAT II Prep:

» ⏱ **FREE full online SAT & ACT practice tests, and practice problems for SAT II Subject Tests**

» 📱 **Sign up to have College Board send *The Official SAT Question of the Day*™ or download the app**

» **Read the free 86-page booklet on ACT test strategies**

Anything and Everything:

» **The blog we found called perfectscoreproject.com has a great article, *SAT Prep on a Budget* which talks about the surefire $218 46-Week SAT Test Prep Plan**

» **Find your own resources online that are catered to your personal needs. Odds are that there's a blog out there that addresses your questions about any and all of the tests**

4. The official test websites—collegboard.org & act.org

» College Board offers all kinds of free SAT prep, but the best part is the free, full practice SAT test. The ACT website offers free test prep, including a full practice test, as well as a free online book for test strategies. You can also download the official ACTStudent app (it's free!) for on-the-go access to their practice material, or The Official College Board SAT Question of The Day™ app.

5. Blogs

» Search online for "free SAT prep blog" or "free ACT prep blog" until you find something that you like.

» We like perfectscoreproject.com, which is a blog run by a mom who took the SAT at the same time as her kids. She provides great resources on SAT prep on a budget and lots of helpful links.

» When you find a blog that you like, sign up for their emails, like them on Facebook, follow them on Twitter—do whatever you have to do that will remind you to continually visit the blog for review and studying inspiration.

15

Completing
COLLEGE
APPLICATIONS

Don't limit your challenges;
challenge your limits.

Completing college applications requires you to schedule some time within your already busy academic and athletic schedule, so you will need to be organized to keep track of all the required materials and deadlines. Students need to start early in senior year to complete their applications, because different schools have different deadlines. If you miss deadlines or forget to attach a document, your application won't be considered, so be careful. Be prepared to spend some time completing all the requirements. It's not difficult, but it is very meticulous.

Obviously, student-athletes will apply to colleges where they want to play, but you might also want to apply to colleges that are above your reach athletically. This is because some high school student-athletes get injured or burned out by the end of their senior year and realize they would rather attend a different type of school more suitable for their academic goals.

The college application process involves taking required standardized tests, writing multiple personal statement essays, asking for letters of recommendation, reporting your family's background and financial information, and completing the online application. This chapter will guide you through this process.

FILLING OUT THE COLLEGE APPLICATION

Today, many colleges prefer that you submit your application online, but whether you apply online or send a hard copy in the mail, there are a few significant documents that you need to collect and refer to in order to complete your college applications. The following checklist will ensure that you include all of these required documents and materials.

☑ APPLICATION "TO DO" CHECKLIST

☐ Gather :

» Academic and activities' log from your blue personal data folder and highlight the accomplishments that you want to include in each application. Different activities may be more appropriate for certain colleges.
» Current transcripts
» SAT and ACT test scores
» Parents' education/background

☐ Complete the actual applications, either online or hard copies for all the schools you want to attend. The Common Application (found at commonapp.org) is the most used process for private schools.

☐ Request letters of recommendation.

☐ Write your college application/personal statement essay for each college.

☐ Pay the application fee.

☐ Write thank you notes to those who helped you edit personal statements and/or wrote letters of recommendation.

☐ Complete the required FAFSA form online

☐ Complete scholarship and financial aid materials, if applicable (Chapter 16)

Gather information requested on college applications

Many colleges (especially private schools) across the nation have students complete online "The Common Application" for undergraduate college admissions. These and all other college applications may require information from the following categories (go back to Chapter 2 if you collected and saved the following):

📁 *Personal and Family Data*

📁 *Education and Academic Honors Information*

📁 *Extracurricular Activities in High School*

📁 *Work Experience and Volunteer Activities*

📁 *Personal and Family Data*

‣ Name
‣ Address
‣ Phone
‣ Email
‣ Social Security number
‣ Parent information (educational level, ethnicity, etc.)

📁 *Education and Academic Honors Information*

‣ Name of high school and possibly school code (see your counselor for this)
‣ List of high school coursework
‣ Grades
‣ Class rank
‣ Academic honors/awards
‣ SAT/ACT scores with test dates
‣ AP or IB test scores with test dates

📁 *Extracurricular Activities in High School*

‣ Clubs/Student government
‣ Athletics

📁 *Work Experience and Volunteer Activities*

‣ Work experience
‣ Community Service/Volunteer work
‣ Church/Youth groups

Many high schools require volunteer community service hours as part of their graduation requirement. Some competitive schools recommend up to 150 hours of community service. If your high school does not have this requirement, you will want to find opportunities to do this on your own. You can work with organizations such as the SPCA, local food banks, and youth sports programs to get the hours you need.

Complete the actual applications

Ideally, you will complete your applications by at least the week before they are due so you have time to make last minute revisions. Furthermore, you want to submit your application before all the procrastinators because thousands of students apply online often, causing servers to crash. However, if you are a typical teenager and wait until the last minute, you will most likely complete applications during Thanksgiving and winter vacations when you have a few days off school. No matter what, check application deadlines, be thorough, and proofread carefully before submitting.

- ‣ Make a list of all college websites and your passwords for future reference, especially when you are forced to use multiple ones. Students have been known to have difficulty retrieving acceptance information later because they forgot their passwords.

- ‣ For "The Common Application" online, all the parts of the application are listed down the left hand column. You simply click on each topic and complete that part. The program tracks where you are in the process (not started, in progress, or completed) for each individual school that you are applying to.

- ‣ Complete the applications for each school; if you get stuck and don't have the information, click "SAVE" NOT "SUBMIT." This will allow you to come back and continue the application. If you have any questions, find out answers from school personnel (high school and/or college), your parents, or online resources. Only hit "SUBMIT" when you have carefully proofread all sections for accuracy. If you get tired or need a break, just hit save, log out and come back another time.

- ‣ Write the required essays for individual schools in a word document and then copy and paste the document in the essay box on the application. Some schools force you to write the essay in the actual box—in this case, be very careful not to hit submit before you have proofread your essay.

- ‣ Print or save a copy of all the pages of your application.

- ‣ Provide credit card information for the application fee.

- ‣ Record on your Admission Log (see next page)

ADMISSION LOG FOR COLLEGE

Keep this log in your college box or crate, stapled on the inside of the file folder for each college you apply to.

Date: Action:
_____   Application deadline:
_____   Application mailed or submitted online
_____   Application fee check sent
_____   SAT/ACT test results sent
_____   High school transcripts sent
_____   Letters of recommendation sent
_____   Interview completed (if applicable)
_____   Admission status: accepted, denied, wait listed, special status
_____   Notify admissions of your decision
_____   Follow-up or appeal (if applicable)

Letters of Recommendation

Generally, private colleges require letters of recommendation for admissions while most state schools do not. However, if you are applying for scholarships at either public or private colleges, you may be required to supply letters.

Today, students submit names of teachers they want to write letters for them and their email addresses to The Common Application website. The teachers will then receive an email and directions on how to submit a letter of recommendation online.

Make a list of people who you think could write a positive letter of recommendation for you. Teachers will generally write the truth, so think carefully about which one can write most effectively to convey your specific contributions to a class and to your teams. It is best to ask teachers from your junior and senior years, ideally ones who taught academic courses. Your letters of recommendation are an opportunity for you to have teachers, counselors, and coaches highlight the attitudes and skills you were unable to convey in your personal statement essay.

You should supply the following items for whomever writes a letter for you:
- A resume that contains your GPA, the course you took with the teacher or years you played with the coach; achievements such as research papers, projects, and activities that they can reference, volunteer work and community service that you have done.
- The due date when the letter must be sent by. (Ask for letters to be finished a week earlier than you really need them.)

For colleges that require application materials in a hard copy form, also give the teacher/coach/counselor the following:

‣ Addressed and stamped envelopes for each letter of recommendation

If you are a borderline candidate, your letters of recommendation could be a determining factor. Help the people who are writing one for you by informing them of projects, activities, papers you wrote, times you were selected as a team captain, etc., so they can provide convincing evidence of your strengths.

LETTERS OF RECOMMENDATION LOG

College	Teacher/coach/counselor to write letter	Date asked to write letter	Date to pick up from teacher/teacher to send	Thank you note sent

Follow up on your requests for letters of recommendation. Make sure teachers have either returned them to you in sealed envelopes or that they have sent them to the colleges. Cross this off on your checklist once they are sent.

Send Thank You Notes

Be sure to send a hand-written thank you to everyone who writes a letter for you. You might want to buy a small gift like a Starbucks gift card or a small box of chocolates.

Write the Personal Statement

The personal statement (sometimes referred to as the application essay) gives the admissions personnel and scholarship officers a chance to get to know you as a person beyond your statistics like your GPA. It gives a clearer picture of who you are in a unique description about yourself. Be honest and sincere.

||||||||||||||||||||||||||||||||||||||||||||||||||||||||||||||||||||||||||||||||||||||||||||||||||||||||||||||||||||||||||||||||||

"Everyone has a story to tell. The personal statement is essentially a college assignment assessing a student's ability to express who they are. It's a formal exercise in self-awareness."

–Walt Wild, 30-year High School Academic Counselor

||||||||||||||||||||||||||||||||||||||||||||||||||||||||||||||||||||||||||||||||||||||||||||||||||||||||||||||||||||||||||||||||||

In the summer after your junior year, write a first draft of your personal statement/application essay. Go to college websites to see their specific essay questions. Most colleges do not change prompts from year to year. Some colleges may require more than one essay. As you begin to think about your personal statement essay, think about your audience: admissions officers that read thousands of essays every year. If you are given some options to write about, select topics that you would enjoy and that show who you really are.

Go to the websites of the colleges that you are applying to and find the prompts. Below are samples of essay prompts.

SAMPLE PERSONAL ESSAY PROMPTS

A. Describe the world you come from—for example, your family, community or school—and tell us how your world has shaped your dreams and aspirations.

B. Tell us about a personal quality, talent, accomplishment, contribution or experience that is important to you. What about this quality or accomplishment makes you proud and how does it relate to the person you are?

C. Describe a character in fiction, a historical figure, or a creative work (as in art, music, science, etc.) that has had an influence on you, and explain that influence.

STEPS TO WRITING A PERSONAL STATEMENT/APPLICATION ESSAY

1. Brainstorm ideas that work with the prompt you select
2. Write your first draft
3. Ask others to read it for feedback—teachers, friends, adults
4. Make final revisions and proofread carefully
5. Submit your application early

Brainstorm: What do you write about?

The following questions will help you generate some ideas on what to write about.

- ✐ What is one of the most difficult decisions you have ever made? Why was it so difficult? How do you feel about the decision now?

- ✐ Do you consider yourself a leader or follower? Does your role change when you are in different groups?

- ✐ What activities have you been involved in? How has this affected your life?

- ✐ What makes you unique? Include your character traits, personality, qualities, philosophies, beliefs and attitudes that make you who you are.

- ✐ What contemporary problem or issue are you passionate about? What is your view?

- ✐ What one of your personality traits could be considered both a strength and a weakness? Explain why and give specific examples.

- ✐ What hardships have you overcome in your life? How did you deal with the situation and how has it impacted your life?

Remember that the essay gives you an opportunity to share your personality with admissions officers. Decide what you want to share with the college admissions officers that will convince them that you belong at their school.

Write: How do you write the personal statement?

There are a few basic guidelines for writing your personal statement/application essay:

- » Read the prompt(s) carefully and respond to all parts
- » Focus on one point or trait and then use specific examples
- » Select one experience that is honest and personal (be yourself)
- » Organize with an outline or graphic organizer
- » Be concise and clear, yet detailed (not easy to do)
- » Keep the focus on you
- » Don't bore your reader
- » Use the essay as an opportunity to explain any irregularity or anomaly (good or bad) in either your transcript or application
- » Use your own words

Avoid:

- » Jokes, sarcasm or being funny
- » Lists of activities, etc.
- » Slang and popular words and phrases
- » Waiting until the last minute to write
- » Poetry

Start writing!

After your first draft, put your essay away for a few days. Then, revise your personal statement to include words that add characteristic specificity, such as "talented, sensible, inventive, trustworthy, exemplary, honest, gracious, cooperative, sympathetic, resourceful, humble, persistent, resilient, self-reliant, determined, self-starter, compassionate, efficient, or clever."

Have a variety of people read and respond to your essay. Maybe even ask an English teacher to give you some feedback. Ask your reader what qualities come through in the essay – make sure those are the qualities you intended to convey to the readers. College admissions personnel want to read about who you are and what you will bring to their school—-not what you think they want to hear. You may also want someone to help you cut down the length of your essay to meet the requirements. Oftentimes, students write too much and have problems being concise. In addition to getting feedback on your qualities and the length of your essay, you might also want to have someone make sure you connect your examples and your evidence.

Here are some categories that colleges use to evaluate the personal statement essays:
- focused
- length requirement met
- developed
- evidence supports claims

Keep a hard copy of all your personal statement essays in your college files and saved on your computer. When you apply for financial aid later, you may be able to use part of or entire essays for those applications.

On the following pages are four examples of student essays to give you an idea of how students responded to the prompts they were given. Chase Dickson wrote the first essay and Kendall Roth wrote the other three.

PERSONAL STATEMENT, UNIVERSITY OF CALIFORNIA PROMPT

Winston Churchill said in a famous graduation speech, "Never, never, never, never, never give up." A personal quality that relates to the person I am is that I never give up.

I am a late bloomer and younger than most of my senior classmates. I am always moving forward at a steady, reliable pace. I don't look back and agonize over the past, and I don't get involved in or gossip about others' personal matters. I especially don't believe all the people in my baseball life that told me I wasn't good enough to play competitive baseball.

I was the kid on the bench in little league. My coach would tell me I was going to pitch the next game. Well, it never happened. I left little league –daddy ball- to join a travel ball team hoping to create that opportunity to pitch. After several months of playing, my coach sat me down in his office and told me I wasn't good enough and couldn't help his travel team. He said I could stay on the team but I wouldn't bat and thought I might pitch one inning in an entire tournament. My mom and I said thank you and walked out with tears streaming down our cheeks. My stomach was coming up through my throat that I couldn't say any words to my mom. And she the same. My mom quickly found another travel club for me and the manager welcomed me with incredibly encouraging words. Coach Sundberg was the first adult coach (other than my parents and grandparents) to believe in me. At every practice and weekly pitching and hitting lesson, he told me I can play—and even more importantly, he told me that I can play college baseball. The way he treated me…I believed. It took us several tournaments to win one game, and then we started winning the next few years. Then, the new coach put me on the bench. Again, I had to find a place to play…next up, high school baseball.

I never gave up on baseball even though most coaches put me on the bench and even though my doctor told me not to pitch because I was too small and would continue to injure my arm. Even my high school freshman coach didn't play me very much and even though I couldn't pitch my sophomore year because of an arm overuse injury, I continued to work on my game in my garage and in my front yard. My mom tossed countless whiffle balls to me to develop as a hitter.

I never gave up on my pitching even though I had to sit out my sophomore season. During my junior year, while we had three great senior pitchers, the varsity coach told me I was good enough to pitch but he never put me on the mound during league play. I played two innings in a pre-season scrimmage and two innings in a spring tournament. I never gave up when I spent countless hours in the bullpen and shagging balls for my teammates.

I never gave up when my teammates were selected this past summer for all-star teams and I wasn't asked. I played senior ball and hit the ball to the fence and struck out plenty of batters. My strength is getting batters to hit ground balls. I just attended a baseball showcase where college coaches watch to see whom they'd like to recruit. I will find a place to play college baseball and to get a good academic education. I will never give up on baseball. It is my passion and gives me purpose to do well in the classroom too. This who I am—a potentially successful college student-athlete who works hard, plays with passion for the game, and will contribute to the university that is the perfect fit.

BROWN UNIVERSITY 500 WORD ESSAY

Tell us about an intellectual experience, project, class, or book that has influenced or inspire you.

Entering the theater, I was expecting the play put on by our family friends to be simply that: a play. The Exonerated was a theatrical reading of the true stories of six men and women forced to endure the unimaginable: face Death Row for crimes that they never committed. Six people who wasted years of their lives behind bars, for merely being in the wrong place at the wrong time. The stage had no sets, no costumes, and no props, just the actors and their words. The script was made entirely of words taken from court documents, interviews and public transcripts, which together, explored the darker aspects of the United States Justice System.

The beauty of the readings was that the audience was drawn into the power of the actors' words. This made the accounts come to life more than I thought possible. After leaving the theater, I was shocked at the effect the stories had on me. Incapable of grasping how those people must have felt, I attempted to imagine how I would feel if it was me who was wrongfully convicted of a crime and imprisoned, all the while knowing I was innocent. I still found the concept impossible. I think that that knowledge that I was wronged would kindle a hatred inside of me for the people responsible for the horrendous mistake. Yet, this does not appear to be the case. I am awed by the whole-hearted forgiveness that the exonerated seem to express. Instead of allowing the ordeal they had to live through beat them down, they demonstrated the strength of the human spirit and the hope that truth will inevitably prevail. Their willpower to cherish life and overwhelming capacity for forgiveness inspires me to do the same.

My mind is unable to wrap itself around the idea that our country is still plagued with these flaws. Although these six were finally released, uncountable others remain behind bars, many times dying in the place of the true criminals. In many cases, when evidence to prove the innocence of the wrongfully convicted person is brought to light, the courts turn a blind eye or deny its existence. In this country of freedom, people's voices continue to be oppressed, just as they were in earlier eras. It helped me to understand that regardless of progress, society as a whole, will never be perfect, yet will always strive for improvement. Their stories made me recognize that the only way change can happen is if individuals, including me, stand up against injustice by keeping an open mind, and by always examining situations from various points of view. At any time, incidents can occur in a person's life that they have no control over; after hearing these stories I realized that the obvious or first interpretation of a situation may not necessarily be the correct one, that I must look deeper into the situation to discover the truth.

PERSONAL ESSAY 500 WORDS

"The years that are gone seem like dreams—if one might go on sleeping and dreaming—but to wake up and find—oh! well! Perhaps it is better to wake up after all, rather than to remain a dupe to illusions all one's life." –Kate Chopin, The Awakening

The Special Olympics swimmer looked up into my eyes with pure, ecstatic joy after I announced that he had beaten his previous race time; I felt as if I had just handed him the gold medal. His happiness filled me with the same unrestrained glee.

Seven years ago, when my mother first suggested that we join the National Charity League (NCL), a mother-daughter philanthropy organization, I replied with a nonchalant, "Sure," never imagining how it would change my perspective on life. At the start, I simply went around on 'cruise control' attending council meetings, signing up to volunteer, putting in the required hours, yet never highly motivated or excited. However, once I began directly interacting with various organizations, everything changed.

There was a significant difference between making one hundred paper flower centerpieces for a fundraiser and physically helping a swimmer out of the pool after he finished a race. When I was able to situate myself in the joyful and giving atmosphere surrounding the Special Olympics event, I felt I had a purpose, one outside myself. I was drawn to these athletes; they represent the true force that the human spirit can have. Despite the conditions they were born with, the handicaps that prevented them from doing tasks others take for granted, they pour their energy and joy into a sport. They have a deep, steadfast determination to better themselves. I am awed by the perseverance and pure happiness that these men and women receive from doing something they love. It is humbling to think of the obstacles that they must overcome and yet to accomplish this with such a thirst for life. Never once do they complain or look downcast. Their spirit inspires me to do the same: to constantly work to better myself, to live in the moment and to find enjoyment in all that I do. Now, an organization that I had resignedly joined has transformed into a source of pride and fulfillment. I race to be the first to sign up for each Special Olympics event or cook spaghetti for the people coming to the Soup Kitchen.

NCL opened a door to my soul and unlocked a passion inside of me that has always been there, the desire to give to others, which in turn nurtures me. Volunteering is now and will always be a priority in my life; it has helped to define a part of me. I look forward to continue volunteering in college and the rest of my life. Giving to the community and spending time with my mother are now both a part of me that I will clasp close to my heart for the rest of my life; I believe it is I who has truly received a gift.

GEORGE WASHINGTON UNIVERSITY HONORS COLLEGE ESSAY

The nineteenth-century philosopher John Stuart Mill once wrote that "one person with a belief is equal to a force of 99 who have only interests." Tell us about one of your beliefs—how you came to it, why you hold on to it, what has challenged it, and what you imagine its influence will be on your education or pursuits.

I very firmly believe that everyone, men, women and children, has the power to be and to do whatever they put there mind to. Through the knowledge I have accumulated over years of history classes, I have see people across the eras oppressed for the color of their skin, their religion and their gender, stopped from controlling their own lives and destinies. Yet, over time, these groups have bonded together and thrown off the dominant collective, showing that the power of ideas and beliefs are strong enough to change the societal rules created by the elite. Seeing the black and white photographs of the women's rights movement to fight for the right to vote, reading the stories of African Americans becoming their own masters, and religious sects working jointly toward a common cause; I have learned that every individual has the right to stand up for what they desire and to support what they believe to be just. For if we do not, we will be stepped-on our entire lives, ignored by those whose voices and opinions are stronger than our own. Through umpiring, especially as a female, the idea of standing my ground has become ingrained in my mind from the first season of training. To gain the respect as the person in charge of the softball field, I need to hold fast to my calls and to assert my authority.

As a female, the remnants of gender prejudice are scattered like ruble throughout my world. Stereotypes, the constant jibes that women belong in the kitchen, that we are neither as strong as men are, nor as smart, I find it infuriating. It is saddening to know that society has come so far and yet the inferiority of women is still an established idea, lurking subtly under the surface. Over the years, various adults and people my own age have attempted to keep me down, telling me that I should not try for something I desire or that it is impossible. Boys did not want me to be on their soccer team for PE because they thought I would be useless. I was told not to take a higher-level class due to the difficulty level. However, instead of these words crushing my spirit, they instill me with the determination to prove everyone wrong, to show anyone who doubted me that I can truly accomplish my goals.

I imagine that this firm resolve, now a part of the mixture that makes up 'me,' will aid in whichever career and life paths that I select. I will not let what others say impede me from attempting new things or exploring unknown realms; I trust myself to decide what I want to aim for. Truly, I believe it will allow me to compete in the world and to hold my own, for I know my worth and am determined not to accept anything less from myself.

ADMISSION DECISION OPTIONS

There are a variety of admissions timetables that you need to be aware of: regular decision, early decision, early action, rolling admission, and wait listing. Many colleges have their own early decision and early action policies, so read carefully and ask questions to make sure this is what you really want to do.

Regular Decision

Most students apply to a number of schools and the colleges review the applications and students are notified no later than April 15 as to whether they are accepted or not.

Rolling Admission

A student applies to colleges that review applications as they are received and offers decisions as applications are reviewed. Colleges may have a recommended deadline or a priority date.

Early Decision

A student applies to his/her first choice college early in the fall (typically by November 1st of senior year) and commits to enroll in that college if admitted. These students will be evaluated on their junior year grades and achievement. Students are required to withdraw their applications to all other colleges once they are accepted. They cannot change their mind if they are admitted.

Early Action

A student applies to his/her first choice, at the same time as early decision, usually around beginning of November. The difference from early decision is that the student does not enter a contract with the college. They still have until May 1st to accept or decline the offer.

Wait list

A student does not initially receive an admission offer or denial, but is offered the possibility of admission in the future. As other students decline admission, spots open up—no later than August 1st. Students do not have to send in a commitment deposit to stay on the wait list.

Last Words...

The application process is vitally important. You really need to pay attention to details and deadlines. Create a calendar with due dates and don't procrastinate. Ask for help along the way with all forms, letters of recommendation and your personal statement (application essay). Complete the applications in the order of the submission deadlines, and remember that some of your essays may be able to be morphed to work for multiple colleges.

> You must accept an admission offer by May 1st in order to secure housing and financial aid. If you do not respond, the college will open up your spot to someone on its wait list.

Chapter 15
Top 10 Plays

1. Be prepared to spend time completing applications

2. Decide if you are going to apply for "early action" or "early decision" and meet the deadlines in October

3. Be careful. If you miss deadlines or forget to attach a document, your application won't be considered

4. Gather your personal information: awards, honors, achievements, any volunteer work, and your student-athlete profile

5. Ask teachers or counselors a month in advance for letters of recommendation and give them your personal information so they can write an outstanding letter

6. Apply online—few universities require hard copies. Save your applications, and have a credit card available for the application fee

7. Send thank you notes to anyone who wrote letters for you

8. Write a draft of your personal essay statement and make sure it reveals who you really are

9. Have a variety of people read your essay and give feedback. Be willing to make revisions. Save your essays on your computer and keep a hard copy just in case

10. Most students apply to 10–15 colleges, however some students only apply to one because they were recruited to their top choice

16

FINANCIAL AID & SCHOLARSHIPS

You miss 100% of the shots you don't take.

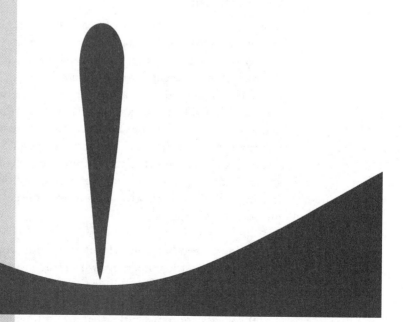

OVERVIEW

This chapter is only an overview description of financial resources and not a complete list of scholarship and financial aid opportunities. There are specific books and websites devoted to financial aid and athletic scholarships that can help you, but be aware of scholarship scams that will guarantee you scholarships for a fee. They cannot make this guarantee, so it is best to look and apply for scholarships yourself.

We found the whole financial aid process to be intimidating. It is not always easy to understand exactly what a financial aid package means. There are all kinds of ways to get money for college. There is financial aid calculated based on financial need, and there are athletic scholarships, academic merit scholarships, grants, and work-study programs—all of which you don't need to repay.

If you do not receive any financial aid or enough to cover the entire cost of college, your family can pay for college in semester or monthly increments or take out a loan. You can also get a student loan, which is offered by the federal government as well as banks and other lenders. Private student loans are normally not a good option since they have higher interest rates and less repayment options. Loans must be paid back once you graduate from college, and it isn't unusual for a student to owe anywhere from $25,000 to a triple-digit debt. Be sure you clearly understand how much you will be paying for school every year, and make sure you and your family can afford the school you want to attend so that you do not go so far into debt that it will be too difficult to repay in the future.

FINANCIAL AID

Most families need some form of financial aid because college is so expensive. Since some financial aid is distributed on a first-come first-serve basis, the key is to apply early to improve your chances of getting financial aid. Be aware of the different federal and state deadlines—some state deadlines are in March, but federal deadlines are in June. Both the federal government and individual colleges/universities offer need-based financial aid determined by your family's income and finances reported on a federal government form called the Free Application for Student Aid (FAFSA). The FAFSA calculates what each family is expected to contribute to the student's educational costs. Some colleges do not offer need-based aid, so it is important to check what options the colleges you are interested in provide for financial aid.

In addition to need-based aid, a lot of financial aid comes in forms of grants, loans, and work-study programs, where students get jobs on campus and their wages go toward their tuition. Blog author, and contributor to *U.S. News and World Report*, Lynn O'Shaughnessy, reveals that only 63 out of 1,700 colleges and universities that award financial aid claim that they meet students' full financial needs. This means that most families have to work with colleges to create packages or find a variety of sources for funding. Families and students may have to apply for grants and/or loans to cover the balance that colleges do not offer in financial aid. Colleges also offer work-study programs where students are given jobs on campus, like working in the cafeteria or library or in the athletic department. Once you know which schools you are interested in, go to their website and look for details on how to apply for loans, grants, and other forms of financial aid. The websites will provide timelines for applications, so make sure you meet all deadlines since late applications are not accepted. Don't confuse financial aid deadlines with scholarship application deadlines. Many scholarship deadlines are earlier and it is recommended by many financial planners to apply early to beat the crowd.

SCHOLARSHIPS

Finally, there are scholarships—there are all kinds of full and partial scholarships. There are academic merit and athletic scholarships, as well as numerous other specific scholarships, many of which go unclaimed since students do not apply for them. Scholarships are offered by private groups and colleges and universities themselves.

Athletic scholarships come in all amounts, depending upon the division, sport, gender, and other factors. Some athletic scholarships are full while others are partial. Athletic scholarships are only good for one year, while other, non-athletic scholarships can be established for four years. Athletic scholarships are found in DI, DII, NAIA, and NJCAA programs. There are almost 2,000 colleges and universities that offer athletic scholarships, and most of them are not DI programs. DI schools do not necessarily offer the best athletic scholarships, or the most opportunities for athletic scholarships for student-athletes.

A long time and well-known baseball recruiting specialist and showcase tournament organizer, Gary Powers of IBAC Baseball, tells athletes that more than 94% of opportunities fall outside of the DI arena.

Besides athletic and academic scholarships, there are a variety of options for financial aid including leadership awards, interview scholarships, academic/honors awards, and also, institutional awards such as presidential awards, trustees awards, and leadership scholarships.

In addition to the variety of ways to get money, there are a variety of creative ways to package financial aid and scholarships. College admission officers do their best to work with athletic directors and coaches to create financial aid packages including, for example, academic merit scholarship money, athletic scholarship money, and work-study program money to total a sum of money to fund a student-athlete's education. So, it is possible to get both athletic aid and financial aid as an athlete.

In general, it has become more competitive to get into college and to earn scholarships and financial aid. Tuition costs have risen significantly, but fortunately, the government wants to help students gain a college education. The federal government offers loan programs for college students and tax breaks for parents of college students. Be persistent and resourceful in looking for options to pay for college, and you will find a way to finance your education.

It is hard work and time consuming to complete applications for financial aid and scholarships. You and your parent must research, seek out, and apply for scholarships and financial aid to get any money. The sooner you start, the more opportunities you will find. One teacher thought of the idea of having his daughter spend the entire summer researching and applying for scholarships as a summer job, hoping she would raise enough scholarship money to pay for much of her college education. With the effort, it can be done.

No matter what, all students must have their parents complete the FAFSA report (available January 1 of their senior year) to get any potential federal financial aid.

OVERVIEW OF FINANCIAL AID & SCHOLARSHIP PROCESS

▸ Start researching early—by the summer after your junior year (or even after your sophomore year) begin by visiting the website collegboard.org and using its invaluable tools for finding scholarships, calculating loans and aid comparisons as well as the resource called Scholarship Search. Check out websites listed in our resources section and search for "scholarships" online, then narrow in on scholarships that fit your interests, talents, and achievements.

▸ Ask your high school counselor and/or your school's college & career center counselor for scholarship information and opportunities during the fall of your senior year.

▸ Create a folder, box, or cabinet file drawer to organize all your scholarship and financial aid application materials and a timeline with deadline dates. Keep copies of everything you send.

▸ Ask your parent to complete the FAFSA (they will need tax returns, income, and financial information) in January of your senior year.

▸ Apply for scholarships and complete the entire application. Proofread and double check for any errors. You will need to refer to your SAT/ACT scores, transcript, extra-curricular activities, community service, and work experience. If required by the application, ask for letters of recommendation and send thank you notes to those who do them for you. Many scholarship applications require an essay. Even though it's painful and time consuming to write these specific essays, it's well worth the money you could receive.

‣ Prepare for an interview—be yourself.

‣ Apply for the financial aid you qualify for based on the FAFSA report and meet with financial aid advisers at the colleges you are applying to. Ask about financial aid and scholarship packages.

‣ Pay attention to and meet all deadlines.

☑ FILLING OUT THE FAFSA

This checklist will help you understand what you need to do to apply for financial aid and/or scholarships. Apply as early as possible, beginning January 1st of each year. Different schools and states have their own deadlines, so contact them for exact due dates.

☐ To find out how much financial aid you qualify for, register with FAFSA (Free Application for Federal Student Aid) and obtain a PIN number. No matter what your family's financial situation is or what athletic/academic scholarship money you plan on receiving, you need to register with FAFSA!

☐ The FAFSA contains questions that ask about you, your financial information, your school plans, and more. Gather your and your parents' personal documents, including Social Security number, driver's license, income tax returns, bank statements, and investment records.

☐ Next, if you want to practice first, print and complete the FAFSA *Web Worksheet* found on the FAFSA website. Write in your answers and your parents' information then transfer the data to FAFSA on the web.

☐ Now, fill out the FAFSA online with your information from the *Web Worksheet*. It is helpful to register online because aid is available through online tools, and answers to specific questions can be found by clicking on "NEED HELP?" There is also customer service. Click on "Live Help" at the top of the FAFSA page. You have access to worksheets that automatically calculate and enter information for you, and you can save your application at any time and return to it later.

☐ Use your PIN to electronically sign your FAFSA on the Web application. Your parent can sign electronically too.

☐ Note the Expected Family Contribution (EFC)—this is a calculation of what you are expected to be able to pay.

☐ Complete the optional, yet beneficial, Financial Aid Estimator (FAE), which is an estimation of what college financial aid is needed in order for you to attend.

☐ To verify the accuracy of your Student Aid Report (SAR), the student access feature allows you to view and print your SAR so you can check your information carefully. Note that the Social Security Administration must verify your PIN information before you can access your SAR. This could take 1-3 days after you submit your application online.

☐ You will verify that your FAFSA form is accurate when you are sent the SAR (Student Aid Report).

☐ If you lose your printed copy, you can call for another free copy of your SAR report—319-337-5665.

☐ Make a copy of your SAR form for every recruiter and visit, even if you think they received it with your FAFSA.

☐ Apply for Federal Financial Aid (fafsa.gov)—check for deadlines in your state, and mark section G of the form to denote which colleges you want forms sent to. Send financial aid requests to all the colleges you want to attend. Visit collegboard.org in order to receive this service for free.

☐ If you are applying for non-federal student aid and **if the college you are applying to requires it**, go to collegboard.org to open an online account and complete the College Board's CSS PROFILE. This profile is used by some colleges to help them award non-federal student aid. Register for the PROFILE as soon as you know what schools you are applying for aid. Gather tax returns and financial documents to complete the application. You can begin the registration process, save it, and return to it later. Plan on spending a few days to complete this. There is an application fee for this profile, in addition to fees for each college or scholarship program you apply to, although there are some fee waivers based on financial need determined by the profile.

☐ Research institutional grants in the scholarship section of college catalogs.

☐ Also apply for grants, loans, and scholarships by searching online and visiting your high school college & career center. There are so many scholarships out there that you can research and apply for.

☐ Complete an Institutional Financial Aid Application Form for private colleges and research specialized scholarships such as alumni, department, or religious scholarships.

☐ If you receive a scholarship for athletic competition that is not from the college where you have been recruited, you need to check with your college's financial aid office regarding NCAA rules BEFORE you accept a scholarship.

SEEK ATHLETIC SCHOLARSHIPS

If your goal is to be a recruited student-athlete earning an athletic scholarship, then you must understand that you can work with coaches and admissions personnel at colleges. Since they are businesses that use scholarships and financial aid to recruit desirable student-athletes, understand that college coaches communicate with admissions officers and financial aid personnel to help recruit athletes. It is in the best interest of the university to build an attractive financial aid package to entice the student-athlete to enroll. By May, most of the financial aid has been distributed.

Recruiting Offers and Scholarships, Grants, and Financial Aid

It is a plus for college programs when the high school student gets, for example, a Pell Grant. Since the federal government pays for the student's college, not the specific college, then coaches don't have to use their limited athletic scholarship money on that student-athlete, meaning they can use the money to recruit another athlete. Coaches can also offer a job and tuition amounting to a work-study program—again saving athletic scholarship money for another athlete.

NCAA institutions cannot guarantee four-year athletic scholarships. NCAA scholarships are limited and are renewable each academic year, and can be reduced or withdrawn.

It is very competitive to gain an athletic scholarship since the NCAA limits the amount of scholarships per sport. Unfortunately, because of the competitive nature of college recruiting, potential student-athletes need to be careful about what recruiters and coaches tell them about playing time, positions and scholarships. Athletic scholarships range from full-ride (including tuition, room & board, and books) to partial scholarships, which might only include books.

In actuality, only about 0.6-0.8% of all high school student-athletes receive a full DI athletic scholarship. Most colleges, especially DII and DIII schools, cannot afford to offer many full-ride. Most sports divide up full-rides among the starters. For example, DI colleges can only offer 11.7 baseball scholarships, 9.9 men's soccer, 12 women's soccer, 4.5 men's volleyball, and 12 women's volleyball, annually per team. DII colleges can only offer 10.8 men's lacrosse scholarships, 9.9 women's lacrosse, 4.5 men's water polo and 8 women's water polo. Many sports offer scholarships that range from 25% to 75% of the cost of college instead of full-rides (ncaa.org).

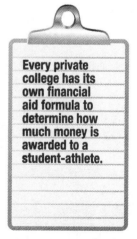

Every private college has its own financial aid formula to determine how much money is awarded to a student-athlete.

Every private college has an institutional financial aid formula to determine how much money is awarded to a student-athlete. The formula is partly based on the institution's needs (such as the need for a baseball, soccer, swim, or rugby student-athlete). The financial aid director exercises professional judgment in awarding packages. **Financial aid is awarded based on merit, academic achievement, potential, athletic ability, special circumstances (to be determined by the financial director's professional judgment), ethnicity, family relationships, and need.**

State colleges and universities do not have this flexibility, as their financial budgets are written in state law. DII and DIII programs offer opportunities for academic scholarships, grants, and other financial aid specifically for successful high school student-athletes.

NAIA schools are not limited to a certain amount of athletic scholarship amounts like NCAA DI and DII schools. NAIA schools can offer what is called "Gap Scholar-shipping" or "Stacking," where there is a supply of money that can be used to supplement the gap between the cost of college and the amount of the financial scholarship a student receives. For example, a student could receive $10,000 for good SAT scores and a high GPA. Then a second stack is the financial aid amount. The third stack is individual scholarships. The fourth stack is the athletic scholarship needed to fill in the gap. The coach and financial aid advisors work together to create a financial aid package for the student-athlete. They keep "stacking" or "filling in the gaps." Obviously, the more desirable an athlete is, the more likely the gap will be filled. A less desirable athlete will probably have to come up with some money on his or her own to pay for college.

SCHOLARSHIPS & NATIONAL LETTER OF INTENT

Once you have come to an agreement with your college coach as to what the school's offer is, whether it is a DI, II, or NAIA program, you will receive two documents from the college that awards you financial aid. These are called an "athletic tender" and an "award letter." The "National Letter of Intent" was covered in Chapter 11, but we are including that information below as well:

Athletic Tender (of Financial Assistance)

‣ Describes amount of athletic financial aid

‣ Commits you to attend that college

‣ Prohibits you from competing at any other NCAA institution

‣ Financial experts say to sign athletic tender and award letter at the same time to be able to continue financial negotiations

Award Letter (for Financial Aid)

‣ This is the letter that explains your complete financial aid package

‣ It is broken down into categories: athletic, academic, work-study, and grant

‣ If you receive two or more award letters, you can go to the College Board website to compare the offers

‣ This is separate from a letter of intent

Gap Scholar-shipping or Stacking involves several financial aid "stacks" at NAIA schools.

For example:
1. academic merit
2. financial aid
3. individual scholarship
4. athletic scholarship that fills the gap

NCAA DI & DII National Letter of Intent (NLI)

‣ A voluntary written agreement sponsored by the Eligibility Center

‣ High school seniors or community college transfers sign in early November. Football, cross country, track & field, soccer, field hockey, and water polo seniors sign in early February

‣ Signing means the athlete agrees to attend the college for one academic year

‣ Signing means the college must provide athletic financial aid for one academic year

‣ Read carefully for any restrictions which can affect eligibility (national-letter.org)

‣ Although it is binding for the student, it is *not* binding to a coach and it does not guarantee an athlete a place on the team or playing time

‣ Do not double sign meaning do not sign a letter of intent with two different schools

You can back out after signing the award letter, but if you sign the Athletic Tender, you are bound to that college and can only compete at that NCAA institution. If you back out, you would be ineligible from competing for a year at another school if the school does not release you. You can appeal to the NCAA with extenuating circumstances if the school does not release you. Go to ncaa.org and the National Letter of Intent page for details of provisions.

Be sure to sign both the athletic tender and award letter at the same time. If you sign the athletic tender without knowing the contents of the financial award letter, you cannot continue to negotiate for more financial aid. Before signing, make sure you have an agreement that meets your family's financial needs.

If your goal is to be a recruited athlete earning a scholarship, then you must understand that colleges are businesses with limited budgets. Coaches and colleges must recruit more than one athlete for each position since students also apply to more than one college. Since most colleges have a depth chart of four potential recruits, prospects don't know where they stand in terms of being offered a scholarship. You need to ask directly where you stand on the depth chart to know how likely it is for you to be recruited, admitted, and offered a scholarship or financial aid. Depth charts are fluid and not set in stone; thus, an athlete's ranking could change from day to day. For example, you might be second on the depth chart and the person who is first could sign with another institution, affecting your position. You now may be the one offered athletic scholarship money.

Before you sign any binding commitment to a college, be sure you understand fully what the college is going to offer you in the way of financial aid.

If you are hoping to earn an athletic scholarship, financial aid package, or academic scholarship, you need to remember that scholarships come in all forms and amounts depending on the sport and the college.

To find scholarships, we suggest that you browse bookstore shelves even though it can be an overwhelming experience. In our research, we have found the book, *The Sports Scholarships Insider's Guide* to be a helpful resource for understanding the complexities of college athletic scholarships and financial aid. There is also a website you can join for a fee: informedathlete.com. The owner-consultant, who has authored two books on recruiting and on transfer athletes, is a former recruiter and compliance officer for two universities and now offers services, guidance, and answers.

In terms of all other scholarships, we highly recommend that you and even your parents visit your high school College & Career Center, if you have one. They have experience and training when it comes to college applications, scholarships, and financial aid, and may have insights that can help you make decisions.

Search the web for scholarships, grants, and financial aid. We recommend the following websites:

If you are hoping to earn an athletic or academic scholarship, first you need to do your research.

Start with these sites:
▸ collegboard.org,
▸ finaid.com
▸ fastweb.com
▸ scholarships.com

▸ collegboard.org
▸ finaid.com
▸ fastweb.com
▸ cappex.com
▸ scholarships.com
▸ collegeanswer.com
▸ whatsMyScore.org
▸ savingforcollege.com

In addition to this overview of college scholarships and financial aid, you could also go to collegboard.org for information on the following *How to* topics:

- ‣ Strategies for Paying for College
- ‣ Finding College Scholarships & Applying for Financial Aid
- ‣ Understanding & Comparing Education Loans
- ‣ Using a Financial Aid Calculator
- ‣ Questions to ask Financial Aid Officers

Some financial planners also offer free college financial planning nights, including online video workshops. Topics include college tax deductions/credits, colleges with best financial aid packages, how to pay for college, and how the federal government calculates your Family Contribution for aid. Be careful, as some of these are merely advertising strategies and are meant to drum up business.

The most important question when you are searching for an athletic scholarship or when you are considering a college to attend is to ask, "Are you a fit academically and athletically for a particular team and particular college?" If you don't make an educated and thoughtful decision now, you may end up dealing with transfer issues. Student-athletes transfer for a variety of reasons including not getting playing time, not getting their athletic scholarship renewed each year, being too far from home, or not doing well academically. There are complex transfer rules that you will want to research such as the rule that you cannot communicate with a coach at a school you want to transfer to until that college has received written permission that releases you from your current college. Be prepared that a college may not release you for the year and you would be unable to compete athletically at another college for a year.

Last Words...

On a final note; remember, this book is designed primarily to help you experience a successful journey through high school and go beyond to help you get into college and ideally to play sports at the next level. **This book offers only a brief overview of how to apply for financial aid and academic & athletic scholarships.** There are countless books written on the topic and numerous websites that can assist you with seeking scholarships and financial aid. The College Board website and Edward B. Fiske's college prep books (published by Sourcebooks and sold on amazon.com and in book stores) are invaluable resources. See additional resources at the back of this book and search "scholarships" online and you will find more resources than you can imagine.

Chapter 16
Top 10 Plays

1. Familiarize yourself with financial aid options. Visit your high school counselor and research online

2. Start researching scholarships and grants by the summer after your junior year—start at collegboard.org

3. Create a folder, box or cabinet file drawer to organize all your scholarship and financial aid application materials and make a timeline with deadline date. Keep copies of everything you send

4. MEET DEADLINES!

5. Ask your parent to complete the Free Application for Student Aid (FAFSA)—they will need tax returns and financial information soon after January 1 of your senior year

6. Apply for scholarships and ask for letters of recommendation

7. Communicate with coaches about potential athletic scholarship offers

8. If you meet with coaches in person, be yourself and attentively listen to what the coach is offering

9. Apply for the financial aid you qualify for based on the FAFSA report and meet with financial aid advisers at the colleges you are applying to ask about financial aid and scholarship packages

10. Don't get caught up in the overwhelming amount of information

Time out!

Take a break and use this space to reflect.

What is important to you? What do you need to do?

17

Narrowing Choices &
SELECTING A COLLEGE

Make the decision, make it with confidence, and the world will be yours.

DECISIONS

During your junior or senior year, you will be faced with many important decisions. As a result, you will probably be asking yourself a lot of important questions:

- Which college should I attend?
- Should I accept my 2nd choice?
- What if at the last minute (weeks before signing day) a new scholarship opportunity comes up?
- What if another opportunity occurs AFTER signing?
- What about my options of redshirt or grayshirt?
- What if I am a recruited "walk-on"?
- Should I go to college or enter the draft?
- Should I go to community college first?
- If I'm not accepted, what do I do now?
- What are the important deadlines I need to remember?

Options

Now is the time *to decide* what you are going to do after high school graduation. If you have been accepted to more than one college, you have to narrow down your choices. You may not gain admission to your top choice—so what will you do then? To complicate matters, some student-athletes may also have to make a decision between being drafted and going to college. Or, unfortunately, you may not get accepted to any of the colleges you applied to.

Megan Erkel was interested in UC Berkeley, but two other soccer goalies were recruited, making her #3 on the depth chart. She chose Rice University in Texas and became the starting goalie. The California girl loved Texas and enjoyed a four-year soccer career, while getting an outstanding education.

Let's look at some other student-athletes' options:

Situation 1: What happens if you verbally commit and then two weeks before signing day find out you can get an ROTC nursing scholarship at a different college that also has a DI soccer program? Do you change your plans at the last minute and go for the scholarship and have to contact the coach to ask to be a walk-on? You have made sacrifices all your life playing with a competitive soccer club and the Olympic Development Program (ODP), and already have been offered a partial scholarship. So, do you settle to walk-on without being recruited, or play at the college that recruited and verbally committed to you?

This is the situation that Caresse Little was faced with. She made the tough decision to call Idaho State University's coach the night before her official signing day to let him know that she was not going to commit.

Instead, she chose to attend Westminster College in Utah on a full-ride ROTC scholarship, even though she had never been a part of the ROTC program in high school. She took the risk of becoming a walk-on for the women's soccer team. While she recieved playing time, she decided the workload of soccer, ROTC, and academics was too much and she did not return to the team her sophomore year. This was not part of her plan, but it worked out for her.

Situation 2: Kayla Karlsson had to make a choice between two excellent options. Kayla was offered scholarship money to two very different DI colleges: UC Davis and University of Cincinnati. She liked that Davis was close to her family and she worried about being so far away in Cincinnati. After taking official visits to both campuses, she clearly realized that the college in Cincinnati was a better fit for her. She liked the coaches, team members and soccer programs at both schools, but once she was on both campuses she realized there was a big difference. She specifically liked the friendly college atmosphere at Cincinnati, while students seemed much more intense and focused at Davis. For her, the campus atmosphere was what determined which school to attend.

These student-athletes were fortunate because they had been accepted to more than one college. What they needed to do was to visualize their choices and use a graphic tool to evaluate their choices. Can you envision yourself attending the college and competing in sports there for 4-5 years?

"I chose Simpson University because, of my four offers, it was the most affordable, it had small class sizes, a really pretty campus and it was far enough away from home for me to feel independent, yet close enough for me to drive home if I need to. They also have a very good softball program which really attracted me to them!"

–Chasteena Determan, college softball player

Write Down Your Deciding Factors

Below are two examples of how to write down the factors to help you narrow your choices.

DECIDING ON SCHOOLS QUESTIONNAIRE

	School #1	School #2	School #3	School #4
Majors				
Proximity to Home				
Setting				
Size				
Cost				
Campus Life				
Team				

Another graphic tool you can use is called a P-M-I chart. You simply write down the qualities that you think are a plus (positive), a minus (negative), and interesting.

P-M-I CHART

	Plus	Minus	Interesting
School #1:			
School #2:			
School #3:			

Using a graphic tool will help you envision yourself on the campus and on the team. Talk to as many people as you can, including your parents, coaches, counselors, teachers and alumni, to help you decide. Reflect on what you want after college and what your goals are while attending college. What are your chances for success in terms of graduation and placement, both academically and athletically? Remember not to make your choice solely based on the coach, since many coaches are transient, and often vying for a better position. There is a good chance that the coach or assistant coaches might not be there the entire time you play for the college. Most importantly, campus visits seem to be the best indicator of whether or not you will fit at a school if you feel good when you step on the campus.

What if You Only Get Accepted To Your 2nd Choice School?

Many student-athletes get accepted to only one school, or to their safe choice but not their dream school. The first decision to make is whether or not you will be happy at a school other than your dream school. If your second or third choice school is a place where you will be content, then your decision is easier. Use the graphic tools to help decide between schools. If you don't get accepted into your dream school, you have some options. (See "Now What?" for your options.)

You also could be offered a grayshirt or redshirt option. Some high school student-athletes are not physically, academically, or socially ready for college sports straight out of high school. They commit to a college of their choice anyway, but declare redshirt or grayshirt status, which will delay their five-year eligibility window for competing in NCAA sports. (See Chapter 8 for more details.)

College or Draft?

Lastly, high school athletes might have to decide between going to college or getting drafted to a professional sports team. Some student-athletes are drafted right out of high school, and the choice between playing pro sports right away or attending college is not an easy decision. Athletes need to take into consideration their draft number, signing bonus money, and the competition. Also consider the option of attending community college for a year or two to improve your draft position. This is a big decision that should include discussions with your parents. The P-M-I chart can also help you make a choice.

Not Accepted—Now What?

What if you don't get accepted to your top choices? You do have options.

Appeals:

Don't give up until you have exhausted all your avenues to gain acceptance. Many students appeal the decision and get into their top choices. Confirm with the admissions office whether or not they received all your required documents. The college admissions office might not have received your letters of recommendation or your most recent high school transcripts. (For example, students who make up or improve a grade in a course, even in the summer after graduation, need to make sure the updated transcripts are sent.)

In terms of appealing, you may need teachers to write you additional letters or perhaps you may need your coach, principal, or school counselor to write about extenuating circumstances.

Wait listed:

Colleges usually have wait listed protocols on their website. If you are wait listed to a college that you really want to attend, then send a letter stating why they should reconsider. Have your high school counselor call for you and inquire what you need to do. Many students gain acceptance for either fall or the spring, so don't give up if you are wait listed.

Delayed Admission:

You could go to community college for a semester or a year and then transfer to the college of your choice. Some student-athletes attend a community college near home for convenience. Others might attend a community college that is a "feeder" school for the specific college they ultimately want to attend.

You might also have an opportunity to gain "delayed admission" meaning you would begin classes during the winter or spring semester, rather than the impacted fall semester. Some colleges can also have you begin during the summer program to meet pre-requisites for attending the college in the fall.

Jamie Bardwil's first choice was UC Berkeley. She did not gain admission but decided to appeal the decision because during her sophomore year she had her appendix taken out and missed a number of school days. Despite the surgery and absences, she worked diligently in all her classes. Her school counselor, journalism teacher, and her AP European History teacher wrote letters for her. UC Berkeley reconsidered and admitted her, not for the fall term, but for winter term. She accepted and completed a degree in journalism.

Deadlines

Students need to commit to a college before the May 1st reply date, unless they applied for early admission. Early decision and early action programs will often have earlier deadlines for commitments. Be sure to check deadlines if you choose one of these options.

Last words...

If you are accepted to multiple colleges you have to make a decision, hopefully with input from people you trust. If you do not get accepted but feel you are qualified and really want to attend a particular school, you have to ask yourself what you are willing to do to get in. You have to follow your dreams, but you also might have to be patient and take a path with some obstacles that will hopefully get you where you want to be.

Gavin Andrews was offered full athletic scholarships for football to all the PAC 12 schools and to many other football programs. He is a unique case in that he didn't make any official visits. He didn't want to go through the stressful experience of making unofficial and official visits—and then trying to decide among lots of good choices. As a kid, Gavin always thought of going to Oregon for college. Since he really liked the head coach when the coach visited Gavin at his high school, Gavin decided early that playing offensive line for the Beavers at Oregon State University was the perfect fit for him.

You have to do what is right for you. Everyone is different. Be sure you will be happy at a college whether you are competing in a sport or not. Will you be happy at that campus if you aren't playing sports anymore?

Remember that ultimately it is your life and your decision. Trust your gut!

Chapter 17
Top 10 Plays

1. Are you a fit academically and athletically?

2. Did you apply to schools that you can get into?

3. Have you really thought about what you want from college?

4. Are you OK with the role you will play on the college team? Will you be happy as a grayshirt, or redshirt if you are not a "true freshman"?

5. Have you considered the distance from home?

6. Have you considered the campus environment and social life?

7. Have you met your potential teammates?

8. Can you afford the costs to attend?

9. What will you do if you don't get into your first choice?

10. Are you willing to be wait listed or make an appeal?

Parting Shot...

Life is a journey, not a destination. Enjoy your high school years and your participation in sports. They're an important episode in your life, but recognize that eventually every athlete's career comes to an end, and so, be able to move on to other pursuits. Tap into the support around you and attack these endeavors and get the most out of them. Sports participation will enrich your life and there is a place for you to play beyond your high school years. It's important to give your best effort academically and athletically; recognize that you'll get the best out of participation by putting the best of yourself into it. Keep a positive attitude. Don't give up on yourself - Ever. Be persistent and bounce back. Have an athlete's short term memory and don't let mistakes be an anchor keeping you in one place. Focus on what went well and how that can help you continue forward – full steam ahead. Thank the people in your life who help you get through as they've also invested time and energy, love and passion in you. One day it will be your job to support and love someone else's pursuit. While you prepare for your future, live in the present and enjoy the moment with your friends and family. May you find your passion. We wish you the best on your journey. Play hard. Play smart.

Play hard. Play Smart.

POST-GAME

RESOURCES

*We found the following resources to be very valuable and re-
ferred to them time and time again.*

Athletic Associations

National Collegiate Athletic Association ✦ www.ncaa.org
National Association of Intercollegiate Athletics ✦ www.naia.org
National Junior College Athletic Association ✦ www.njcaa.org

College Planning Resource

The College Board ✦ www.collegboard.org

Test Prep & Testing

SAT Test ✦ www.collegboard.org
ACT Test ✦ www.ACT.org

College Applications

The Common Application ✦ www.commonapp.org

Scholarship Search & Financial Aid

Free Application for Federal Student Aid ✦ www.fasfa.ed.gov
Scholarship and College Search ✦ www.fastweb.com
Student Guide to Financial Aid ✦ www.finaid.org
College Scholarships ✦ www.scholarships.com
Free Education Guide ✦ www.freeeducationguide.com

Recruiting Information Sites

Informed Athlete ✦ www.informedathlete.com
Stack ✦ www.stack.com

WORKS CONSULTED

Brown, Bruce. Coach Quotes for Basketball. Monterey, CA: Coaches Choice, 2003.

Covey, Sean. The 7 Habits of Highly Effective Teens, 36th ed. New York: Simon & Schuster, 1998.

Davis, Jaren L. "Inspirational Quotes." The Foundation for a Better Life, 2012. Web. 30 July 2012.
    http://www.values.com/inspirational-quote-authors/1128-Jaren-L-Davis

Fiske, Edward B. Fiske Guide to Colleges, 27th ed. Naperville, IL: Sourcebooks, 2010.

Garabedian, Craig. "Concussions." Powerpoint. Roseville, California. 2006.

Jacobson, Jennifer. "Focusing on the Forgotten: How to Put More Kids on the Track to College
    Success." American Educator. (Fall 2007): 30-33.

Jones, Niven. "A Numbers Game." Blogspot. Rounding Third: How to Play Baseball at the Next Level.
    RoundingThird. December 2008. Web. 12 Dec. 2010.
    http://roundthird.blogspot.com/2008/12/numbers-game.html

Lombardi, Vince. "Famous Quotes by Vince Lombardi." Luminary Group,
    2010. Web. 1 Aug. 2012. http://www.vincelombardi.com/quotes.html

NCAA Eligibility Center. "2011-12 Guide for the College-Bound Student-
    Athlete." NCAA Eligibility Center, Aug. 2010. Web. 17 June 2012. www.elibilitycenter.org

Openshaw, Jennifer. "It's Not Too Early to Apply for Financial Aid." Sacramento Bee. 8 Jan. 2012: D6.
    Print.

Orlick, Terry. In Pursuit of Excellence, 4th ed. Champaign: Human Kinetics, 2008.

O'Shaughnessy, Lynn. "63 Colleges with the Best Financial Aid." CBSMoneyWatch. CBS Interactive,
    Inc., 18 Feb. 2011. Web. 2 March 2011.
    http://www.cbsnews.com/8301-505145_162-37244545/63-colleges-with-the-best-financial-aid/

Pope, Loren. Colleges That Change Lives. 2nd edition. The Penguin Group: New York, 2006.

Scarborough, Karen, Ph.D. "Peak Performance." Workbook for Sport Psychology. California State
    University, Sacramento. 1997.

"Selecting a College Where I can be a Student-Athlete." UC Davis Athletics: Student-Athlete Guidance
    Services. 5 Dec. 2003. Web. 11 July 2012.
    http://athletics.ucdavis.edu/academicservices/Old/SAGS/Where.htm

Wheeler, Dion. The Sports Scholarships Insider's Guide: Getting Money for College at any Division.
    Naperville, IL: Sourcebooks, 2009.

Wooden, John and Jamison, Steve. Wooden: A Lifetime of Observations and Reflections on and off the
    Court. Chicago: Contemporary Books, 1997.

INDEX